WILD AND WOOLLY

WILD AND WOOLLY

Tails from a Woodland Studio

LINDA JOHNS

M&S

Canadian Cataloguing in Publication Data

Johns, Linda
　　Wild and woolly: tails from a woodland studio

ISBN: 0-7710-4412-7

1. Wild animals as pets. 2. Wild birds as pets. 3. Johns, Linda. I. Title.

SF416.J63 2000　　C818'.5403　　C00-931237-4

We acknowledge the financial support of the Government of Canada through the Book Publishing Industry Development Program for our publishing activities. We further acknowledge the support of the Canada Council for the Arts and the Ontario Arts Council for our publishing program.

Brush drawings throughout by Linda Johns

Typeset in Sabon by M&S, Toronto
Printed and bound in Canada

McClelland & Stewart Inc.
The Canadian Publishers
481 University Avenue
Toronto, Ontario
M5G 2E9

1 2 3 4 5　　04 03 02 01 00

For the wildlings –
and all who take time
to help them

CONTENTS

1. In the Beginning Were Cats   1

2. Winged and Woolly   14

3. Old Cars and a New House   37

4. Woods and Wildlings   50

5. Studio Personalities   62

6. Meat or Tofu?   73

7. Spring in Winter   85

8. Perplexities with Pigeons   97

9. Not Always Man's Best Friend   110

10. The Awakening Land   124

11. Tree Personalities and Dwellings   131

12. Caught in the Coils of Spring   141

13. Spring Unsprung   158

14. Raising Eyebrows   164

15. Tails of Wonder, Tales of Woe   177

16. Lord of the Rings   194

17. Family Feelings   209

18. The Ringleader   224

19. Butting In   233

20. Butting Out   254

21. Faux Paws   263

22. Transience and Thresholds   277

23. Woolly Pull Buns   292

24. Another Bill Arrives   300

25. An Unwise Fling Before Spring   312

26. Remembering   321

CHAPTER 1

IN THE BEGINNING WERE CATS

O urs is *not* a household for the faint-hearted.

Wild creatures, winged or woolly, arrive often and unexpectedly at our woodland home, where we do our best to heal them. Like relations, they remain for unpredictable lengths of time, absorbing deluxe care and nourishment before departing with seldom a backward glance. However, *unlike* relations, our wildlings, when they go, leave a poignant feeling of regret as well as relief.

Whether the *regret* is mutual, only the creatures themselves can affirm. However, I think it's safe to assume the *relief* – not only do they return to their familiar element, but they finally escape the unpredictable emotional minefield that surrounds every artist.

And her nearest and dearest.

My saner half, Mack, committed voluntarily to such a lifestyle, deserves the highest commendation – although he claims he wouldn't have missed this for anything. For unguessable endings, gripping plots, and continual amusement, our world leaves the entertainment industry nowhere. Fortunately, he's a patient man. And blessed with such abundant energy that, even after an arduous day gardening under a pitiless sun – punishment that would reduce me to a faint after-image – his natural gait up a flight of stairs is a vigorous trot.

Before we met, I lived with an ever-changing cavalcade of birds and animals in a small house and studio wriggled comfortably into the woods near the northern shore of Nova Scotia. The dwelling grew a little broader here and there as it matured – like so many of us, alas – each facelift contingent upon my financial status at that moment. But twenty-one years of persistence created a simple home that sheltered diverse creatures in need – myself among the rarest – and nurtured my art.

One of the biggest struggles in those early years was in supplying household water, and I survived eight years of hauling it from springs and other people's houses, an experience which I'm told builds character as well as calluses. Even today, I can recall with a shudder those superhuman efforts to stretch a limited quantity of water beyond all reasonable bounds. The last bucketful would be used to wash my hair, then the dishes, then the floor – in that order.

At the university library in Antigonish where I worked on weekends, I would arrive early, wash at the kitchen sink in the coffee room, dry my hair over the stove burners, and finally gallop upstairs to unlock the main door for disgruntled waiting students – most of whom had had the luxury of a hot morning shower. When I descended to the coffee room later for my mid-morning break, I was usually met with the lingering reek of burnt hair.

During each winter, whenever a sudden thaw set in, I'd run outside with every utensil I possessed and align them under the dripping eaves, creating water music that in my ears rivalled even Handel's magnificent effort.

One summer day, during a lengthy dry spell, I drove determinedly to a distant spring, hoping to return with enough water to – with care – last at least a week. I wore old clothes and high rubber boots, since lugged water always seeks its lowest level – usually down my pant leg and around my feet on its way back home to underground springs. My crumbling second-hand Volkswagen, which had known better days but seemed resigned to its present fate, bore a jumble of lidless tubs, buckets, and large plastic bags heaped carelessly on the back seat. Together, we presented an alluring spectacle to the other people lined up at the spring, who were carrying single, more elegant containers designed for drinking-water only.

I filled every receptacle I had, including the bags, which I stacked optimistically on top of one another on the back seat and on the floor below. They sagged and lolled about in a drunken manner, but seemed reasonably secure. Then I set off for home at a moderate speed.

A mile later, a bird dashed in front of the car and I braked suddenly – and disastrously. Rigid containers lurched and slopped, and some toppled. Bags pitched forward, crushing others and splitting instantly. Swirls of water sloshed around my feet.

I leaped out, leaving my door ajar and jerking open the other one as well. Water gushed out both doors and spewed out innumerable holes elsewhere, as though I'd been driving a colander. Little rivers ran off the road in spidery trails, carrying my hard-won liquid gold away to the ditches. Passing cars veered erratically as drivers and passengers goggled at the windows.

Fortunately, the tears that created similar rivulets on my face sprang from laughter rather than frustration.

When finally I had a well dug, and a hand pump attached, my lifestyle definitely improved, though I recall with clarity the aftermath of a major blizzard. Needing water, I forced open the door of the house only to see dramatic whiteness unbroken by the familiar dark silhouette of the well pump.

Leaning against the house was the shovel, with the handle still visible. Twisting the rest of it free, I began to clear a path – which could be described more accurately as a half-tunnel – to the snowladen duck house. It stood twenty feet away and housed "Wattle" and "Daub," who would no doubt be suffering from cabin fever after this three-day blow. I banged the shovel against the frozen latch to loosen it, wrenched open the small door, and was warmly greeted, despite the cold. Then I began shovelling in the general direction of the well, both ducks following excitedly in my wake and grabbing thirstily at the snowy walls that rose up beside them.

Half an hour later, my shovel clunked into the side of the invisible well and, when it was finally cleared of snow, I pumped up a bucket of water for the ducks. They drank eagerly, plunging their heads in as far as they could reach and blowing out gurgling streams of bubbles. Then they lifted their heads, bright-eyed and gasping with shrill honks, and tried ludicrously to rub water all over their backs.

Two years later, when water was piped into the house, I gambolled just as joyously in my own celebratory bath.

Although birds came to predominate in my home, in the earliest days I'd also cared for two cats who'd been born in a city. One of them, "Rogue," was blind.

As a grey kitten, with unusually small eyes and a chronically myopic expression, he was endearing – if homely. But it was only when he began to scamper that I realized something was wrong. He'd crash into *anything* that loomed up too quickly for him to stop – sharp corners of doorways, boots, bags of groceries, legs belonging to humans or furniture.

Then I understood that those tiny eyes possessed minimal vision.

I padded all obstacles, but Rogue developed such a hesitation about running, which seemed unfortunate in a naturally exuberant youngster, that I often took him to solitary beaches. There, on the open sands, unable to see enough to cower in vulnerability beneath the enormous sky, Rogue ran and jumped ecstatically, twitching his tail and maintaining contact with me through questioning calls.

It was during one such excursion that he unwisely outdistanced me and I watched helplessly as he ran headlong into the protruding end of a wooden lobster trap, partially buried in the sand – the *sole projection* on the beach.

The injustice of the gods . . .

As Rogue matured, his vestigial eyesight disappeared, leaving him in darkness, but he gained a compensatory lifestyle unusual for a cat. His auditory dependence converted him into an ideal companion during woodland walks. There, among mixed trees, shrubs and wildflowers, he followed my voice in utter security, experiencing to the full sounds and fragrances around him that, conversely, I was sensing only minimally. How amazing it would be to wander in Rogue's inner landscape, I mused. How utterly unfamiliar my familiar world would become.

When I canoed on the nearby lake, Rogue rode with ease in the unfamiliar conveyance, often sitting like a feline figurehead on the bow or stalking meditatively along the narrow edge of the gunwale. He also relished drives in the car, either dozing by himself on a seat, or lolling languidly in someone's lap – sometimes behind the wheel in mine. I recall driving home after a day-long trip with a tired Rogue lying across my lap, his head on my arm, his useless eyes closed, but a steady purr of contentment vibrating his body.

Though he spent summer days outside, ears and nose registering sounds and smells, the wild birds easily discerned his infirmity. On our walks, chickadees teased him mercilessly, brazenly swooping near his ears with "cat calls."

One afternoon, I watched from a window as grackles tried to feed on scattered seed in an open yard, while Rogue, as visible as a flashing light, stalked them hopefully. Finally, a couple of grackles lured him away from the others by fluttering and pausing right before him, over and over, while he crept after them steadily, blinking and trying to focus. When he had been enticed at least twenty-five feet away from the flock, the two culprits lifted up onto a breeze, glided soundlessly over Rogue to their companions, then dropped back down to the ground and began to feed hungrily.

Rogue was left peering irritably in all directions, still searching for his prey, while I chuckled shamelessly.

Even then, I was on the side of the birds.

Unfortunately, Rogue discovered that, by smelling out mouse or chipmunk pathways in the hayfields, and waiting patiently to one side despite the insistent summer sun pressing down on him, he could eventually catch a victim – a deplorable habit, and one which I tried relentlessly to dispel by lugging him indoors as soon as I spotted him hunting.

The upstairs sleeping loft, in the early days of the house, was reached by a rough ladder with odd sizes of boards for steps. These were nailed to the supports with varying gaps between them, a hazard even for the sighted. Rogue, however, conquered this challenge – but only when climbing *up*. When he wanted back down, he stood at the edge of the loft loudly demanding assistance, and was lifted to the bottom like royalty.

One day I left the ladder leaning not against the loft floor, but against the wall of the living room, which curved up and over into a cathedral ceiling. I arrived home to find Rogue marooned stiffly and helplessly at the top of the ladder after untold hours, rigid with alarm at the unprecedented disappearance of the entire upstairs.

Rogue's sister, Saffron, possessed such enormous, golden eyes that I sometimes fancied she had garnered Rogue's share of vision as well as her own. Being sighted, she preferred the more usual forms of feline life rather than the questionable pursuits followed by Rogue. Cars, in particular, were anathema to her.

I still recall – with visible shudders – the day I drove her to the vet's office. Saffron braced her hind feet on the back of my seat, her front paws on my shoulders, and alternated piercing howls with cascades of warm, sticky drool that trickled down the back of my neck and soaked my blouse.

I never even considered offering her a canoe ride.

Despite that memorable performance, her natural demeanour was undeniably ladylike, her body small, and her fur a sleek "basic black." She disliked "roughing it." Those cold winters in a house inadequately insulated, where frost not only encrusted the windows but created undesirable crystals on the inside of the visible roof-boards, were *not* to her liking.

A true city cat, Saffron liked her "creature comforts."

When electricity was finally installed, I often returned home, after several hours' absence, to the tantalizing, but perplexing, aroma of *toast*.

I couldn't understand it.

I'd ponder this new enigma as I quickly kindled a fire to dispel the cold. Both Rogue and Saffron, huddled in obvious chilly displeasure, would wait for heat with slitted eyes of reproach at such barbaric living conditions. Later when I climbed into bed in the warmed loft, I knew they'd quickly join me, dreading the cooling hours before morning.

However, one night the thermometer plunged drastically and strong winds shook the bones of the little house. I awoke in the cold dawn to the fragrance, *again*, of fresh toast.

How could this be?

As noiselessly as possible, I crept down the ladder and spotted Saffron in the kitchen, warming herself over the new electric toaster. As the glorious heat faded into the prevailing chilliness, she lifted one dainty paw and pressed it down firmly on the switch. Again the coils glowed, internal crumbs kindled, and once more the odour of fresh toast rose as Saffron draped herself contentedly over her personal fire.

Not for her the rustic pleasures of our pioneer life.

Saffron's desire for the luxuries suitable to her station also led her to dip her paw coyly into the spout of the electric kettle when the water was still pleasantly warm, ignoring the cold water in her dish. She'd lick the heated water off her paw, eyes closed in bliss, then dip it again.

Altogether, we were a resourceful family.

Living on one's own for the first time can, of course, create anxiety – especially for a woman. I remember one night, before I had a lock on the only door, hearing a suspicious sound. I looked nervously at the doorknob and, to my horror, watched it wiggle.

My throat tightened instantly, and my heart began to gallop. I seized the poker with trembling hands. Braced with the desperation of one cornered, I *jerked open the door.*

Only to see a startled Saffron, paw still in the air, sitting on a stack of firewood beside the knob, her mild eyes wide with astonishment.

One day, when I was waiting beside the railway station for the train that would bring an old friend for a visit, I became aware of desperate mewings on the other side of the tracks. The cries never ceased. Finally, I crossed over to investigate.

I found a tiny kitten, eyes just open, crawling with shaky limbs in a grassy yard. When I picked the creature up, I saw that fleas were milling so thickly through its fur that they looked like an aerial view of rush-hour traffic.

I was sickened.

I knocked on the door of the nearby house, but the gaunt woman who answered muttered nervously that she'd *had* to throw the kittens away – her man was coming home. The cat had carried off the rest, she added, and closed the door.

Her situation seemed as bleak as the kitten's.

There was no sign of the cat, though I waited hopefully. Then the train pulled in and my friend descended, looking incredibly fresh and cool after such a long journey. I greeted her, gingerly holding out a screaming, flea-infested kitten. It was gift-wrapped in toilet paper from the station washroom.

"You haven't changed a bit!" she laughed, after the initial shock.

Fortunately, she loved cats.

Later, we undressed to our underwear in the kitchen – to avoid taking on any undesirable passengers. Gently, we immersed the tiny kitten – with room to spare – in a two-cup liquid measure of pine oil, which is *lethal* to fleas. And they very quickly realized it.

The nimbler ones leaped off their sinking ship, only to be caught and crushed instantly by any available fingers. The kitten, who'd suffered enough trauma for one day, wailed heartbreakingly. Not until he was cuddled in warmed towels did his cries finally dwindle to an exhausted, and tentative, purr.

But this crisis was the first step in his rise to good fortune. Another friend took the kitten from the wrong side of the tracks, and he became a contented, cosseted cat in a posh city apartment. With *no* access to wild birds.

Gradually, the house gained more comforts. Insulation was completed, clapboard replaced the rough slab siding, and real stairs connected the main floor to the loft. Bookcases crept across the golden spruce walls of the living room and rugs added almost a note of elegance to the painted plywood subfloors.

A studio with double-glazed north windows jutted out of the east end of the house. A carving studio, which gradually transformed into a bird hospice, clung to the west end, connected by a door to the living room. The eventual change-over to a bird "family" led to the creation of an indoor garden, which dominated the living room. Here, among arching plants, woodland soil, and tall, leafless trees suitable for perching, many injured or orphaned wild birds found a semi-natural environment in which to recuperate before release. Or, if unreleasable, to live out their days.

A capacious "Grandma Bear" woodstove, standing foursquare on cast-iron paws, and referred to fondly as "Grannie," warmed us, dried mittens and boots, thawed frozen suppers, and simmered soup. Birds perched near her, wings and tails spread, basking in warmth.

Outdoors we lived surrounded by forest, wooded hills, crop fields, meadows, and lakes, each offering its own special beauty through the changing seasons, its own particular glimpse into the great mystery of which we are all a part. Small vegetable gardens in raised beds struggled for survival among the trees, producing cucumber vines that climbed spruces, and tomatoes that ripened quickly against the south wall of the studio.

Mack and I, joining forces in our fifties, therefore began our life together in a small house designed more for the comfort of birds than of humans. A place where perches and tree branches were more plentiful than chairs. A tiny kitchen, with ample room for me, shrank awkwardly when Mack attempted to knead bread while I was cooking.

One evening, he passed through, carrying several boards. As he turned into the living room, the boards swung into a heavy steel rack on top of the woodstove. The rack shot off the stove and slammed violently into a metallic heat shield before crashing to the brick platform below. The uproar made shunting freight cars sound like bumping grocery carts.

But this was not the worst of it.

A week earlier, I had placed a gallon bottle of solid honey on top of the rack to melt in the rising warmth. The last lump had dissolved that morning, and now we had a glass jar full of warm liquid honey.

That is, we had it briefly.

When the rack was suddenly swept away, the jar flew off. It bounced on the edge of the stove and exploded.

Honey sank between the bricks below. Honey splattered the nearby cookbooks on their shelf. Honey – embedded with shards of glass – coated the small kitchen floor and permeated part of the dining-room carpet. Mack, in understandable exasperation, flung down his boards with a final clatter on the living-room floor.

The outbreak of mysterious crashes, punctuated by Mack's blasphemy and my dwindling wails, brought Bubble, my loyal rooster-in-residence, on the run from the studio to rescue his "hen." But I was trapped in a corner of the kitchen, separated from Mack by a sea of honey. Neither of us could get at the other.

Which was probably just as well.

Bubbs, with hackles flaring, rounded the corner of the dining room and skidded unexpectedly in golden goo. Now I wailed even louder, horrified at visions of cut feet and sticky trails of blood and honey meandering throughout the house. Clutching the counter on one side and the fridge on the other, I skated awkwardly through the honey and scooped up Bubbs, thereby coating my blouse as well.

I struggled out of my honeyed shoes and carried Bubbs into the bathroom, where I washed his feet. Then I hugged him and locked him in the studio. Resisting a wild impulse to run out the back door, leap in the car, and keep driving, I returned reluctantly to the kitchen.

Across a gulf of honey and broken glass, Mack and I stared helplessly at each other.

Where to begin?

With no precedent to guide us, we followed the dictates of our own desperation. We lifted dripping gobs of honey between spatulas and transferred them to plastic bags. We gathered handfuls of honey and glass while wearing oven mitts – which were later discarded. We chose our most worn hand towels, dampened them, and wiped the floor, bricks, carpet, and lower cupboards over and over again. We mopped off each cookbook several times. We gingerly rinsed out the towels every few seconds, washing honey down the sink to sweeten the drain.

We worked in ominous silence.

Despite our caution, we were pricked continually with hidden shards of glass, till we felt like we'd been playing handball with cactuses. Sweat dripped off our noses, trickled down our backs and combined with the ubiquitous honey to plaster our clothes to our clammy bodies.

Mack wasn't sure he ever wanted to see honey again.

I wasn't sure I ever wanted to see *him* again.

Somehow, order was restored. But "honey" was one term of endearment he dropped for good.

The house was definitely too cramped for both of us. Even my steep narrow stairs forced Mack to descend sideways, while ducking to avoid hitting his head on one of the floor joists supporting the loft. He often just backed down clutching the stairs, there being no rail. The diminutive loft with its modest closet and single dresser gave him no place to store his clothes. But the room which, in a moment of enthusiasm, I called a bathroom, presented his biggest challenge.

Or, more correctly perhaps, his smallest.

The money to pay for a septic field and indoor toilet still eluded me, at this point. Thus, in a room six feet by six feet, I had fitted an old-fashioned, four-footed tub with shower, which occupied exactly half the space. Next to it was wedged a portable chemical toilet – without chemicals – and, in front of that, a tiny washer/spin dryer which nearly touched the knees of anyone sitting on the "throne." There was no room for a sink.

There was certainly no room for someone nearly six feet tall. Mack often had to step outside the room to dry himself after a shower.

One evening, as I was preparing supper, I heard a resounding *klunk!* from the bathroom, followed by a stifled moan.

"Are you all right?" I called out, with that touching concern so characteristic of a new relationship, when even a simple hangnail troubling the beloved seems important.

"Just backing out of the stall," he mumbled as he reappeared, stepping backwards out of the bathroom, and ruefully rubbing his head.

We decided that major renovations were needed.

CHAPTER 2

WINGED AND WOOLLY

Accordingly, plans were laid to retain the adjoining studio and hospice, but to demolish the house that lay between them and erect a more commodious shelter.

One with a *standard*-sized bathroom.

Such a major upheaval, however, had to be arranged harmoniously with the current indoor bird family. At that time, this included Chip, a five-year-old grackle, whose black plumage shone with bronze iridescence on her back, and with teal on her head. Her dark eyes never did lighten to the familiar gold of wild grackles, but remained dark in conjunction with her devilish nature.

Though I'd tried several times to release Chip, her latent pulmonary condition always flared up, driving her back to me for treatment. Fortunately for her, if not always for the rest of us, Chip's busy mind usually contrived enough entertainment to compensate for her more limited indoor life.

Molly, an irascible domestic pigeon with beautiful burnt-sienna back and wings and the purest white face, front, feathered feet, and tail, had lived with me for eleven years. She'd been a sick squab, ten days old, with an impacted crop, when she'd arrived, but a dose of mineral oil and a gentle massage had resolved that difficulty.

Whenever I worked in the silence of the studio, Molly would lie on her high shelf, eyes warm in unmistakable contentment. (Pigeons prefer shelves to perches in the home, just as in cities they seek building ledges instead of trees. So on Molly's shelf, I kept her water dish and mixed seeds.) But, if another bird flew into the room, Molly would stand up, cooing irritably, and march back and forth territorially, bristling with belligerence.

An endearing Japanese quail named, appropriately, Bashō, after an ancient haiku poet, was another important member of the family. Two and a half years earlier, he had arrived, a three-week-old youngster considered expendable in a laboratory. The indoor garden became his home base, from which he made frequent forays on busy feet, exploring other rooms. He seldom resorted to flight, being by nature a ground bird, but was fully capable of suddenly rocketing up to the ceiling if he so desired.

Bashō adored being cuddled, especially if his feet were cold. Mack, who suffered equally from cold feet, would sympathetically pick up Bashō and hold him before the fire in his large, gentle hands. Bashō would snuggle down happily, then tip onto one side, spread his upper wing and thrust both feet out towards the blaze. His obvious pleasure easily compensated Mack for the eventual ache in his extended arms.

Bashō's plumage, growing in complex patterns of rich golds and dark browns and accented by creamy white, merged readily with the plant world of the indoor garden. He adored dustbathing wherever the soil was dry, and dozing in a warm sunpatch. Transient birds have come and gone steadily during Bashō's reign, and he's taken them all in his short stride.

In the two leafless trees of the indoor garden, high above Bashō's head, lived Beejay, a blue jay mutilated – for sport – by a fed housecat. One bitten wing had healed enough to allow level flying or a gentle descent, but instant flight upwards, so necessary to elude predators, remained only a memory for Beejay. One leg had escaped damage, but the chewed one, once it had healed, protruded at an awkward angle from his body, serving more as a brace.

Eventually, Beejay had developed impressive speed leaping from branch to branch through his trees, using his wings as well. He created familiar routes through the lofty maze, and descended quite easily to the soft earth to bathe in the communal waterdish. He tended to stay in the garden area, but whenever the upstairs beckoned, Beejay would hop up, one stair at a time, awkwardly but effectually. Returning, however, he was able to glide easily from the top of the stairs to his favoured tree – surely a brief moment of delight for one with such reduced mobility.

Sadly, his mate still lived near the house, and the two jays would call over and over to one another every evening. Beejay, for me, was a living plea for restricting the outdoor activities of housecats.

Last of the birds, but far from least, was the aforementioned Bubble, an aging but handsome rooster, with reddish-gold plumage dominated by a magnificent arched tail of iridescent dark green. He lived mostly in the studio but spent each evening lying cozily in my lap, drooling happily when I stroked his silky feathers, or snoring gently.

Bubble was ever loyal and affectionate towards me. Mack, being another "rooster," remained *persona non grata* in Bubble's opinion. Caught between them at crucial moments, I can state decisively that being loved by two males isn't all jam.

Or even by *three* males.

A second rooster, named Squeak, had also been a major part of our lives, but had succumbed a few months before to an aneurysm, a blow which had devastated Bubble and me.

Both Bubble and Squeak had been staunchly loyal, and unwavering in their mutual condemnation of Mack – although they shamelessly wolfed down his homemade bread. They'd glare coldly at him from the sanctuary of my lap, daring him to come near. Or suddenly leap at him, long spurs foremost. Or chase him, with bristling hackles, around the living room. Finally they would tree him on the staircase, where he'd crouch halfway up, shouting unmentionables at his pursuers circling below.

They almost seemed *aware* that Mack's last name, Kohout, meant, in Czechoslovakian, "rooster." And they brooked *no* rivals.

When Squeak so sadly died, dividing the challengers by half, Bubble's energies against Mack appeared to double, as though Squeak were still supporting the cause.

Mack, to his great credit, remained very understanding, and often commended Bubble for his loyalty – though sometimes through gritted teeth.

It was only when speaking to strangers on the telephone that I'd see the eccentricity of our lifestyle with the eyes – and ears – of others. Any verbal communications would have to be strained through a screen of chirps, squawks, and barnyard crowings. Inevitably, questions would be asked.

"So realistic, these nature tapes, don't you agree?" I'd purr, wickedly. "You'd almost think those were *real* bird calls."

The remaining member of our family was neither winged nor wild. But she was definitely woolly. And unlike the others, she had come after Mack and I were together.

One morning, we were in the feed store buying birdseed when I spotted a small notice on the crowded bulletin board.

"Baby Meat Rabbits Free."

I have always had a soft spot in my heart for rabbits. When I was a child, a big white rabbit – predictably named "Thumper" – was one of my favourite companions. He lived in a large wire cage with an enclosed wooden hutch, which I shifted from place to place on the lawn. This allowed fresh grass to push through the floor caging for Thumper to eat. But his activities, aside from frequent escapes when he'd pillage neighbouring gardens, encompassed broader realms.

When I skied or tobogganed down the snowy hills, Thumper's head would peer out of the chest pocket of my ski jacket.

When I pedalled my ponderous "balloon-tired" bicycle through all the streets and byways of my town, Thumper rode like a king in the carrier attached to the handlebars.

Mack, on the other hand, had grown up in a large rural family where all creatures, including rabbits, were viewed through strictly utilitarian eyes. He'd never been privileged to share friendship with a rabbit.

In short, he *needed* a rabbit. Or so I told him as we drove to the address listed in the notice.

Only when we arrived did we discover the real reason we'd come: the rabbit needed *us*.

Two remaining babies, one brown and one black, were incarcerated with their mother in a tiny cage fixed, several feet above ground, to the side of a shed. Though acres of leafy wild greens lay beyond the yard, the rabbits' nourishment was limited to pellets in one dirty dish and discoloured water in another.

The surrounding yard was littered with decaying cars, worn tires, and rusting chunks of unidentifiable machinery. We picked our way through the mud and rubble with great care, as did a couple of thin, filthy cows with no visible forage. In a miserable pen of mud and manure huddled a few disconsolate sheep. A similar pen to one side enclosed pigs. To the other side, in a cage floored with mud, manure, and mouldy seed, a flock of chickens pressed to the wire in hopes of food as soon as we approached.

The smell of mixed manures was appalling.

In a separate shed, we were shown three male rabbits. As we walked through the doorway, I nearly stumbled over a cage. No windows or electric lights relieved the monotony of darkness, and a reek of urine stung our eyes. One cage, only about four times the size of the inmate, and with an adjoining hutch, held a grossly obese rabbit lying on a solid bed of compressed dung. His food pellets were mouldy, his water filthy, and no fresh greens were visible. For exercise, he had his dreams.

Two more cages nearby repeated the horror.

Yet the woman proudly showing us these creatures was pleasant and soft-spoken. She "just loved animals"!

Mack and I were sickened.

She never noticed their misery. Never thought of them as being forced to endure dirt, reek, and darkness, without even the luxury of movement, while she, also unthinkingly, accepted light, clean food, and entertainment as her rightful due, as well as the freedom to spend her day as she chose.

I know of no creature who would *choose* such deplorable conditions in which to live.

Anxious to leave, Mack decided to "rescue" one of the baby rabbits and chose the female. The male, he suspected, might be inclined to stake out his territory with urine, and we planned to keep the rabbit indoors. I climbed behind the wheel and we drove home, Mack gently cradling a baby rabbit so frightened of humans that her eyes were ringed with white.

One of our favourite friends being Edna Staebler, a well-known author, we honoured our young rabbit with the name "Edna."

The original Edna was quite delighted.

That night we settled Edna in the studio, leaving her loose to make herself comfortable. In a little box we put rolled oats, a dog biscuit, cornmeal, sunflower seeds, and commercial pellets. Heaped beside this lay an *enormous* mound of mixed fresh food – some wild, some from the garden. Not yet knowing her preferences, we'd brought in a complete selection: clover, dandelions, carrots, carrot tops, yellow beans, lettuce, and grass. Nearby stood a flat bowl of sparkling clean water and under the table a litterbox of earth.

Mack cuddled her in his lap for most of the evening, but Edna was too timid to eat more than a few carrot tops while we were present.

However, when I opened the studio door in the morning, I laughed aloud. Anxious perhaps that such bounty might not come her way again, Edna had eaten *everything* – except the cornmeal and the dog biscuit. Only half her water remained. Droppings rolled merrily from one end of the studio to the other between two pools of carrot-coloured urine.

Only the litter was untouched.

I scooped her up with a final chuckle and tucked her into bed beside a drowsy Mack. When I peeked later, they were both sound asleep, Edna under Mack's chin.

Following the advice of an experienced friend, we confined Edna to an area of the studio four feet square by using waist-high walls of plywood. We added the litterbox, foodbox, water, and another heap of fresh food. Still she persisted in using the floor as her litter, and her litter as a bed. Puzzled, we changed the earth litter to a commercial cat litter and, from that moment on, Edna used her litter for its intended purpose.

We could only wonder if she'd been a cat in one of her previous lives, since she'd certainly never seen litter in this one. After a few days, we doubled her space but left the litter in its original spot. She continued to use it.

We doubled her space for the second time, with the same excellent results, and after a couple of days, we removed all the plywood barriers so that she could again enjoy the freedom of the studio. The litter remained in its original spot, and Edna never again soiled the floor.

With triumph one day, I announced to a friend that "Edna wasn't peeing on the floor anymore." The confounded expression on his face reminded me – *too late* – that he *also* was a friend of Edna Staebler.

When I related the story to Edna herself, she not only laughed with gracious humour, but relayed it to her friends.

The birds, as usual, tolerated this new featherless arrival. Chip longed to tease, and stalked Edna curiously, but in the end remained too intimidated to try anything. Bashō, cuddled into my shirt while Edna lay in my lap with her head near him, remained totally unperturbed. Later, when I set Bashō down on the floor, Edna was fascinated.

Ears curved forward with ardent curiosity, she thumped slowly along behind Bashō, following his every move, while he trotted in a blur before her. With such a (relatively) large creature on his trail, he showed a touch of anxiety and tried to shake off her pursuit by dodging under the woodstove. Edna, however, merely pushed under too, propelling herself on her belly. They both emerged from the other side, with Bashō still trotting hard and Edna lumbering in his wake.

Fortunately, at this point her food dish distracted her, and she veered away to enjoy a feed of rolled oats. Bashō, relieved and triumphant, stood on tiptoe and crowed.

Each time we introduced Edna – the *rabbit*, that is – to our various friends, Mack would assert with mock gravity that, although we'd been told she was a meat rabbit, such was not the case. We'd been *had*.

"Oh really . . . ?" his victim would murmur, puzzled. And taking the bait.

"Nope. We tried her on steak, chicken, veal – even spareribs with all that extra chewing in the bones – and all she wanted was lettuce, carrots, clover . . . you know, that veggie stuff!"

I never failed to enjoy the sudden light that would dawn on visitors' faces at this point, transforming perplexity to laughter as they realized just *who'd* been had.

Edna's sanctum became the corner behind the woodstove and she'd scamper back there to hide whenever she was startled. We laid out her food dishes beside the woodstove and soon, whenever we rustled fresh greens, heaping them up, she'd hop timidly towards us out of hiding.

We patted Edna often, trying to win her confidence, and gradually her fear of us lessened. As her trust grew, she began to show happiness, kicking up her heels in play. Considering her former treatment, and the collective fear of humans all those creatures must have shared, we knew she'd need time to adjust to her new surroundings.

To our lasting delight, only twenty days after she'd begun her new life with us wide-eyed with fear, Edna began jumping into our laps to be patted. Like magic, her personality unfolded.

Soon *she* was the teacher and we her pupils.

She taught us "mutual grooming," a natural activity between rabbits but adapted, in our case, to include humans. We would pat her and rub her head for a while, then she would rouse herself out of her blissful trance and reciprocate. She'd assiduously wash our faces or our hands with her dry, pink tongue, her whiskers tickling our skin. All too soon she'd stop abruptly, nudge her head under our hands and wait.

It was our turn to do *her* again.

Never will I forget Mack's delighted expression, his closed eyes and beaming smile, as Edna vigorously washed his face. It matched the delight on my own when it was my turn.

We finalized our design for a new house, to be built on the same site as the present one. The existing studio and hospice would remain standing when the old house was demolished, and then be attached to the new when it was built. But we would all have to move elsewhere till the project was completed. In a town forty miles distant, Mack owned a rental house, and there, in an unsettled atmosphere of unpacked boxes and restless traffic, we made our temporary home. We arrived in mid-August, and would remain for the next four and a half months.

A former dining room was converted into a bird room, with layers of heavy plastic protecting the mellow hardwood floors and newly painted walls. One end was fenced off for Bubble, so Mack could enter the room safely. Another indoor garden, complete with trees, was created for Chip, Beejay, and Bashō. Clusters of chokecherries hung alluringly from the branches, and a bird feeder beyond the large window attracted wild birds for further interest.

Edna, too, had her own area sectioned off, and, despite the trauma of another car ride, she adjusted with surprising ease to this new arrangement.

Above the garden, a plate rail was converted to a broad ledge for Molly. It held her food and water dishes and provided her with a familiar roost – and with more company than her unsociable heart desired, but that couldn't be helped.

We all had to bite the bullet until we could return to our woodland home.

The birds not only settled in well after their move, they seemed stimulated by their new surroundings. Beejay vigorously plotted out routes in his new trees, descended for frequent baths, and wolfed down chokecherries. Chip also tackled the chokecherries, adding her own clean pits to those of Beejay's, which lay scattered all over the floors, from the living room to the kitchen.

Bashō, after thoroughly inspecting a different garden that mysteriously grew exactly the same plants as the old one, slipped through a gap in the sheet that draped the doorway and pattered off to explore the rest of his new domain. We came across him later, threading his way cautiously through stacked boxes like a tiny boat hemmed in by massive icebergs.

Molly lay on her new shelf, eyes open to their fullest, rumbling comments on all the activities below her. When we left early each morning for another exhausting day at the building site, she watched us innocently from her roost, and was there when we returned at suppertime.

But, to our surprise, pigeon droppings began to appear upstairs.

Only once, when unrelenting rain drove us home unexpectedly in mid-afternoon, did we interrupt her on the hall stairs, returning after hours of blissful solitude in the empty rooms above.

Bubble adapted just as easily to his new surroundings and travelled back and forth each day riding in my lap. Mack did the driving, so I pointed Bubble's head towards the window on my right. I had begun to do this after one memorable trip, when Bubble, who was facing Mack, had been unable to resist suddenly lunging at his old enemy, seizing his arm in his beak.

Once back in familiar territory at the building site, Bubble scratched happily for bugs in the earth, and dustbathed in the warm sunshine while we dismantled the house, board by board. When we sat under the trees to eat lunch, he eyed our sandwiches so longingly that I'd lower mine to his level. Then Bubbs would devour one side, eagerly swallowing veggies, mayonnaise, and black pepper, while I worked on the opposite side, trying to get my share but rarely succeeding.

Bubble's advantage was clear: unhampered by teeth, he didn't have to chew.

During evenings in the bird room, as I sat in the armchair with my supper in my lap, Bubbs would watch hopefully for one of his favourite foods – cooked, long green beans. I'd hold them out, one at a time, and he'd seize the end, propelling the entire bean down his throat like a human sucking back a long strand of spaghetti. How many he could eat in one session remained a mystery, because he never refused any, and I always insisted on at least a few for myself.

After supper, I'd carry Bubbs into the living room, where he'd squat down tensely in my lap, tail arched high while he remained on guard, eyes watching Mack on the couch. But as Mack seemed disinclined to offer a challenge – being, in fact, too weary to challenge a housefly – Bubbs would gradually relax. I'd stroke his soft plumage over and over, and rub his head coaxingly, my eyes on that barometer of a tail. The slow descent of his tailfeathers exactly paralleled the easing of his emotional tensions. By the time those long green plumes spilled across my lap and down to the floor like a waterfall, Bubble's eyes were closed in bliss.

"Wish you'd save a little of that for me," Mack would murmur enviously.

To which I'd reply, lightly but callously, "Bubbs has seniority."

The woodland house dissolved quickly under our inexorable hammers and levers, and we saved most of the wood for future use.

But we and the birds hadn't been the only residents.

Mack gently released a startled bat that he unexpectedly exposed one day. And I popped off an angled board above a long window only to reveal four beautiful deer mice huddled together, blinking in the sudden light. One trotted unhurriedly away as I cooed over them, then another also departed. But the last two remained longer, one washing its face and ears as though not feeling presentable at this unforeseen arrival of company.

Despite our exhausting task, which had to be completed on schedule so that the builders could begin the new house, we both paused in our labours to enjoy watching the mice.

One morning when we arrived to work, I picked up a tiny, baby deer mouse in the rooster run, grateful that I'd spotted it before Bubble. Chilled, naked, and blind, it lay in my hand twitching feebly, no doubt bewildered and fearful at this drastic separation from its mother's care. Perhaps she had been killed en route to a new nest, and had dropped her babe when struck. She may have become a necessary meal to nourish an owl. Though we warmed and fed her babe, we were unable to save it. Or to locate the rest of her litter. So we resumed work on the house, using extra caution.

But this youngster was just the forerunner.

Two days later, I found three older baby mice – too young to be on their own – crawling around the partially dismantled kitchen. We set them up in a little box, with a nest of cotton batting on top of a litter of shavings. Then we added one dish of mixed seeds, chopped apple, and cornmeal, and another of easily digestible goats' milk, which I tore into town to buy, and in which I soaked crackers. We also included a lump of peanut butter mixed with ground sunflower seeds and more cornmeal.

Mack lifted each baby in turn, their bodies looking drastically tiny and frail in his large fingers, and dipped each muzzle lightly into the warmed milk. The babes sneezed and blew bubbles but responded enthusiastically to the milky taste, licking valiantly in this novel method of nourishment. Afterwards, they washed themselves and each other to perfection and fell asleep in an enchanting warm huddle. Then we set them out of harm's way while we worked on.

The next day, we found three more babies wandering in search of their mother, fed them and added them to the slumbering heap. With growing concern, we combed the kitchen area until we

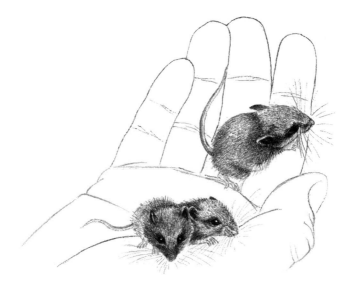

located the nest, still clean but now mercifully empty. Perhaps the mother had ventured outside to the bird feeders and been killed. In the wild, many youngsters vainly await their mothers, dwindling away finally from dehydration and starvation.

But these ones were lucky.

After several days, we released all the mice except the smallest, whom we felt was dying. He was so much tinier than the others that we were convinced that he originated from a different litter. We carried him back to the greater comfort of our temporary town home, and settled him into a corner of the bird room.

Unlike the others, he'd become sticky all over from milk and was suffering from diarrhea. He felt chilled, and seemed too weak to clean himself. Under a warm lamp, we washed him gently with cotton batting dipped in heated water, and kept him under the lamp until he was dry. But not close to the bulb lest he become overheated.

We also eliminated milk from his diet and offered bread soaked in water. He licked it half-heartedly, but when we offered peanut butter, mixed with cornmeal to lessen the stickiness, he *adored* it. He clutched it tightly in his minute paws, licking and chewing with great eagerness. After this response, we began to feel he'd survive.

We freshened his box, provided a shallow glass caster to hold his water so he couldn't soak himself as before, and built a thicker nest to substitute for the warmth of siblings. We also maintained the lamp, but only at one end, so he could move away from it if he wished.

He was obviously fighting so hard to live that we could do no less than support his effort.

Days passed and "Winner" gradually grew stronger. Most of his fur mysteriously fell out in patches, but his skin looked pink and healthy. He ate well, cleaned himself fastidiously as mice do, and eventually grew a beautiful coat. His eyes brightened and became knowing, and he scampered energetically around his box.

At last, a couple of weeks after we'd found him lost and hungry, we brought Winner back to the woods one morning. There, we released him in the stored hay of the old goatshed, and wished him well.

Then Mack and I resumed our daily labours of destruction, while Bubble scratched contentedly in the soil under the trees, devouring bugs with clucks of joy.

Mice do have a great measure of my sympathy, particularly because they're fated to have top billing on nearly every carnivorous menu in the natural world. But I've also always found them attractive as individuals. As an adolescent hemmed in by the sterile confines of city apartments, I found my narrow world brightened by my pet mice, who produced enchanting babies from time to time. I admired their shining eyes, soft glossy coats, and fastidious habits.

One lovely black creature and her snow-white mate produced a family of eleven brown babies *three times* in succession. Like all mouse mothers I've known, she was wonderfully caring. Her warm huddle of babies always smelled clean and fragrant whenever I laid my face gently next to them.

Built on a larger scale, "Barney," my white rat, was another of those clean, sweet-tempered rodents that are generally feared or despised. Barney, however, was one of my best friends during my teen years. Tucked warmly into the hooded collar of my jacket, he rode the subways and streetcars, travelled up and down escalators and elevators, and "shopped" in multi-level department stores. I delighted in his whiskery tickle against my neck and, when I turned my head, he'd lick my face affectionately.

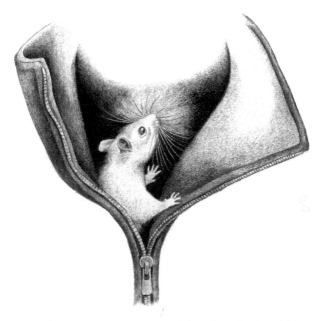

If I stopped in a restaurant to indulge that deplorable teenage craving for hot chips and gravy, Barney would slide down onto my lap, my opened jacket shielding him on either side from the "vulgar gaze." There he'd sit up, his nose twitching expectantly. I'd sneak him a chip, which he'd hold between his paws and nibble eagerly until it was finished. Then he'd wash his paws and face and stand up, sniffing hopefully for another.

Whenever he travelled inside my jacket, he'd restrain his basic needs until we returned home. Then he'd scamper over to the bathroom corner of his cage, where for one long minute he'd relieve himself with half-closed eyes of bliss.

Often he'd let himself out of his cage when I was asleep, root through the covers hanging over the sides of my bed, and push his way up between the sheets till he reached my head. Then he'd lick my face, curl up beside me, and fall asleep.

Once, when I was in a bank, the teller noticed Barney's peering face and questioning whiskers emerge from my hood. She seemed genuinely intrigued, which was a welcome change, since Barney's admirers were few.

"Isn't he sweet!" she exclaimed.

Just then Barney reversed and burrowed back behind my head, his long, bare tail braced briefly against my face for balance. The teller's eyes widened.

"But . . . what is he?" she asked uncertainly.

"A rat," I murmured fondly.

She screamed. And I fled.

The word, not Barney's appearance, was the problem. A rat by any other name would be sweeter in her eyes.

Once, Mack and I had to live-trap a wild rat that was gnawing great holes in the wall of the present bird hospice. The tested lure of peanut butter worked yet again, and in the morning a large rat with soft, brown fur and bright, anxious eyes awaited his fate. We drove him to a riverbank several miles away to continue his life, but what saddened me was the automatic response of loathing from other humans who heard about him. Their reaction was mixed with bewilderment that we didn't joyfully slay the creature when we had the chance. Our reply – that the rat was just another woodland rodent – fell on deaf ears.

Throughout the years, I've grown accustomed to sharing my house with mice. However, when other people complain about nighttime gnawings that rob them of sleep, or about clean clothes being soiled in dresser drawers by mouse urine, or about packages of food being chewed apart, I genuinely sympathize. An overrun of mice can be *wearing*. One compassionate solution is to live-trap and release them several miles away.

Some friends of mine, avid supporters of this last method, installed a large aquarium, liberally provided with food and water, as a "holding tank." When the numbers of captured mice in the tank bordered on crowding, they'd load it into the car and release them a long way from their farm. I enjoyed sharing supper at their table while several charming deer mice jostled each other for a good view of us through the glass tank. Enchanted, I would drop in savory tidbits as treats.

There was a particular female mouse, in the last stages of her pregnancy when captured, who responded to her sudden change of circumstances by producing a litter of minute babies. Her release had to be delayed till the youngsters were mature enough to handle the move.

One winter's evening, when the tank was brimming with mice, the woman was preparing to leave for an important meeting. She decided that emptying the tank, however inconvenient, could not be delayed much longer, lest the inmates create yet more inmates. She was supported by a female friend, and both women, suppressing their chronic nervousness around rodents, bravely lugged out the tumbling tankful, pressing the lid down securely.

Barely a mile down the road, she was forced to brake suddenly. The tank immediately lurched off the back seat, pitching the lid clear. In a triumphant burst, mice of every size and description poured down between the front seats like marbles out of a bag.

Both women screamed.

Then they clawed frantically out of the car, abandoning it in the middle of the road, doors wide and headlights blazing. Between their leaping feet, escaping mice fled into the darkness in all directions.

So much for the best-laid plans of mice and women.

I remember one evening, many years ago, deciding to go to bed early. I was unusually tired and out of sorts as I climbed the stairs to my sleeping loft above the living room. As I began to undress, I became aware of a peculiar scuffling, punctuated by soft squeaks. I peered in all directions, seeing nothing unusual, until I focussed beyond the railing above the expanse of living room.

There, set into the end gable of the house, just below the cathedral ceiling, was a six-foot-tall stained-glass window. The different colours of glass were not united, as is usual, by thin strips of metal. Instead, I had cut an intricate design out of wood and inset glass into each section. Now, scrambling desperately among the curves of wood from one section to another, unable to escape, was an adolescent deer mouse.

I groaned irritably. I just wanted to go to sleep. I did *not* want to spend the next hour devising some method of rescuing a mouse from such an outlandish situation.

But there was no choice. A ten-foot drop lay below him.

After several minutes of intense reflection, I finally dismantled my easel, strapped the three legs together in tandem to form one long pole, and improvised a net at one end out of a coathanger and a pillowslip. Then I grudgingly thrust the apparatus out over the railing towards the stained-glass window, manoeuvring the net awkwardly beneath the scrambling mouse.

Soon, I managed to joggle him into losing his foothold, but he failed to fall *into* the net as I had intended. Instead, he remained upright, clinging to the rim. I began carelessly to pull back the pole, the little mouse clutching helplessly to the rim of the net like a shipwrecked soul, watching me with wide, alarmed eyes.

Suddenly his vulnerability touched me. And his fear. I felt his dilemma from *his* viewpoint and my chilly self-centredness thawed.

With extreme care, I guided the pole with its trembling passenger until I could nudge him into a large jar. Then I released him outside.

The episode ended happily, but a touch of shame lingered in my memory as a gentle reminder that helping even the least of creatures is a privilege, *not* a nuisance.

Mice are an integral part of country life. I recall Mack and I driving home late one snowy night. At least two inches of pristine snow, unmarred by tire tracks, sparkled on the roadway. Ahead suddenly, in the full glow of the headlights, we saw a snowy lump cross the road rapidly before us, creating a long mound.

An unseen mouse was travelling below the snow's surface for protection from owls.

I remember, too, releasing a mouse near the woods. An enormous puddle lay before him as he scampered away from us. Without the slightest hesitation, he plunged in, swam to the other side, and emerged, still trotting as nimbly as ever, to blend immediately into the mouse-coloured terrain.

I've also spotted mice occasionally in the indoor garden. Sometimes I see a preoccupied mother with a mouthful of small baby, transferring her family to a new nest for reasons best known to herself.

One afternoon, many years ago, I was cleaning out the goatshed. A deep, well-packed base of hay, spotted with dry droppings, covered the floor. I dug and forked load after load onto the wheelbarrow, trucked it off, and dumped it nearby.

The work was heavy, the air warm and dusty, and I worked rapidly, longing to be finished. As I tipped one wheelbarrow load onto the outside heap, I paused – and stared at it unbelievingly.

Amid the musty litter, tiny forms were moving.

I peered closer, blowing off the chaff. To my acute dismay, I saw two baby mice, eyes still unopened, bodies barely furred.

I immediately nestled them within one sweaty hand while, with the other, I searched through the old hay, finally rescuing a third. Then I ran back into the goatshed, only to find a distraught mother mouse searching for her family.

I knelt down and placed the babies gently before her. She gave them a quick sniff, lifted one carefully in her mouth, and tottered away, tail angled high for balance. Twice she returned, each time lugging away yet another baby. When she returned the third time,

I was feeling carefully through the rubble of her home for more babies and she joined me in the search.

Knowing there *had* to be more, but not discovering any, was amplifying my anxiety.

Despite her own desperation, the mother showed not the slightest hesitancy in being beside me. In fact, at one point, she paused and sat up, one front paw touching my knee as I knelt, her eyes fixed compellingly on my face as I tried to speak reassuringly to her.

It was a moment I've never forgotten.

Shortly afterward, I found four more and she immediately carried them away. I'll never feel certain that all her babies were rescued, but the manifest way in which that mother mouse and I worked together to restore her uprooted family remains a special moment in my life.

Only a few years ago, I decided to take the axe and split a heap of old board ends into kindling for the winter. I had left these remnants from an earlier building project in the wheelbarrow, which I had rolled into the woodshed.

One after another, I split the boards into narrow lengths, gathered up the pieces, and dropped them into an empty feedbag. Nearly halfway through the heap, I was tugging another board free when a fleeting movement inside the wheelbarrow caught my eye.

I gently lifted a few pieces and discovered a very young mouse, agitated by the noisy shifting boards. A mouse too young to be alone.

That meant there were others.

Sure enough, a little more searching revealed a lovely, soft, clean nest with a round entrance. I probed cautiously into the nest and found, as I had expected, several warm, furry babies moving around restlessly.

The mother was absent, perhaps foraging, and I gently pushed the first mouse inside with the others. Then I carefully rearranged boards to disguise the nest from preying eyes until the mother's return.

My early years with pet mice had taught me that in two or three days those youngsters would be on their own. When I did check days later, the nest was empty, and I finished splitting my kindling. Thereafter I found a droll significance in the cuplike resemblance between nests and wheelbarrows.

Surprisingly, both could be cradles.

Not until the unwelcome appearance of two adult weasels in my living room did I absolutely *draw the line* at resident mice. The weasels, beady-eyed and hungry, had slipped through a mousehole, seeking their prey.

But weasels also eat birds.

With a constant, though ever-changing, feathered family to consider, I had to stop weasels being lured indoors by the scent of mice.

In one mammoth undertaking, I searched through the outside eaves and dismantled sections of inside walls, plugging every mousehole and crevice with metal screening and crack-filler. Then I began baiting the live-trap each evening with peanut butter, and releasing the inmates (sometimes two at a time) outdoors.

I realized I'd missed an entry somewhere after freeing one small mouse. He looked as though he'd been rolling all night in the too-generous dollop of peanut butter – his fur stuck up in greasy tufts and he looked distinctly annoyed. Later that morning, when I was busy in the kitchen, the very same mouse passed me, trotting hurriedly in a preoccupied manner – and still greasy.

Evidently, washing peanut butter out of fur is as difficult as removing chewing gum from hair.

I searched for that last mousehole, stopped it, and waited with growing satisfaction as the trap remained empty. Then followed three cameo performances by determined mice chewing through the dining-room ceiling at ungodly hours of the night, while I shivered in my nightgown on top of the table, contriving hasty repairs.

But eventually, the mice and I reached a compromise.

I lived, undisturbed, in the rooms, while they ruled, unchallenged, in the walls.

In this way, years of mutual peace had prevailed. But when Mack and I, in typical human style, broke the treaty and began pulling down the walls, we spent days enveloped in clouds of dust and mould as pounds of seed fell out repeatedly all over us – most of it a mixture of oats, barley, and cracked corn known as "chicken scratch." After one particular avalanche caught Mack broadside, he backed away coughing and croaked out, "You really *meant* it when you said you built this house from scratch!"

However, stored seeds were the least of our burdens. Worse was the chewed insulation from old nests that clung to our clothes and hair till we doubted if we'd ever get clear of the reek of mouse urine.

But two weeks of persistence pulled us through the gigantic task, and the fast-approaching date on which the builders would start pushed us from the rear.

By the eleventh hour, the site was cleared for action.

CHAPTER 3

OLD CARS AND A NEW HOUSE

When the new house began in September, Mack and I found ourselves busy from early morning until the workers dropped their tools at the end of the day. Sometimes, on our way back to the birds, and supper, we were too tired even to speak. The difficulties that naturally accompany such an undertaking were further intensified by unrelenting bad weather for four months.

Rain only ceased when the thermometer was so low that snow fell instead.

Thanks to the generosity of a neighbour, who had recently dismantled an old barn, we collected a number of handhewn hemlock beams to add ancient dignity to our new home. I'd had two in the old house, and these we had carefully saved. Varying in sizes, from six-by-six inches to fourteen-by-twelve inches, and in different lengths, these beams lay heaped in an empty pasture. We climbed excitedly all over them, running our hands lovingly over the gentle undulations shaped by adze and broad axe, selecting those that would fit the house we had designed.

Then the neighbour good-naturedly loaded our chosen beams carefully onto a decrepit flatbed, which was held together by pure optimism, and set off for the site. Mack and I followed in our car, our anxious eyes on the load ahead.

The flatbed lurched and tugged at the frail pin in the hitch as though trying to break free, which one jolting pothole could easily have achieved. The whole body hung askew, with each wheel pointing in a slightly different direction. Our precious beams, sturdy, but liable to shiver if struck violently, bounced and lolled like matchsticks.

It was the only time we regretted the beautiful – but unending – hills and curves that grace our road.

And the only time we drove it without breathing.

But the gods were gracious to us that day, and we crawled to a stop near the site, with the load intact. Then we leaped out and wedged rocks around the flatbed's bald tires. Almost drunk with relief, we triumphantly levered and pivoted the great beams off, and stacked them neatly, numbering each one with chalk to correspond with numbered positions on the blueprint.

The beams were a noble gift, and even non-stop drizzle couldn't extinguish our glow.

Then Bubble appeared, having searched the vegetable garden for bugs, and flapped loudly up on top of our treasures, where he delivered ear-ringing crows – "fowl language" we could *all* understand.

We definitely had something to crow about.

That disjointed vehicle, which nevertheless served us well, released several memories of second-hand vehicles I had driven in my earlier, impecunious days, when ingenuity – not to say desperation – was my chief currency.

Foremost was a Volkswagen bug named "Lurch," whose impeccable body disguised an aging car with an expensive appetite for rebuilt engines – it devoured *three* while I had it. The shock-absorbers were non-existent, and every trip down my dirt road rattled the teeth in my head. Unable to afford new shocks – *or* new teeth – I hung tiny brass bells here and there inside, so that every bone-crunching jolt released a peal of delightful chimes that eased the physical torment.

Every vehicle has its foibles, and the next one, "Clementine," was liberally endowed. Having frequently denounced her lineage in graphic terms, I found her easy to classify:

Kingdom: mechanical enemies
Phylum: internal combustion engines
Class: passenger vehicles
Order: Volkswagen
Family: family car
Genus: bug
Species: beetle

Clemmie's windshield wipers were prone to Chronic Fatigue Syndrome and, after one arduous trip across the windshield, refused to rise again to the occasion. Only if I reached out the side window while driving, and *prodded* them, could I convince them to make one more trip across and back.

On rainy days, this method left half my body soaked, so I devised a solution to fit my scant finances. I attached a cord to the left wiper, ran it up the windshield behind the roof rack and in through the passenger window. As I drove, I pulled the cord in a continual rhythm to activate the wipers.

Unfortunately, driving in town traffic during rainfalls or snowstorms was a trifle cumbersome – I could either shift gears, or see where I was going, but not both.

Then the brake pedal began to stick, often refusing to rise after it had been pushed down. My mother unwisely borrowed the car at this point – fortunately during sunny weather – and drove into town. At the main intersection, during the noon rush, she braked to a halt before the red light.

And there she remained.

Nobody could budge that car, although various irate male drivers swaggered up, only to back away, baffled, before I got a frantic, teary call for help. Being without a vehicle, I had to hitch-hike ten miles into town, an hour-long feat which further inflamed the situation.

By the time I arrived, the local traffic had created unusual solutions to the congestion, and cars were milling everywhere. My mother, mortified to her soul, was standing near Clementine, trying unsuccessfully to appear a mere onlooker. Several red-faced men were also on hand, and they stared contemptuously as I hastily slid behind the wheel.

As I suspected, the brake pedal was flat on the floor. I hooked it up with my toe, started the engine, and drove around the corner – to the collective astonishment of my male audience. My mother soon joined me, and we fled the scene of the crime.

Flushed from my victory over the windshield wipers, I used the same solution for the recalcitrant brake pedal, and tied a cord to it, so I could jerk it back up as needed. Clemmie, not to be outdone, began withholding her gas pedal as well – so I added another cord.

Now I drove with two reins in my hands to control the *mechanized* horsepower, as well as a steering wheel and a manual shift. The system was further complicated when downpours forced me to operate the wipers as well.

I felt as though I were challenging the dexterity of Shiva, the four-armed Hindu god.

I'll never forget driving my mother to a distant weekend convention. When the day of departure arrived, rain – of course – fell steadily. My mother climbed in beside me, looking askance at all the cords, and I put one in her hand.

"Just keep pulling," I remarked cheerfully. And so she did. For two hundred and fifty miles, she operated the wipers, pulling down the cord over and over with a rhythm similar to that used in milking a cow, while determined rains hammered on the windshield. Meanwhile, I continually pulled a second cord to adjust the gas, and a third to release the brake, disentangling myself as necessary in order to move the gearshift by hand as well.

Only when our destination finally rose before us did she mutter that universal complaint of overtaxed parents everywhere, as she stared unbelievingly at her offspring.

"This is what I get for rolling my own instead of adopting!"

The names of the North American car that followed Clemmie were numerous – and unrepeatable. The engine started not when I turned the key, but when it felt inclined to do so. Usually, I had my better clothes on and was in town, trying to remain presentable. But as soon as the car, which had been operating normally for several hours, silently ignored me after I turned the key, I knew there was just one solution – to open the hood, reach down through a maze of unidentifiable, dirty, greasy machinery, and twiddle the starter.

Not until I had filthy stains up to my shoulder would the brute start.

That car definitely *craved* attention. Not for it the gracious anonymity of those who serve. I recall driving absentmindedly along the Trans-Canada Highway when the hood suddenly flew up before me and crashed into the top of the windshield, completely blocking my view of the road. By some miracle I kept cool, slowed down immediately, and guided myself over to the shoulder by watching the centre line through my side window. Only when stopped did I begin shaking from head to toe from shock.

When I had recovered to the point when I could fluidly curse that car and all its forebears, one by one – and *did* – I climbed out on watery legs and tied the hood down with shoelaces.

Cars, if not woolly, can certainly be wild.

By comparison, the day that car dropped part of its exhaust system on the highway was a breeze. A sudden, shrill scraping noise had broken out as I was driving, alerting me to yet another move by my antagonist in that endless struggle between us for supremacy. I pulled over, assessed the situation, then lay on the roadside, cars and transfer trucks roaring past only a few feet from my legs. Grim-faced and muttering ominously, I tied up the dragging pipe with my belt.

"Check!" I snarled, as I climbed back in – although, having relinquished my belt and shoelaces to that car, I felt more like I was playing a game of strip poker than chess.

I had better luck, mechanically, when I switched to a truck, and more room to lug paintings. But the body rusted so badly that, as I glanced down at the road whizzing past between my feet, I predicted that soon the whole truck would look more like a sit-down lawn mower.

I rivetted sheet metal all over the floor, and covered rusty eruptions and gaping holes on the body with duct tape in order to pass inspection. But the tape gradually disintegrated in silvery flutters, leaving patches of white adhesive over the affected areas. It also needed to be renewed a year later, when vehicle inspection time again approached.

The roof leaked so persistently that I needed a raincoat and hood inside on wet days, even *after* the sun began to shine outside – a problem I solved by tarring the top of the entire roof.

The standard shift on yet another truck jammed periodically between first and second gears, utterly immobilizing me. The occasion that left the deepest scar occurred at the toll gate of the Halifax–Dartmouth bridge just after I'd flung my money into the receptacle and the light had switched to green. At rush hour, naturally.

With this difficulty, the clutch pedal had to be depressed constantly while, with the hood up, I climbed up onto the bumper, reached down into the bowels of the engine (why is the solution always at the *bottom* of the engine?) and released a lever – a mechanism that, in my more frantic moments, received a number of unprintable appellations.

Being inside the cab and under the hood simultaneously was beyond my ingenuity, so I always kept a short board in the truck. Wedged between the seat and the clutch pedal, the board gave me the time needed to disengage the lever in the engine.

The next vehicle was a cargo van which tore along the roads so enthusiastically that I frequently had to replace the brake linings. It was the epitome of dependability, but of course each vehicle has its chronic problem – in this case, it was the back doors. For the first year, they were so inoperable that at last they became *seized* shut, squealing shrilly when attempts were made to disturb them. Their stubbornness was beyond any of my homegrown solutions, and not until a professional mechanic battled with them for three hours did the hinges function properly.

The handle, however, retained a mind of its own.

Only too clearly do I recall arriving in Halifax with the van packed to the ceiling with large canvases for a show. Any remaining spaces held boxed sculptures. Mack and I were together by that time, and when he walked around to the back of the van, grasped the handle, and pulled, it came off in his hand.

There was the show, ready to hang, and no way to get at it.

Another time, we had a complete show loaded into the van for an exhibit in a distant town. I had stopped at our local gallery to pick up one last piece, when the entire exhaust system fell off on Main Street.

Sometimes I think a llama, accustomed to lugging packloads in the Andes, would be the solution. Mechanized vehicles, though equally endowed with personality, don't seem to possess the necessary stamina.

Fortunately, that same van proved invaluable during our house-building project, hauling loaded cardboard boxes to our temporary home day after day, as well as rubbish to the landfill site. Innumerable trips were made to town when various needs arose, and even a few smaller beams were transported safely. The van was a godsend.

And *nothing* fell off.

Our new house rose steadily, despite the unending drizzle, which was varied by downpours and blowing sleet. We all wore rain gear resignedly, but mitts and gloves never stay dry, and I, for one, despaired of ever having warm hands again. With the weather so much worse, we left Bubble, disappointed but infinitely more comfortable, in his section of the bird room when we departed each morning.

Near the stacked beams, I worked at carving a great dragon out of basswood to use as a railing for our staircase. Flurries whirling past on a north wind numbed my hands as I chiselled steadily, day after day. My old studio, with its large north windows, had been warmed more by the vibrant colours on the canvases than by the portable electric heater by my booted feet.

Though I'd often worked with an insulated jacket on as well as mitts, in comparison with this outdoor arrangement, the old studio seemed luxurious.

"To think," I wailed mockingly to a passing carpenter, who glanced commiseratingly at my red nose and stamping feet, "that I *believed* him when he promised me a warmer studio. Men are such deceivers!"

The weeks slogged on.

One by one, the great, grey beams were cut and set skilfully into their designated places, where they remained in unassailable dignity, admired by visitors and workers alike. The second storey was eventually topped by rafters and roofing which, to everyone's relief, gave shelter from the rain and snow, if not from the cold. On bitter days, snow blew in through the window openings, creating drifts in the corners. When actual windows were finally put in, the relief from the elements was tremendous – except for those hammering on the board-and-batten siding outdoors.

As soon as a chimney was installed in the new studio, above the old one, "Grannie" the woodstove was set in place. When the warmth of the first fires began to offset the chill, the carpenters thankfully took all their breaks around the stove. I moved the dragon carving inside for electric sanding, utilizing the coils of loose wires with attached multiple outlets that lay underfoot everywhere. Slowly a sense of home began to emerge from the upheaval.

Beyond the windows, great trees that had withstood all challenges for decades radiated strength and stability, and even comfort – reminding me that calm always follows chaos.

Ancient lamps, formerly from a convent, eventually hung from the pine ceiling. Our collection of solid, panelled doors, in birch and maple, would mellow the stark walls. After the dragon, I carved a rooster's head, beak open and crowing a challenge. The carpenters built it into the portico over the front door – which actually opens on the *back* of the house. Two more hewn beams were set below the rooster, on either side of the door.

A skilled mason, working with local sandstone, built a masonry stove that resembled a fireplace for beauty, but far surpassed it in efficiency. In the depth of winter, only two short – but hot – fires a day would be needed to heat the great mass of stone so that it could radiate warmth for twelve hours, or longer. In the front of the stove, the mason set a circular stone carving that Mack and I had completed, depicting a mother robin and her youngster amid the spiralling energies of fiddlehead ferns.

The six-foot stained-glass window that I'd created and built into my previous home had been carefully preserved and installed high in the western wall of our living room. Even the dreary, grey light outside was transformed as it passed through the rich colours. It glowed on the new walls and enriched the pine cathedral ceiling.

When the sun finally shone again, I knew that a mingling of vibrant colours would glide silently, imperceptibly, through the new house, like a welcoming aura.

During one weekend, Mack and I coated the ceiling with mellowing linseed oil, while moving cautiously along rickety staging ten feet above the floor. Looking down with trepidation, I decided that the thought of falling was rendered even more undesirable by the great chunks of stone that still littered the floor from the unfinished chimney.

As the year drizzled to a close, the final stages were completed. Stonework was pointed, and the cement began its necessary drying before the first fire could be lit. Brown maple flooring – appropriately with "birds' eyes" gleaming here and there – was laid, then sanded and urethaned. Walls were painted, a more durable floor covering installed in the studio, and a roof deck added. The hospice and the old studio (which would be transformed into a workshop) had been reattached and sealed to the main house – no doubt delighting the mice who were sheltered in them. In the living room, under a southwest window as before, Mack and I built another indoor garden with two tall trees, in readiness for the birds.

The new kitchen bore little resemblance to the old. Now I was surrounded by multiple cupboards, acres of counter space, drawers that glided open with a smile instead of being *levered* open with curses and brute strength.

Best of all, there was enough room for both Mack and *any number* of jars of honey.

In our temporary home each night, we chafed with impatience to be back permanently in our woodland world, and even the birds seemed subdued, as though dispirited by the continual rumble of traffic.

Then tragedy struck.

Bubble jumped down from my lap one night and fell on his back, dead instantly. In professional consultations later, it was considered a brain death, like an aneurysm – the same disorder that had killed Squeak. There'd been no struggle, no gasping, and his eyes remained closed, not half-open as is usual when dying is slower. Stricken, I froze his body so I could return it to the country world he'd loved.

The blow was terrible. Bubbs and I were *so close.*

Aching with loss, I saw him everywhere: outside, his long green tailfeathers held high and twisting in the wind – or on wet days, sloped to the ground, so the rain could run off. I missed his reddish-gold eyes, edged dramatically in dark, with a constant star in each, always seeking contact with mine. The touches of sun on his brilliant plumage.

His congenial warmth in my lap, his closed eyes and soft snores. The times he drooled with bliss as I patted him, his head

lying on my shoulder. Or other occasions when he'd thrust his head under my arm, like a chick under a mother's wing, needing extra hugging.

His own obvious grief when Squeak died.

Every evening, I missed Bubbs standing on my lap so he could press his face close to mine. Missed the great warmth of comb and wattles against my cool cheek.

Missed, too, the way he'd come on the run if I called or whistled, his eyes alight, knowing he'd be scooped up and hugged in a whirl of fun.

Our last night together lingered in my memory, when he stood on a stool by the kitchen counter at suppertime, eating strips of cucumber seeds while I tossed a salad. The warm pasta he loved was already planned for his breakfast.

How difficult for people, who have never experienced chickens on such a personal level, to comprehend such a loss. If Bubble had been a dog, they could tolerate my sorrow. And, if they were dog lovers themselves, could even empathize sadly.

But if Bubbs had been a dog, he couldn't have been a more loyal, loving companion. How irrelevant, after all, are our external appearances.

I recall a woman, with the furtive manner necessary to any admirer of chickens, telling me about one of her hens who used to come into the house, jump up on a chair, and sit there beside the cat, watching television. The delight that lit the woman's eyes was equalled only by her sadness that the hen, too, was no more.

And by her relief that she could speak freely, without fear of ridicule.

Bubble's death in the town house accelerated our longing to return to our own home. As soon as the urethaned floors were dry, we began the arduous task of moving carloads of boxes and furniture once again, distributing them to their designated rooms. Friends pitched in and helped, working long hours packing and unpacking vehicles, eating sandwiches hastily at odd moments, bringing us closer to home with each trip.

On New Year's Day, when the cement in the masonry stove had finally dried enough to allow fires to be laid, we took the birds, a box of groceries (mostly mixed birdseed and mealworms), and our clothes, and fled the urban world.

As though in celebration, the persistent clouds finally dissolved, and sunshine sparkled on the snow-laden trees around us, like a welcome.

We had come home.

CHAPTER 4

WOODS AND WILDLINGS

The birds were delighted with their new surroundings, but their obvious perplexity amused us. After all, the indoors was entirely different, yet the familiar views outside the new, bigger windows remained unchanged.

And judging by Beejay's sudden enthusiastic screeches, answered with equal intensity from a wild jay outdoors, his mate still survived. It was in hope of just such a reunion that we'd maintained our bird feeders during the long months of building.

Chip *adored* her new domain. Though in some ways similar to her old home, the new one was bigger, with more flyways. And brighter, with more windows facing in different directions. She had been caught and thrust, gently but ignominiously, into a medium-sized cardboard box, with one solid side replaced by screening. Throughout the ride home, just as during her previous journey to the town, she'd periodically squawked her outrage at such treatment. Then in the living room, as soon as I opened the box, she shot out, and up, up, *up* – into the glorious new space.

Around and around above our heads she swooped before clutching onto the heavy chain suspended from the centre of the pine ceiling. The chain held our long, narrow cathedral lamp that glowed like a blessing when illuminated. Wide-eyed, Chip clung to the chain, peering in all directions: at the two tall trees in the indoor garden, with Beejay leaping from branch to branch. At Bashō puttering among the plants under the trees. At Mack and I below, watching her with upturned faces of delight. But most of all, at the spaciousness everywhere, so perfect for flight.

And so perfect for getaways after causing mischief.

Bashō, after checking out the new garden, popped out of it like a grasshopper and set off for a quail's-eye view of the rest of his kingdom. Only when his elderly legs had exhausted themselves trotting through the kitchen, laundry room, hallway, and bathroom, did he avail himself of the little "seniors'" ramp that assisted him back over the wall of the garden. There, he restored his tissues with a satisfying drink. But often, during the next few days, we caught glimpses of Bashō diligently "checking his fences," exploring rooms that, from the eyes of one only six inches from the floor, must have seemed vast.

One night, Mack woke up and padded downstairs, past the undulating dragon stair rail, on his way to the bathroom for the usual reason – only to discover Bashō standing in the dark, facing the toilet.

Mack confessed later that he almost felt he had to wait in line.

As though Bubble had passed on his stewardship, Bashō now crowed every morning at dawn, his surprisingly powerful call bursting out of the dawnlit garden to prod insistently at our slumbering forms. Soon afterward, Chip would be up and doing, shattering gentle sunrises with her strident shrieks. She was followed very quickly by Beejay's shrill outbursts responding to the outside jays as they arrived in good appetite at the feeders. Unlike the other house birds, Beejay's vocalizations were reserved strictly for his own kind.

Except when he sang.

Never had I associated such melodic beauty with blue jays – soft, rippling trills and warbles, often harmonizing as though *two* birds were singing, and accented with sudden resonant notes from the percussion section. His song flowed out gently as though he'd been transformed into a choir of warblers, and we'd stop our activities to listen, entranced.

The unsociable Molly was installed on a wide shelf in the new, upstairs studio. This removed her from the other birds, not only because she preferred it, but also because of her deplorable tendency to bully. Chip and Beejay being out of reach, Molly celebrated the new home by invading the indoor garden and intimidating Bashō. We quickly hung a door on the studio to restrict her villainous forays.

But to Molly's annoyance, even "her" studio had to be shared.

And in mild-mannered Edna, Molly met her match.

Though she swooped down two or three times to register her disapproval of bunking with a *rodent*, Molly was intimidated by Edna's large, furry form. Edna would hop over, ears erect with curiosity, until Molly, backing up hastily, would finally turn and take wing. Edna would hop to a surprised standstill, her long ears monitoring Molly's flight like two radar dishes.

Not being power-hungry, Edna enjoyed her new studio life.

Unfortunately, she also enjoyed new *chewing* sensations, and one day, she discovered my shelf of art books, which I had lovingly collected over many years. She hopped along, sniffing the various book spines, until she came to one with MUNCH in bold letters.

And immediately *obeyed*.

Though Edvard Munch's last name, being Norwegian, is *not* pronounced like a command to eat, Edna was convinced otherwise, and half the spine fell victim to her vigorous teeth before I discovered her. Soon, I was devising barriers before my books that would prevent her from destroying them, yet still allow me to find each one as it was needed.

Though both Ednas of our acquaintance obviously had a penchant for books, only Edna Staebler could be trusted near them.

The studio soon became our favourite rendezvous in the evenings. With Grannie's doors opened wide, like arms held out in welcome, and bright flames dancing fluidly before us, we cozied down in our chairs with books, birds, Edna, and a pot of home-grown herbal tea. Beyond the great studio windows, stars gleamed between dark splotches of spruce foliage or among the netted branches of birches.

One quiet night, with Bashō tucked under my shirt and Chip perched on my knee, I offered them a drink of water. As usual Bashō swallowed a few times, as though waking his throat muscles, then took several drinks, seizing the water each time in jabs. Chip, too, accepted a drink, but her playful nature immediately exploited the moment. She lifted another beakful of water and dropped it on my fleece sleeve, her eyes glinting as she watched the water break into beads which she then pursued, one by one, until she'd imbibed them all.

Edna's delight, at times like these, was to lie beside our chair while we rubbed her fur, over and over. Like bookends, her ears would be vertical and back to back, facing east and west. After a while, she'd flip over onto one side in order to get the upper side "done." Then onto that side, so as not to neglect the first.

Our "easy over" rabbit, done to perfection.

But her absolute preference was to be rubbed up and down her face between her eyes, with occasional detours behind her whiskers. During such ecstasy, her ears would droop to half-mast and her eyes, nearly closed, would glaze over drunkenly.

Even her nose would cease its tireless twitching.

As dogs convey happiness by wagging their tails, and cats by purring, so Edna's contentment was expressed by *licking*. After her back rubs, the rug below her chin would bear damp testimony to her delight. Or, if she'd been lying on the floor, we could be assured of *one* clean patch to shame the rest.

But if other activities should drastically reduce our attentions to Edna, she'd bring this omission to our notice – emphatically. She'd toss cushions onto the floor, or – worse – chew holes in them. She'd seize a small chunk of firewood on the stack near the stove, and hurl the wood again and again into the metal heat shield. If this ruse failed to get results, she'd "play poker" by seizing the heavy poker *in her teeth* and flipping it repeatedly onto the bricks that support the stove. This created an uproar that terrified me the first time I heard it – while I was showering. I thought someone was breaking into the house.

With minimal rehearsing, Edna could provide plausible sound effects for Handel's "The Harmonious Blacksmith."

Hell hath no fury like a rabbit ignored.

One of Edna's most avid admirers was a little seven-year-old girl. As soon as she met Edna, the girl crouched eye-to-eye with the rabbit and began wiggling her nose up and down with deep gravity. Intrigued, Edna sniffed all over the young face before her, causing convulsive giggles with those tickly whiskers. Then she gave the girl a brief licking on the nose and began to hop back to the food dish.

Entranced, the little girl crouched down and followed Edna, hop for hop. Around and around the studio, even under furniture, they hopped in tandem, Edna obviously puzzled but seemingly unalarmed, her follower convinced in her own imagination that she was no longer human.

It was a charming encounter between rabbits.

Living in the woods again was marvellous. There was so much to *see*. So much to *absorb*.

We rose early one morning and looked into a huge pink shell of a sunrise, barred with purple clouds, that glowed at the bottom of the ocean of sky – but in the *south*. Such an auspicious beginning *had* to lead into an unusual day, and so it proved.

We breakfasted with open windows, planning a hike in this remarkably warm, sunny weather. Only shallow snow whitened the land, and we were eager to see again our familiar trails and favourite trees. As the sweet air freshened the house, it almost seemed as though spring, longing, as we had, to return to these northern hills, had sneaked back before her proper season.

But Janus, the two-headed god of January, was looking both ways and spotted the usurper.

A huge, black cloudbank swept in rapidly from the northwest, as though in response to Janus's command, and the temperature dropped five degrees in ten minutes. The landscape darkened with disquieting speed, while the mercury still plummeted. We closed all the windows with regret. The freshness sweeping in caressingly had sharpened into biting teeth when the cold registered triumphantly at zero.

However, by the time we'd donned long underwear to augment our thick boots and insulated mitts, the sky had rebelled and chased the clouds away. Sunshine kindled the snow once more and the thermometer ventured cautiously up again, like a white flag in the celestial tumult.

Truly, we were in for one of those yo-yo winters.

We left the house and stepped into the hayfield, plunging immediately into white brilliance that stabbed our narrowed eyes with needles of light. The usual sense of dark solidity under our feet was obliterated by sudden brightness, as though the ground had fallen away, making us feel almost weightless. Blue-jay calls resonated in the crystalline air till we marvelled that it didn't shatter into glittering splinters. Millions of tiny suns shone out from the warmed snow as though newly hatched by the parental orb brooding above.

We swam through the blinding glitter to the top of the drumlin that rises so abruptly and steadfastly in a neighbouring field, and paused on the summit, turning in slow circles on our snowy pivot. Our aching eyes sought the quieter beauty of the wooded hills that undulated all around us like great caterpillars, the dense spires of dark spruces probing the open fretwork of leafless hardwood trees.

Then we dove back down into the engulfing dazzle and surfaced by the path that flowed unobtrusively through the woven blue shadows of the trees.

Deer tracks tattooed the snow on established trails; other, erratic, ones branched spontaneously in response to good browsing. Or to pressure from predators. Double perforations of mouse tracks, entwined with the larger leaps of squirrels, led out from and vanished under stumps, overhanging banks, and fallen trees. Or sometimes ventured to the edge of a cupping of meltwater for a drink. Snowshoe-hare tracks congregated in thickets where nibbles were plentiful, or struck the areas of open snow in six-foot bounds, seeking cover from the threatening sky. The occasional tread of a fox or a wildcat evoked an aura of stealthy silence in the bustling community. The stately steps of a passing grouse lent quiet dignity.

We wandered contentedly through the woods, weaving our own footprints into the intricate web around us, Mack eagerly leading the way while I dawdled behind, distracted by subjects for potential drawings.

A clean set of prints crossed the trail before me, having miraculously escaped Mack's canoe feet.

"Look!" I called out. "Donkey tracks!"

Mack peered round at me questioningly.

"Really!" I added, nodding vigorously. He took the bait and retraced his steps to where I was standing, pointing at the snow.

"That's a *deer* track," he scoffed – but suspiciously – trying to spot the snare that experience taught him *had* to be hidden in my words.

"Not at all," I remarked serenely, reeling in my victim. "Watch!"

I pulled off my mitt, crouched down and traced a muzzle below the print with my finger. Then two eyes and a neck out to the side. Suddenly the elongated curves of the deer's hoof became long ears on a donkey's face turned benignly towards us.

"Donkeys are everywhere," I added wickedly, and stepped past him, leading the way down the trail.

Stiffened, bleached beech leaves trembled on saplings in the breezes, their sound reminding me irreverently of Bubble and Squeak when, each with one lowered, rigid wing vibrating against the nearest spur, they'd advance on Mack, buzzing like rattlesnakes.

Or, more pleasantly perhaps, the leaves rustled like a peacock's tail spread alluringly – and fruitlessly – before the disinterested eyes of his hens.

Brook waters, always rushing away yet always present, jolted frenetically between their icy banks, disappeared under unmarred snow that lay like visible silence, burst out again further away – dark, sparkling, and wholly irrepressible – only to submerge once more.

Above our heads, descending branch by branch for a closer scrutiny, chickadees called, their black caps worn so low that only twinkles revealed their curious, dark eyes. Higher still, flitting about in the spruce tops, chimed the kinglets, whose round, even-tinier bodies make the chickadees look large. Almost clumsy.

As we turned towards home finally, one more straggle of deer tracks crossed before us. "Another donkey," Mack chuckled.

"Rabbit," I corrected.

"I mean these ones," he added, pointing to a clear hoof print at his feet.

"Exactly. A rabbit." And I leaned down, drew a circle below the "ears," added whiskers, eyes, and a round body, while Mack laughed delightedly at animal tracks turning into animals.

"To think that at your age you can't tell a donkey from a rabbit." I shook my head, and began the homeward trek.

"At *your* age," I repeated, sadly.

We floated home through the beauty around us, back to an austere, new house where raw windows called out for oiled wood framing; where bookcases needed to be built before more books, alas, could be unpacked; where the big painting table had to be attached to the studio wall before I could begin work for an upcoming show; where plywood scraps waited to be amalgamated hastily into a temporary writing desk.

And where inside doors still demanded to be hung – especially the one for the new, "Mack-sized" bathroom. Although, as a friend suggested, if I required privacy while using the facilities, I could always put a bag over my head.

But sightings of wild creatures from the windows often lured us from our tasks. What at first glance we'd taken for a smallish grackle with a tail still lengthening after a moult turned out to be an immature rusty blackbird – a rarer bird in our area. After Mack scattered seed each day and filled the feeders, nine red squirrels descended from the trees to join the jays, evening grosbeaks, tree sparrows, and grey voles in a communal feast. Deer ventured close most days in small groups, anywhere from five to thirteen, seeking the apples we often tossed outside the door for them.

Up in the studio, I raised my eyes to encounter the calm stare of a ruffed grouse on a branch only a few feet from the window. In the fields beyond, a flurry of snowbirds swirled past just as real snowflakes began to drift down. Outside the studio window, redpolls, tree sparrows, and pine siskins vied for the tantalizing mixture of canary and niger seeds in the silo feeder. There were goldfinches, too, mingled with the others, looking in their dull winter plumage as though their brilliant summertime yellows had been washed out in the autumn rains.

But *some* of the wildlings wanted indoors.

One day, while I was unpacking my paints in the disorder of the studio, Mack arrived with a feedbag stuffed with kindling. When he upended the bag over the large woodbox, tugging at the wedged wood chunks to loosen them, a mouse leaped out. Then another, and another.

One – with literary leanings – dashed across the floor and disappeared into a bookcase. A second eluded Mack's sudden grab and vanished like spilt water to the bottom of the half-filled woodbox. The third, sensing the lack of welcome, sprang about like a frenetic ping-pong ball in a bingo cage, while Mack clutched handfuls of air and I laughed helplessly. Then it, too, darted to the bottom of the woodbox.

Molly, from her royal shelf, watched with indignant eyes this intrusion of "vermin" into her domain, while Chip, ever ready to exploit situations for her own amusement, swooped after the first runaway as it scrambled among the books. Edna sat bolt upright, her ears like two black question marks and her nose twitching double-time.

Our primary concern was: *in which box had we packed the live-trap?*

Mice soon dominated our lives. Despite the illusion of a new, mouse-proof house, we were overrun. During the fall, they had nested in the old studio and hospice buildings while the new house rose in between, replacing the old one. When the three units once again became one, the mice – and all their enthusiastic progeny – flooded into the central living quarters with the rest of us.

Mice burrowed into the compost bucket under the sink, rode on the Lazy Susan like children on a merry-go-round, and boldly raided seed dishes in the indoor garden – often before our very eyes – where they were chased by a gleeful Chip. They trotted openly across floors, dodged in and out of rooms, and nested in bookcases. They stashed sunflower seeds in the toe of one of Mack's boots.

One evening, visitors stopped in. They were planning renovations of their own, especially in the kitchen. As Mack was demonstrating some of the desirable features of our own – the easy glide of drawers, two-sided access in a pull-out pantry – he chanced to open the cupboard under the sink in order to elaborate on the adjustable hinges.

Fortunately, at that moment the visitors' eyes were on Mack's face as he spoke.

But I, watching light flood into the dark cupboard as the door swung open, was treated to a perfect view of a multitude of agile mice suddenly springing like grasshoppers out of the compost bucket. They vanished just before the visitors looked inside – wondering, no doubt, why we left the lid lying *beside* a container with such noisome contents strewn about. Not knowing if the visitors had any fear of mice, I remained silent and turned away, eyes streaming with suppressed mirth.

During another memorable evening, we watched a mouse gingerly making its way down a bamboo wall directly behind a visitor's head. For the same reason, we both refrained from exposing our little woolly neighbour, but the sheer comedy of the situation reduced our conversational exchanges to watery-eyed incoherence.

Using one live-trap against such odds seemed comparable to bailing out the well with a teacup, so we borrowed several more and launched into a concentrated catch-and-release program that went on for months.

Often, we caught two in a trap simultaneously – bonus points for us.

Oftener, a trap was sprung, but empty – one point for the mice.

Despite our desire to vanquish them, we held to our rule of freeing a nursing mother *inside* the house, so she could tend to her babies. Thus, when we caught a youngster just setting out in his career, we knew we were in for a dozen more from that litter alone.

Releasing a pregnant female *outdoors* called for a celebratory drink.

Not until all the traps remained empty for weeks and the cupboards stayed clean did we feel that the house had finally become ours.

CHAPTER 5

STUDIO PERSONALITIES

The new studio, though closely surrounded with tall, elderly trees, was illuminated by seven windows and two skylights, creating a bower of light – even when herds of dark clouds wandered over to lie moodily above, day after day. But although I rejoiced in the increased brightness, it made Chip feel too vulnerable.

No matter which direction she faced, she felt invisible predators behind her. All perching possibilities seemed to expose her like a spotlight. Even when she was sitting in familiar safety on my shoulder, her eyes would be saucer-round, her head in constant movement to catch the enemy leering over her shoulder.

In such a room, only three-headed Cerberus could have maintained perfect vigilance.

But Chip, never one to surrender, persisted in making nervous forays into the studio, scuttling under chairs suddenly, or vanishing under the woodstove at the slightest alarm. Her loud, abrupt flights, accompanied by shrill squawks, disrupted the peace I needed for creative work. When she finally began to sense protection, not just visibility, from the surrounding glass, and to relax in consequence, I was greatly relieved – for *both* of us.

But Chip's returning equanimity meant creating entertainment for herself – usually by making victims of the rest of us. She began one day by raiding Molly's sanctuary, throwing seeds out of her dish all over the floor until Molly, rumbling irritably, marched along her shelf and drove her away. But later, while Molly padded about the floor, exploring her new studio home, Chip swooped back up to the forbidden shelf. There she climbed into Molly's waterdish and churned up a bath, spraying water all over the rest of the seeds as well as trickling it down the walls to form little puddles on the floor. Even the ceiling was splattered.

When she was satisfactorily saturated, Chip flapped heavily over to the drying rack above the woodstove. But not in a straight flight. Instead, she detoured through my side of the room in order to scatter droplets all over the painting in progress – a ploy guaranteed to raise a howl and waving arms from me. Then she perched smugly above the heat, preening her feathers with satisfaction.

I suspect both Molly and I harboured a certain regret at the restoration of Chip's confidence.

Many creatures have shared studio space with me, though not all were wildlife.

In earlier years I was joined by a beautiful grey cockatiel, possessing expertise in destruction that would shame a skilled rodent twice his size. What that bird could do to a painted, varnished canvas during a moment's reflective nibble doesn't bear remembering. His cheery whistles – which were more enjoyable when they didn't erupt without warning during my times of intense concentration – together with his studio home, earned him the name "Whistler."

Determined to enjoy his piercing blasts, I decided to direct his raw talent into more harmonious channels and began whistling, over and over, one of the catchier parts of the *1812 Overture*. Before long, to the amusement of others besides me, Whistler too could deliver the *1812* perfectly. Later, he began to create his own "Goldberg Variations."

The famous legal battle between the artist Whistler and the critic Ruskin provided an appropriate name for a second cockatiel who joined us a few months later. As though they were indeed incarnations of the original antagonists, both namesakes became immediate rivals. Even their personalities seemed to be polarized. Whistler exhibited a fluctuating temperament that was stereotypically artistic, whereas Ruskin, openly critical of Whistler's behaviour, was more culturally oriented, with a particular inclination towards languages.

When he arrived, he peered up at me out of the travelling cage and murmured politely, "Good morning. How are you?" It was the only time I've ever been floored by such a commonplace query. When I began setting out his food dishes, he climbed up my arm to my shoulder. There, with every evidence of interest in my actions, he inquired casually, "What are you *doing?*"

Ruskin ignored Whistler's obsessive renderings of the *1812 Overture* – perhaps having no ear for music – but Whistler, like an artist whose technical ability exceeds his originality, soon copied Ruskin's distinctive vocabulary. Often, after I separated the two, following yet one more skirmish, they would hiss at each other, with crests raised, while asking in solicitous tones, "How *are* you?" Or perhaps indignantly, "What are you *doing?*"

Then, as likely as not, the *1812 Overture* would ring out as a final challenge in duet form.

Even mornings began like the opening farce of a burlesque. When my frumpy, middle-aged self lumbered on stage, enthusiastic cries of "Hello! Hello!" would ring out with that peculiar parrot nasality, like an insistent voice out of a telephone. This was quickly followed by rakish wolf whistles that, if wasted on my grey hairs, would have gotten instant results on any corner downtown.

I felt I was living with repressed street urchins.

Another studio character from the past was Busybill, a duck – or, more correctly, a drake. He was obsessed with shoelaces, tugging and chewing on any that came his way, and I suspect my habit of wearing sandals winter and summer dates from my days with Busybill. But, like the cockatiels, he too could behave in ways that seemed more human than duck.

One evening, I had many hours of printmaking ahead of me – a process that consisted of taking an incised plate, rolling ink evenly all over the image, laying a sheet of hand-made paper on top, and rubbing the back of it carefully with a large spoon. This transferred the inked image to the paper, but was a slow, exacting job.

If the result was successful, forty-five minutes would produce a print, which was then blotted carefully and hung to dry. Later, each one would be signed and numbered in a limited edition.

If a mistake caused ink to spoil areas that should have remained blank, the whole sheet was discarded, the plate re-inked, and another effort made.

As most printmakers will attest, compared to the lively tensions involved in cutting the original plate, actual printing is *tedious*. Many artists hire someone else to do it. Not having that option, I was resigned to my fate.

Determined to alleviate the boredom somehow, I brought in my small black-and-white television from the living room and turned on the one available channel. Luckily, a nature program was in progress, and soon featured wild ducks. I glanced around inquiringly at Busybill, who was rooting through his mixed seeds, selecting favourites and transferring them to his water rather than eating them dry.

Ducks quacked. Ducks splashed. Ducks upon ducks flew calling above lakes on the television, but Busybill took not the slightest notice. He turned his back and preened.

I shrugged and carried on with my work. No one could tell me *anything* about the unpredictability of birds. But when the nature show was followed by Walt Disney cartoons, even *I* was surprised.

On came the famous Donald Duck, sailor suit and all, gabbling incessantly. Busybill, who'd fallen into a doze by my feet, leaped up as though electrified. In a flash he was at the screen, grabbing over and over at Donald Duck and quacking almost hysterically, while I laughed helplessly.

I can only hope that what he was expressing was annoyance at the parody, not the affinity of a long-lost brother.

One of the more unusual creatures to share my studio – though only briefly – was a brown bat, injured by a housecat seeking entertainment.

I tucked "Dingbat" into a small, dark box with a light towel spread over the top, and screened holes in the side for ventilation. Towelling inside gave him soft bedding on which to recuperate. Then I loaded an eyedropper with honey water.

When I held the dropper before him the first time, there was no response. Reflecting on the incredible auditory skills of bats, with their famous echolocation system for finding flying insects in darkness, I blew gently into one of his ears. Instantly, Dingbat lifted his head, and I touched the dropper to his mouth. To my delight, he swallowed some of the nourishing sweetness, then licked down the rest while I gently squeezed it out.

At the next feeding, I again blew in his ear and he followed me, if not "anywhere," at least to the dropper as before – with the same excellent results. Thereafter, whenever I lifted the towel, he turned his head and began licking the air till I touched the dropper to his tongue.

A day and a half later, Ding exhibited so much energy climbing around in his box that I carried it outside at dusk and freed him – with my blessing.

And with my hope that he wouldn't begin licking the air whenever a breeze tickled his ear. Like humans, conventional bats might resent original expression.

Mostly birds, however, have reigned in my studio, distracting me from my work by means fair and "fowl," so that by now I almost *need* some level of avian bedlam to further my concentration.

Even those familiar household budgies have contributed their share.

I first fell under their spell as a youngster trapped hopelessly in city apartments. Between one such character, "Carmen," and myself, a bond existed that still awes me.

Carmie climbed all over me like a feathered acrobat, and woke me each morning by walking all over my face and nibbling my eyelashes. She endured my nightly homework sessions better than I by turning them into play and chasing my pen as I wrote. She climbed down curiously into laden grocery bags, or up into kitchen cupboards when doors were left ajar. Once, when I'd been frantically searching for her for half an hour, I found her inside the *fridge*. She rode on the back of "Benny," my hamster, like a trick bareback rider at a circus – when she wasn't chasing him on foot and mercilessly tweaking his pink, half-inch-long tail.

I found Carmie utterly delightful, but my Siamese fighting fish, cruising moodily in his tank, thought otherwise. Between Carmie and "Buster" lay that unbridgeable gulf of cultural differences that has contributed to so many of our human wars.

She'd prance cockily along the edge of the aquarium, pausing frequently to lean down and sauce him, budgie-style. Roused, Buster would flare out his gill plate and fins, and his rich blue and wine-red colouring would deepen in intensity as he lashed about angrily. Then he'd break the water surface repeatedly, snapping at her, while Carmie hooked her claws firmly under the steel edging, leaned down, and snapped back.

I didn't actually witness Carmie delivering the long scratch that appeared mysteriously on Buster's head when I was away at school. But circumstantial evidence was definitely against her.

For the safety of both, I screened the top of the tank.

Between Buster and me, harmony prevailed. I often stuck my finger into his water to watch him glide gracefully over for our own special interaction. I'd gently turn my finger in circles and he'd twine around it with beautifully flaring fins, as though we were dancing together. Perhaps indeed there was an element of piscine courtship involved, despite the sterility of my eggless finger. But I had no reason to doubt his favourable feelings towards me. Or that he sensed they were mutual.

Then one day his budgerigar rival was nearly vanquished.

My mother, dashing off precipitately to work one winter morning, failed to notice Carmie perched on the thick collar of her coat. Only when Carmie, alarmed at the traffic and open sky that suddenly surrounded her, flew up into a tree, was the calamity realized.

My horrified mother, after racing back inside to explode her bombshell – thereby annihilating my languorous, pre-school torpor – wisely fled the scene.

Left to navigate my own way through the disaster, I instantly discarded all excess baggage – such as going to school that day, a decision to which I was always partial. Without thought of coat or wrap – fortunately I had already dressed – I bolted outside, calling desperately for Carmen.

Just as I finally spotted her in a tree, she took wing to another, and I galloped to the scene. But as I leaped up to grasp the lower branch, determined at all hazard to climb up, she flitted off to a third tree, alighting on a branch just outside the dormer window of a house.

I darted up the porch steps and banged peremptorily on the door. Then, without further hesitation, I barged inside, almost knocking down an old woman in the hall who had been approaching the door.

"My budgie!" I shrilled, pushing rudely past her and bolting up the stairs, two at a time. I chose what I guessed would be the correct bedroom door, jerked it wide open and burst in on an old man just pulling up his trousers.

His heavy eyebrows leaped so high that even in my own agitation I wondered fleetingly if they'd slide over the top of his bare dome and down the back.

He clutched his trousers defensively.

Gasping "My budgie! My budgie!" like one demented, I bounded past him to the sash window and jerked it up. There before me, perched calmly on a close branch, and twinkling with the novelty of this moment, was Carmie.

Ignoring the old man's roars, I climbed partially out the window, holding out my finger and chirping beguilingly. Behind me, I could hear the woman shouting as well – no doubt the old fellow was hard of hearing – but all I cared about was the tiny blue bird, so vulnerable in the chill, wintry damp. So endangered by the reckless speed of indifferent drivers whizzing past below.

Finally, as though tiring abruptly of her great adventure, Carmie shook her feathers, peered endearingly at me, and landed lightly on my finger.

Bubbling with sudden joy, I backed carefully into the room – not without growing trepidation as my anxieties shrank. I closed the window, then turned to face the outraged faces, keeping one hand cupped protectively around Carmie's fragile form lest we be parted again.

But even being curtly escorted to the street door failed to submerge my floating relief.

Thus my initiation into budgie personalities.

Years later, I would rescue sick budgies from those ghastly, multi-department stores, where birds were crowded into cages, neglected and languishing. Succumbing to their unhappy eyes (and thereby endorsing the shameful practice), I'd buy ailing individuals at a discount. Then I'd doctor them at home; often cleanliness, freedom, and warmth were their greatest needs. Before long, I'd be rewarded by their exuberant flights and cheery songs as they gradually took over my painting room.

They busied themselves everywhere. Career-oriented females dropped eggs indiscriminately on windowsills, but showed not the slightest interest in establishing nuclear families. Budgies sang on swings suspended from the ceiling. Budgies shredded wallpaper, chewed plants and books, and ruined paintbrushes. Budgies flung droppings into my paints or, alas, onto finished paintings.

In a word, they were *adorable*.

Occasionally, an ailing newcomer would fail to respond to my usual treatment but would hunch morosely in a corner, dozing and disinterested in food. Then my bacteriologist mother would be called out of retirement to create a makeshift lab.

She'd swab a dropping across the growing medium in a petri dish, then cover it and slide it into her bed with the heating pad on low. The organisms, which she was able to identify, would breed rapidly. Then she'd add samples of human medicine.

Those which possessed no resistance – that is, no antibiotic power specific to the bacteria present – would be overrun. But perhaps the culture would *avoid* one pill, showing great sensitivity to it. This pill, then, would contain the antibiotic needed by the bird to restrain the bacteria that was causing its sickness.

There was such beautiful logic involved.

I would take my findings to the vet, who would transpose them into avian medicine containing the proper antibiotic, and determine the dosage according to the weight of the bird. And the bird would be cured.

Not surprisingly.

My mother was a top-level bacteriologist, albeit retired at that time, who had worked with Charles Best, of the famed Banting and Best duo.

She knew her stuff.

But, gradually, budgies gave way in my studio to a steady succession of wild birds. Winged neighbours arrived with urgent needs – chicks of all kinds. Adults recovering from window or vehicle collisions. Victims of cats.

Through the years, I doggedly painted with sparrows in my lap, pigeons on my head, and grackles sabotaging my paints. One female starling explored the nesting possibilities inside one of my hollow, clay sculptures as it lay recumbent on a cushion, waiting for me to incise the title on its base.

A female robin *did* build nests and raise young – on top of a cow skull on the wall.

But far from obliterating my artistic aspirations, the birds added their own dimension to it, and enlarged my vision, time and time again.

I can't imagine any of my work without their vitality in it.

And I can't relate to a studio without droppings.

CHAPTER 6

MEAT OR TOFU?

The erratic weather patterns that had greeted our return to the woods – after the four months of rain and sleet *daily* during our building project – maintained their high standard of eccentricity.

One wonderful snowfall launched us on cross-country skis through soft silence, where dark spruce tops retreated under undulating shapes of white, and their contrasting, criss-crossed fingers hung like bright netting around their dark hidden trunks. Only the sharp staccatos of arctic three-toed woodpeckers and the pealing of unseen kinglets betrayed the hidden bird world that was always busy around us.

But next morning, the temperature soared upwards and a silver thaw set in. Sparks of sunshine kindled rimed branches into prismatic fires that were too feeble to consume their frozen fuel. For two days, the trees bowed under their brilliant burdens before an overnight rain released them. Then they eased thankfully out of the rigid girdles of their icy casings, relaxed, and slowly righted themselves again.

The third morning roared in with a driving blizzard so thick that the beleaguered trees were lost to view.

When the winds finally ceased a day later, sheltered trees were once again bowed – this time under snow – while others, standing in the full blast of the winds, remained relatively clear-eyed and upright, if dishevelled from broken, scattered branches.

Friends dropped by at this time, and we all headed for the woods to visit the great hemlocks. There are two areas of them, both on tilted hilltops, with rapid brooks below sending up their greetings. The trees are very tall, with enormous trunks, some of which spiral upwards. High above our heads, the first branches open. Below, the boles stand well-spaced in quiet dignity, without undergrowth – like ancient pillars remaining long after the temple roof has disappeared.

Even a few hemlocks together create a special aura that I sense immediately – like an invisible veil of protection – and we often see deer lying down or browsing in hidden hollows hooded by hemlocks.

I recall hiking a trail across a steep hillside in Algonquin Park, Ontario. We entered an area dominated by several massive hemlocks, and Mack strode ahead of me, at one place stepping over a huge root that crossed the path. A few moments later, I too stepped over – then stopped immediately, overcome.

As I'd passed over the root, I'd felt an incredible charge of energy so palpable that I cried out involuntarily. Mack turned, and retraced his steps to where I stood transfixed, gazing up in reverence at the great tree beside the path.

A hemlock.

Mack, too, admitted that he'd felt something when he crossed over the root. We gazed at each other, awed.

This day, on our walk, we all offered homage to the hemlocks around us, as to wise elders. Then we sat on our bottoms and slid at least a hundred yards down the steep, undulating hillside of wind-polished snow, pushing awkwardly around trunks and roots, till we slammed into a heap at the bottom, giggling and rosy as children. A nearby brook, with its rhythms frozen in edgings of rippled ice, sounded as jubilant and as youthful as we did.

I was reminded of a tale I'd heard in the local feed store. Some children on a distant farm had raised a pig, converting it from potential pork into the family ham. When the kids went coasting in the winter, the pig – now a hundred pounds of pure enthusiasm – not only rode down the hills on the toboggan with his buddies but heaved himself back up the slope for the next ride.

Clambering to our collective feet, with less grace probably than the pig, we sought out a dell sheltered from the winds that now tugged the treetops and swooped along the trails. Fallen trunks provided us with seats and we kindled a fire with dry "witches' brooms," those great clumps of dense, spruce twiggery that erupt suddenly out of the ends of branches like clusters of fingers.

With contented murmurs, we sat back, sipping hot chocolate from our knapsacks. When a good bed of glowing coals lay ready, Mack toasted slices of his homemade bread for us all.

Nothing can surpass the smoky sweetness of buttered toast, hot from an open fire in a snowy woodland setting.

On our way home, we left the protection of the woods and staggered across fields against icy blasts of wind that struck and tore at our faces as though determined to flay us. But thoughts of homemade soup simmering on the stove beckoned us onward, and soon we were gathered around the hearth, willing the newly kindled fire into blazing billows of warmth.

One bitter morning, I sat up in bed, writing determinedly, and ignoring Mack's comfortable slumbers beside me – the easy, rhythmic breathing and soft whistles that exercised such hypnotic persuasion on me to close my own eyes and slide into a deep doze. A cup of cocoa lay near to hand, fuelling my efforts. Beyond the window hung a waning gibbous moon, like a sagging spotlight.

The moon and I both looked a little the worse for wear for being past the full.

The night, even older than we, began with enviable grace to retire before the youthful beauty of the sunrise that now tinted the eastern sky. Then a sudden snow squall rudely slammed the door, blotting out the light.

But as though a challenge had been flung down, the swirling snow flurries and charred cloudbank were eclipsed, in turn, by a second, more obstinate, sunrise – yellow, this time – and *not* to be vanquished. Before long, sunbright fields emerged out of dusky valleys while I watched, pen in hand, musing.

A day with *two* sunrises had to be special.

Another witness to this silent struggle sat in the birch tree near my window: a great raven. The universal trickster.

And a messenger, if I'd only realized it.

Later, after breakfast, as I was sweeping out the studio upstairs, the telephone rang downstairs. I shot out of the room like a thoroughbred out of a starting gate, and the race was on to answer *before* the answering machine did. It kicked in after only the third ring, and neither Mack nor I knew how to adjust it. We just knew how to run.

Why does the staircase suddenly lengthen at such times?

I feel as if I'm trapped on an endless treadmill, condemned to listen over and over to the imperative summons of a telephone I can never answer. Steps whizz past in a blur under all my feet, which clatter like I've strapped boards to them, while high above, where my head floats, time stands still.

Unlike the Red Queen with Alice, running to stay in one place, I seem to be staying in one place *in spite of* running to get somewhere else.

The elasticity of reality fascinates me, as does our feeble attempt to control it with the invention of time – our mechanically spaced intervals called seconds, minutes, hours, etc. In truth, shovelling out the car for ten minutes takes hours longer than ten minutes spent working on a painting that's going well. Conversely, ten minutes wrestling with an intractable painting can make shovelling out the car for two hours look good.

Driving for twenty minutes to a paralysing opening of one of my art exhibits takes only a moment, while a similar twenty minutes extends forever when I want to arrive at the ocean in time to watch the sun sink sizzling into the water – a sight that even the endless wind pauses each night to watch.

Distance and weight are affected too. I find, after a hard day's work in the garden, lugging buckets of cast-iron manure and wrestling with weeds that seem to have someone else hanging on to the other end, that even picking up half a carrot from the kitchen floor is beyond me. The carrot is too heavy, and the floor too far down to reach.

I recall Mack, whose elastic mind functions easily in this fluctuating existence, teasing an old man who was *just able* to get about, his body stiffened with arthritis.

"Don't you find you're getting stronger as you get older?" Mack queried, lightly.

"Jeez, no!" the old fellow grumbled. "Don't I *wish*!"

"I am," Mack resumed, with a twinkle. "Used to be, I'd need both arms and a cart to carry a hundred dollars' worth of groceries. Now I can carry it all in one hand!"

The old fellow's mirth was delightful.

I escaped the stairs finally, seized the phone, and gasped out a wheezy "Hello." I'm told I answer the phone like I've just been shot, and no wonder.

The caller, a stranger, was concerned about a flightless raven who'd been scrounging for food under her bird feeder – for a couple of months.

And she was concerned only *now*?

He also rooted each day through their compost, and ventured occasionally into their barn to steal dry kibble from the cat's dish. Surprisingly to me, no scraps seemed to have been set out specifically to help the struggling bird. The woman felt that the raven looked a little worse, and wondered if we wanted to help him. I noted down the directions to her rural home, rounded up Mack, and we were off.

As we drove into the yard, we looked about in vain for the raven. Getting out of the car by the house, we noticed his tracks dwarfing those of other birds below the bird feeder; then we spotted him near the barn. The raven, seeing us approach, immediately turned and began walking rapidly away towards the base of a hill, eyeing us nervously over his shoulder.

Although he couldn't fly, his mobility was impressive, and he wasn't hampered, as we were, by breaking through the crusty snow with each step.

He also had a hundred-yard advantage.

We lengthened our strides and moved steadily towards him, reluctant to stress him but seeing no other solution. Determined to evade us at all costs, the raven broke into a lope and fled to the hills.

The chase was on.

Mack strode quickly ahead of me, then swung out to the left to try to head off the raven's escape. Seeing this, the raven bore right and started up the hill. Mack broke into a run and scrambled up the crusty slope, still too far behind to cut off the raven's path, but closing rapidly. They both gained the hilltop simultaneously, but there the wily raven veered suddenly to the right.

Mack, charging uphill through clutching snow, broke out of it abruptly on the wind-hardened summit, where he found himself out of control on pure ice. He skidded erratically in the same direction as the raven, both arms flailing, as he scrambled desperately for traction.

The raven, meanwhile, floundered more easily across the ice

and slithered under a fence. Righting himself, he began loping downhill again, but *away* from where I waited at the bottom, watching anxiously. Holding his wings open for balance, he began widening the gap between himself and his pursuer. Mack, breathless and miraculously still upright, slid into the same fence and clutched it gratefully.

It was an *electric* fence.

Energized instantly by a charge that stuck him like a clenched fist, Mack hastily let go of the wire, rolled under the fence, and began leaping down the hillside, helped finally by the steadying grip of the deeper snow. The raven, already halfway to the bottom, loped doggedly towards a paddock.

At this point I saw I could help by cutting off the raven's escape. Three electric fences separated me from his trajectory and I rolled rapidly under each one. Then I scrambled dizzily to my feet and staggered towards the bird, which had just entered the same paddock from the other side.

Only then did I realize that the enclosure was already occupied.

By a stallion. A very *powerful*-looking stallion.

I slowed, eyeing him uncertainly. He stood alert, ears up, tail slightly raised and nostrils flaring as he tossed his head with nervous jerks. Caught in between us, he rolled his eyes at me approaching from one side and the gallant raven with spread wings, still hotly pursued by Mack, converging from the other side. Then, flinging up his head, the stallion spun around and fled to the farthest reaches of his domain.

I almost whinnied with relief.

The raven now found himself between Mack and me, and we closed in. Desperately, the bird dodged this way and that, while we countered each feint. At last, Mack was able to seize the hapless creature. Composing the wings and lifting him up, he held the bird gently in his arms.

I spoke soothingly and quietly, trying to ease the raven's fears, and allowed the great beak to seize and hold my fingers in silent rebuke – a gesture that I hoped would communicate our lack of aggressive response, our willingness to submit as well as control. Our desire to return his dignity. He was too weak to seriously hurt me, although his grip was impressive, but I felt that it was important for him to assert himself somehow.

With Mack's winded state and my own agitation, it was more than a challenge to convey feelings of friendliness and calm – especially after such a dramatic capture.

And especially when we were representing a species that bares its teeth as a greeting.

To our dismay, each of the raven's breaths came in laboured, wheezy gurgles, indicating bronchial congestion, if not pneumonia. His breast was bone-thin from malnutrition, but his wonderful eyes showed great depth and clarity – which gave me hope.

The caller, too, was delighted with our success, and wished us well as we departed.

Mack held the noble creature on his lap while I drove us to town. On our way, we marvelled that, despite his illness and the unavoidable discourtesy to which he'd been subjected, the raven still possessed that inherent royalty and intelligence which had elevated him to creator status in traditional cultures.

It was left to our own "superior" scientific culture to reduce the great ravens to a clutter of biological facts and meaningless statistics, to judge them by our own limited standard.

And to slay them needlessly.

We paused briefly at a store so I could dash in and purchase one stewing hen and a package of chicken livers – repulsive fare to one who has maintained vegetarian habits for over thirty years.

And has hugged chickens with mutual enthusiasm.

As we resumed our journey, we began discussing Edgar Allan Poe's famous poem, "The Raven," so that, when we finally arrived, Mack carried "Poe" into the aviary shed. There we dosed him with three-quarters of a c.c. of Panmycin, a tetracycline-based medicine that, in my experience, is very effective with birds. Our method

was simple: Mack offered a finger, Poe seized it, and I trickled the medicine into the side of his open beak with a dropper. Then I popped in a small chunk of liver as a reward.

And as a bribe to release the finger.

Mack set Poe down on the largest perch, where he instantly shuffled as far away as possible – understandably. Next, Mack loaded a food dish with three chunks of raw chicken and two grisly lumps of liver, reminding me inevitably of my own revolted reaction as a child, when someone else's liver was served up on my plate.

To this day, liver – raw or cooked – disgusts me, the appearance and the smell equally repulsive.

In later years, even someone else's *muscles* on the end of my fork would repel me, and the seed of vegetarianism took root. Since then, it's just been my fate that most of my best friends, be they woolly or winged, are considered edible by nearly everyone else.

Mack topped up Poe's dish with moistened dog kibble, poultry grains, grit, and crumbled oatcakes. Then I completed the culinary preparations with hard-boiled egg mashed with avian vitamins and cod liver oil – *more* liver, alas – and a large dish of water.

Poe, at last, was left in solitude.

When we peeked in later, the offerings had been well spread out and examined, and all the meat, *including the liver*, devoured.

I sensed, somehow, that tofu wouldn't have the same charisma for him.

The indoor birds, meanwhile, were flourishing in their new abode, as every morning attested.

I had finally whacked together a makeshift desk out of scraps of plywood, a pair of kitchen cupboard doors from the former house, and a chest of drawers. The desk was wedged comfortably into a corner of our bedroom. A window on each side looked through trees to wooded hills both east and south.

Here each morning, at five o'clock, I'd work on my writing. And here Chip often joined me, guided through the darkened house by the glow from my study lamp. She'd roost on my shoulder like a witch's familiar, dozing lightly while I pondered and wrote, erased and wrote again, consulted journals or dictionaries, and wrote some more – stirring the verbal concoction in my mental cauldron.

The light rising in the eastern sky and dimming the stars rose simultaneously in Chip's eyes, igniting her chronic nefarious gleam. At some point, usually when I was groping for one of those shooting-star words that flare enticingly, then fade maddeningly, she'd *erupt*.

A hair-lifting screech would burst out, saluting the new day – and obliterating every word I'd ever known. Mack, asleep behind us, would moan plaintively and bury his head in the covers, but there was no stopping Chip. When the day began, so did she. It would be easier to stop the sun.

Bashō, from the dusky foliage of the indoor garden downstairs, would crow with almost equal volume, if less shrilly, his calls, like a cricket's, out of all proportion to his size.

Beejay, not to be outdone, would rout any remaining silence with piercing cries answered by the outside blue jays, who sounded some mornings as though they were inside. Edna, restlessly awaiting her backrubs, would begin banging the poker against the metal heat shield around the woodstove, or flinging the iron trivets off the cold stove-top onto the bricks.

Only Molly's salutation, a gentle cooing in the studio next to the bedroom, and strangely at variance with her churlish nature, seemed kind to our vulnerable morning ears.

Eventually, we began to hear Poe's guttural responses to each brightening day mingle with the general cacophony.

He was progressing well, eating enthusiastically, and often venturing through the small, floor-level door into the outside aviary. But when fair weather soon gave way to bone-chilling sleet, we confined him to his shed and changed the ceiling bulb for a red, two-hundred-and-fifty-watt brooder lamp on a short cord. Since the shed measured only eight feet by eight feet, the air soon gained the drier, warmer quality necessary to offset his congestion.

Twice a day we dosed Poe with medicine and dusted his meat with avian vitamin powder until, a week after his arrival, his breathing sounded normal. Then we eliminated the antibiotic and, with drier weather outdoors, allowed him into the aviary again.

As the weeks passed, Poe gained weight and energy, and leaped vigorously from perch to perch, often with partly spread wings. Mack studied his movements daily, adding or adjusting extra perches as needed. And Poe grew stronger almost visibly.

Unfortunately, one wing had been damaged, perhaps by a power line or a rifle shot. This had probably grounded him initially. Lack of flight and proper food consequently led to illness.

Now, despite his returning health, we suspected that the original injury, though healed, would prevent him from flying again.

Time would tell.

Meanwhile, Mack had noticed that Poe's favourite food was beef heart. Anxious to help to his utmost, Mack returned from the abattoir one day with three *enormous* hearts for Poe.

Noting the date, I commented drily that our relationship must be deteriorating. Poe got three *real* hearts for Valentine's Day, while I didn't even score a single, heart-shaped chocolate.

Soon, in the freezer, we had dozens of little bags containing chunks of heart, liver, and muscles. In the aviary, several bones rich with marrow hung within easy reach of Poe's restless bill. At any time of the day, unidentifiable parts of carcasses would be thawing slowly on the kitchen counter, or waiting, chilled and accessible, in the fridge. A reek of raw flesh often hung in the air until I almost fancied I was seeing a vulture when I looked at Poe.

Or, more disturbingly, when I looked at Mack.

Barring display counters in supermarkets, I'd never been surrounded by so much carrion in my life.

And I'd never been so creative with tofu.

CHAPTER 7

Spring in Winter

As the winter days sped by, we worked hard on the finishing touches in our new home. Baseboards were nailed in place. A pine woodbox replaced a dilapidated cardboard box. Inside shutters with rich red glass hung in the bathroom window. Working together, we created an unusual wooden casing of circling birds to frame our round window. Tatters of pink insulation desecrating the stained-glass window in the living room were finally boarded in. A desk for Mack utilized space under the staircase.

We were almost civilized.

But when I recall local lore about the resourcefulness of earlier generations, our own exhausting efforts seem feeble in comparison. One man, a house painter by trade, washed out his empty paint cans, removed the bottoms, hammered the cans flat, then roofed his house with them.

I've *seen* the roof.

A husband and wife, near neighbours, jacked up their great post-and-beam barn with a *cheese press*, one corner at a time. Then they mixed their own cement, and replaced the entire stone foundation.

I've *seen* the barn.

As my equally resourceful mother put it, when she was culturing budgie droppings in her bedclothes for lack of a proper laboratory, "It's what you do with what you've got!"

My sentiments exactly.

But insistence of indoor chores, many of which still beckoned in every direction, had a serious competitor in the lure of the outdoor world.

One dark morning unfurled into a day of bright snow rippled with blue shadows, like a flag. As one, we dropped our tools, drove to a coastal cape, and hiked through the hushed woods to the shore. We followed a deep gorge cleaving the hills and chanced upon an exquisite spring welling up under a tangle of roots.

Entranced, we followed the singing stream as it bounded down to the ocean.

Wherever the motion slowed, ripples froze on the surface, while the chastened waters crept on below. Then a sudden drop over a rock would speed the flow, and the escaping waters would burst out with renewed vigour, bubbling in breathless haste. Fallen trees occasionally linked the narrow banks of rich green moss that glowed in living contrast to the whitened woodland surrounding them. Everywhere, the precision of fox tracks mingled with the erratic leaps of snowshoe hares.

As we scrambled and slid down the bluff cresting the frozen beach, the melodious waters sprang down lightly beside us, then sank suddenly out of sight and sound.

On the silent shore, massed with tumbled ice floes, we heard the distant, eerie moans of calling seals.

Edna, meanwhile, in these late winter days, was living the life of a privileged rabbit in the studio. Though she persistently chewed plants, electric cords, the string on my reading glasses, and any book forgotten on a chair, *still* she was cuddled. As I painted, she often stood up beside me, her front paws on my knee, her busy tongue licking my jeans – a compelling reminder that it was time to pat her again.

Edna's sense of humour also began to emerge. One morning, I set two pieces of hardwood in the studio stove, then walked to the other end of the room for kindling. I scrunched up papers, thrust them between the logs and piled kindling on top. Then I reached for the matches.

Suddenly the kindling *jumped*!

And so did I.

It heaved violently and I leaped back, matches in hand, just as Edna pushed her head out of the stove. With the interior of the stove as black as Edna's fur, I'd failed to see her when I'd laid the fire.

At the thought of what nearly transpired, I broke into a cold sweat that felt as if it would stick to me for the rest of my life.

From that time on, Edna and I engaged in a battle of wits at stove-lighting times. I'd try to gather all the necessary materials before opening the stove door, but often something was needed. If I left the opening unguarded for even an instant, Edna darted inside, and I'd come thundering back, scolding. By then, clouds would be enshrouding the stove, and ashes would be spewing out all over the floor from between her hind legs as her front paws dug down joyfully.

Often she'd feign disinterest when I opened the stove, and would sit demurely nearby, chewing a carrot. Standing up, I'd glide backwards towards the kindling box, watching her warningly, but she'd seem utterly indifferent. Beguiled by those innocent eyes, I'd turn to gather up the extra kindling.

Bang! She'd be into the stove, hurling out ashes.

During warm days, when the stove wasn't in use, Edna, scorning the cushioned lounge chair, would recline casually *on top* of the stove, her hind legs stretched well back and an unmistakable smirk on her face.

No wonder rabbits are tricksters in traditional lore.

Mack's innate trickster humour soon joined forces with Edna's and they began each day with hilarious games. Mack would drum his feet loudly and make aggressive "grabs" at Edna, growling ferociously the while.

Edna, though initially taken aback, soon recognized a new game and retaliated with gusto. Often *she* challenged *him* to play. She'd crouch under the stove while he "grabbed" and "growled" at her, biding her time. But as soon as a hand came too close, she'd dart out and back like a cuckoo clock, growling and lunging with her sharp front claws and trying very convincingly to bite.

When her teeth *did* make contact, they just brushed the skin harmlessly. But for a vegetarian, she flashed an impressive set of choppers.

Soon I, too, was playing the same game with Edna, chasing her around the stove and under the furniture. Sometimes she'd leap up on the lounge chair, gallop to the other end, and leap off, all in a split second. Or she'd spring up suddenly, kick her heels in a spin, and land facing in the other direction. Then she'd dodge behind the stove and face out, growling like a mastiff.

In response to astonished friends doubtful that rabbits could growl, I replied that Mack – in trickster mode – could hoist growls out of a tulip.

Mack and I often returned from our walks with fresh branches, choosing varieties favoured by local snowshoe hares, and heaped them beside the studio woodstove. Edna's first move was to snip off any projections blocking her "escape route" to her lair at the back of the stove. In her high-speed games with us, a clear path was essential.

Then she'd settle down to eating the buds and branches, sitting solemnly before us and steadily chewing on the end of a long twig, while it slid slowly up into her mouth and disappeared – an accomplishment carried out with such dignity and finesse that it never failed to inspire our admiration. Dried, bleached beech leaves she ate with the noisy gusto of a human enjoying potato chips.

She also nibbled the stacked hardwood nearby, favouring curls of birch bark and clumps of moss. Or she'd burrow happily into the box of softwood kindling, pausing often to chew the bark. Therefore I was surprised when she developed constipation and quickly lost weight.

We were advised to dose her with mineral oil and provide her with fresh hay as an essential to her diet, a procedure which restored Edna's health almost immediately.

But the hay also gave her other ideas.

Edna had come into heat with delightful mannerisms. She became *obsessed* with being patted. When we rubbed her flour-soft fur, she released a pungent aroma – no doubt inspiring to male rabbits, though more readily associated in our culture with the eye-watering cologne favoured by "hussies."

Also, during her heat, she'd spin. If we gave her short touches over and over on her left side, she'd spin round and round to the left. If we suddenly switched to patting her right side, she spun to the right. We'd wind and unwind her, Edna in ecstasy and Mack and me in giggles.

Thus, when I placed an armful of sweet-smelling hay in her corner, Edna began nibbling it, but deeper plans were forming in her head. When we returned after a day's absence, the hay had disappeared – except for a trail of wisps leading to a large cabinet of drawers and shelves that I used for storing artwork. One deep bottom shelf had been rudely emptied of oil pastels and wood-engraving supplies. At the very back, Edna had created a nest by hauling hay, mouthful by mouthful, across the room. Her smug expression seemed to suggest, "If I build it, they will come."

Edna wanted *babies*.

Somehow, we had to convince her to be a career rabbit instead – in any season but spring, that is.

Easter Bunnies are traditionally male.

Rain suddenly lashed out at our snowbound beauty overnight, thudding on the skylights and spraying the windows like blasts from firemen's hoses. Clumps of sodden snow were wrenched off the nearest trees and hurled onto the metal roof with resounding smacks. Ice pellets rattled like flung handfuls of gravel, as though the elements had a grudge against us. Thoughts of trees, close to the house, snapping like matchsticks, began to take shape in both our minds as we cozied down by the studio fire with our books.

Chip preened drowsily on Mack's knee, while Bashō slumbered in the cup of my hand and Edna stretched out beside me, licking the rug while I rubbed her back. In his tree, Beejay slept, head under wing. Even Molly dozed benignly on her shelf.

At times like these, the indoor birds, like their wise counterparts outdoors, set an excellent example – one cannot govern the weather, so one rejoices in shelter.

Therefore, we went to bed.

Morning emerged cautiously, a pale, tumbled sunrise amid the ragged remnants of clouds. Light crept through the exhausted stillness that bound our world as we peered curiously out the steamy windows. Beads of water clung to the glass, or trickled down like tears. Beyond the house, chequered fields of dead grass and snow faded away into the low, heavy mist that blotted out hills and distance. Pale puddles gazed up blindly into the growing light. The empty dirt road, no longer packed with snow, now lay encased in ice.

We felt like the lone human survivors of a primal flood.

Only the echoing rush of unseen swollen brooks and the unquenchable calls of jays at the feeder disturbed the stillness.

Later, we ventured out for a walk, sloshing through meltwater and slipping on hidden ice. With quiet dignity, Poe watched us pass his aviary. Perched in a bare elm tree, a red-tailed hawk held out his great wings to dry. A robin's nest, miraculously intact – perhaps from the combination of saliva with mud in the building of it – still clung to a fallen tree. A hare eyed us covertly from an alder thicket, depending on his camouflage to disguise his whereabouts, but his pale winter coat shone against the dark, woven branches. Two deer bounded away soundlessly into the mist. The image of their white, waving tails, like the Cheshire Cat's smile, lingered on alone before disappearing.

The pervading silence was uncanny. We almost resorted to whispers.

But though calm was restored outdoors, an underlying unrest still permeated the atmosphere, and both of us felt chilly and sweaty at the same time. In the studio, condensation from a skylight suddenly dribbled all over a painting as I was working on it – creating *another* storm.

Indoors this time.

Mack fled to the saner – and quieter – outdoor world, where he busied himself cutting drainage channels in the saturated banks of heavy snow edging the driveway. The last shovel cuts released *six inches* of standing water from around the car.

At least one of us gained a feeling of accomplishment.

Raccoons emerged each night from under the house during the sudden thaw, looking as bedraggled as though they'd been swimming. They squatted among the muddy seeds and hulls left by the dissolving snow and felt through them carefully, stuffing the solid ones into their mouths, and chewing energetically. Their masked eyes wandered about, vague and preoccupied – like a child's in school – but their noses and ears were always alert.

Noises I would never detect, or a passing scent, would hoist them up on their collective feet, all noses sniffing in the same direction, all ears at attention. One or two of the more submissive raccoons would hastily retreat a few steps, then pause and turn, retreat and turn again, everyone peering earnestly into the darkness beyond the porch light.

Watching them, all my senses would also be wary and prickling with anticipation.

What on earth could be out there?

What monster, disturbed by the chaotic elements?

All my eyes – and at times like this, I seemed *covered* with unblinking eyes – would be trained like spotlights on an empty stage, when into view would come . . .

Just another raccoon.

As though the hard shell of winter had broken open, waking dormant energies and releasing a sudden burst of spring, we spotted occasional robins foraging between remaining snow patches. Pussywillows swelled, and during one whole day, even the unmistakable fragrance of spring permeated the air.

Not the scent of a mild winter day, but *real spring* – the essence of warmed earth, loosening buds, rotting vegetation, running water. And over all, we could hear the annual bird songs that celebrate the end of short, cold days.

In the trees surrounding the feeders, blue jay couples passed each other seeds, strengthening their mutual bonds, and indoors Beejay seemed unusually animated. His ringing calls seemed full of fervour and urgency – sadly so.

How interwoven are the characteristics of the seasons. In the woods, we saw ferns, though flattened by the now-vanished snow, appear even greener and more pliable than during the summer. Whereas, on a rainy July day, I remember seeing a fragment of flat white lichen resting lightly on mossy ground. Roughly circular, and possessing an intricate design, its paleness was further intensified by the vivid green of the wet moss. Chanced upon suddenly, the lichen looked like a large snowflake.

Following our woodland trails, we noticed little stockpiles of spruce cones everywhere, food caches that had been hidden under the snow. Small heaps of deer droppings, which had settled down through the dissolving snow, also spotted the forest floor.

They completed the equation: seeds and manure, the catalyst of a future forest.

Wind blew, and above our heads, spruce trees, ragged with trailing lichens, swayed restlessly, moaning and creaking eerily. With each gust, their needles hissed.

Only the greatest of the hardwoods resisted the lure of this artificial spring. They remained dormant, with all their buds set out and waiting, like people asleep indoors with bottles ready on their doorsteps for the milkman.

As we drove to town one morning, during almost summery warmth, we passed a tall, dead spruce, needleless and broken. On the top branch, two crows sat side by side – one with its head tilted back, its beak pointed up, while the second crow carefully groomed the first bird's throat feathers. In a pasture, two beef cows stood close to each other in the sunshine – one with lowered head and closed eyes, the second licking the first one behind the ears. Crowding the puddles of a stubbled field, a flock of starlings splashed and bathed with communal enthusiasm. In town, two pigeons were *actually copulating* high up on the ledges of a building.

Being human, and supposedly more intelligent, we almost felt we should scream warnings that this halcyon lull would *soon be gone*. But taking our cue, instead, from the contented creatures around us, we decided to follow their wiser example: enjoy it while it lasts.

And we were glad we did.

Before long, cold winds swung down from the north as though winter, having been repaired, was in good working order again. Temperatures dropped drastically each night and rose minimally each day. Ice encrusted all exposed water. As puddles continued to seep, their frozen tops fell in, unmasking water that froze again, till layers of ice filled the hollows. Accumulated moisture crystallized on branches, so that the icy, rounded top of hardwood hills resembled cumulus clouds.

Mack's amazing creation – a vegetable garden shaped like a flying robin, with a ninety-foot wingspan – lay white with frosted mulch early each morning. Surrounded by dark ground, the garden almost seemed transformed into a great white dove, hovering.

And marking the end of our floods.

One morning, we left the house in response to a phone call from another town about a robin that had struck a window. Being better equipped than our caller to house a robin temporarily – if necessary – we set off, ready for anything.

The wooden boardwalk from our house to the road was encrusted with glittering crystals of frost. The boards squealed shrilly under our footsteps, drowning my own squeals as I skidded on beauty.

Just as I stepped off the boardwalk, there was an explosive CRASH!, echoed internally by my heart striking the top of my head. In a sinkhole beside the road, trapped water had seeped down slowly but steadily until the thick slab of ice on top, still clinging to the stalks of bushes, suddenly collapsed. A tinkling of shattered ice faded into silence.

After an hour's drive, we found ourselves in an intriguing home. Throughout the living room and kitchen, fish and amphibians watched us expressionlessly from various glass tanks, while we looked in at them with fascination. We appeared to find *them* more interesting than they found *us*. Plants everywhere added to the almost tropical ambience.

The young couple who had called, concerned about the robin's welfare, had isolated it in a dark box with adequate ventilation from airholes. So often, would-be rescuers selfishly stress a bird because it's a novelty. They handle it frequently, subject it to flash photos, allow children to lug it about, or force it to eat incorrect food. Hours of such treatment can do more damage than the original injury. For nestlings, it's frequently lethal.

When I cautiously opened one end of the box and peered in, the white-ringed eyes of a lovely female robin watched me, alert with alarm. She sprang to life, thrashing violently until I managed to grasp her gently and lift her out. I murmured soothingly, sending calmness, and she instantly quieted in my hands.

Her eyes were deep and bright, and her wings and legs obviously undamaged. Best of all, her breast was not thin at all. Despite foraging through the winter months, when most of her kind were inhabiting warmer climes, she was feeding very well – which I was relieved to see. I'd often worried about the occasional robins one sees during the winter months.

To everyone's relief, she was ready to go, and, when I released her outdoors, she swooped up easily into the grove of trees sheltering the house.

On our way home, snow began at last, whirling crazily in front of the headlights but falling steadily and soberly on the passing fields. Distances shrank. Solid hills were replaced by constant movement.

When we woke next morning, soft white beauty surrounded us, yet fine snow hovered still, catching the hidden sunlight and creating what seemed almost a bright mist. Tiny flakes flew upwards, sideways, into our nostrils – in every direction but down. Trees faded into shimmering silhouettes like fine Japanese ink paintings.

In the early light, a ruffed grouse balanced his rotundity with great precision on the thin branches of the serviceberry tree, eating buds. Tree sparrows lined up at the silo feeder. Voles emerged cautiously from under the doorstep, dark eyes bright in silvery fur. They ploughed rapidly through inches of fluff to snatch up seeds below the feeder, then dashed back under the protective step. A brown creeper spiralled up the trunk of a great spruce. Chickadees and blue jays alternated on the swinging suet feeder.

Mouse trails disappeared into visible snow holes beside the house and woodshed. Bird tracks cross-hatched light snow under the deck, where sand could still be dug up for grit. Squirrel leaps bounded everywhere.

But those springlike days that had broken loose in midwinter had planted seeds – quite literally.

Only a few weeks later, though deep snow stifled the land, we received our first baby bird of the year.

CHAPTER 8

PERPLEXITIES WITH PIGEONS

The March lion blew in with roaring winds that lashed the sky-lights all night and clawed at the laden trees. Clumps of hardened snow hurtled off pitching branches like stones out of slingshots. We tossed and turned restlessly all night as though storms were heaving the deep waters of our dream worlds.

Then morning rose, exhausted and leaden-eyed.

In the uncanny stillness, mist drifted uneasily over the fields as I drowsed, equally leaden-eyed, in the kitchen, assembling break-fast mostly by touch. Near me, Mack yawned as he filled the kettle to make tea.

Suddenly, great brilliance burst through the windows, fol-lowed instantly by a BANG! that shot me straight off my feet into Mack's arms. Moments later, chuckles of thunder rumbled across the vast belly of the sky, fading finally into satisfied silence.

Silence broken only by Mack's own chuckles when I glanced down shakily between my feet to see if the floor needed mopping.

Sudden noises have *always* been my downfall. They're the curse of any high-strung nature, and through the years I've developed spontaneous leaps that would inspire the National Ballet – if they *could* be inspired by a middle-aged ballerina with raw nerves instead of raw talent.

Mack, blessed with an even disposition, and the added bonus of being slightly hard of hearing, usually becomes aware that he's launched yet another rocket only when he notices the shadow of my descending parachute. Years earlier, when he still lived in his home in town amid continual traffic noise, he sneezed – and a neighbour in the next house telephoned with a surefire cold remedy.

He's learned – in self-defence – to warn me about imminent sneezes, but with his energy, he considers a door fully closed only when the walls shake on impact. I can be sound asleep upstairs at the far end of the house, but find myself suddenly airborne when he closes a door.

Mercifully, he never slams one in anger. I don't think the doors, being only solid hardwood, could survive it.

I *know* I couldn't.

My gratitude that Mack regularly washes the dishes is somewhat tempered by wondering how long they'll survive being clattered cheerfully into the sink or hurled into cupboards. Since he tends to do them just before he goes to bed – *long* after I've fallen peacefully asleep – I'm invariably wakened by the opening crescendoes of the dishwashing chorus.

Perhaps in time, my hearing will be deadened enough to match his, and the problems will resolve themselves.

Mack's explosive reports from his "other end" are equally impressive. Once, during a still morning, he "backfired" while walking out on a wharf. *Fifteen startled ducks* shot out of the reeds into quacking hysteria and instant flight, convinced that hunters had arrived by stealth.

Our difficulties in finding a comfortable setting on our mutual volume control were compounded by my habitual extremes in the opposite direction. After years of living only with birds, padding silently through darkened rooms where they were sleeping, and being constantly concerned lest I startle them, I don't just live in the house.

I *haunt* it like a ghost.

Rather than risk closing the kitchen cupboards with a bang, I tend to leave them open, thereby risking our eyes instead. I shut house doors in utter silence, as though I've crept in to steal the silver we don't have. I set dishes down on the counter as though they might explode on contact. The morning an untouched pot lid suddenly slid off a stack of washed dishes and clattered violently around the metal sink beside me, my nervous system was nearly destroyed for the day.

Accustomed to murmuring companionably, even inarticulately, to birds, I mumble comments Mack can't possibly hear – then accuse him of not listening.

"Did you make the bread?"

"The sheets need to be washed."

"No-o-o, *bread!*"

"I know there isn't – I still have to make some."

Friends dining with us compare it to dinner theatre.

Late one afternoon, I was making supper, "helped" by Chip, who had her gleaming eyes fixed on the onions I was chopping. Whenever I strayed to the stove to check on the soup as it simmered, or to peer through the oven door, she'd snatch up a chunk of onion and swoop off triumphantly to the garden. There she'd crush it with her beak, releasing more pungency, and rub it all over her feathers – her indoor version of the anting ritual indulged in by wild birds, in which black ants are rubbed through plumage, supposedly to deter parasites. Fresh garlic also inspired her, and I still shudder when I recall the day she wallowed in both.

She smelled like a hamburger with "the works."

Unfortunately, one piece of onion never sufficed. As though embracing the use-it-once-then-throw-it-away attitude of our human culture, she'd toss the onion aside almost immediately, then flit back to the kitchen for more. Knowing from grim experience that Chip, unrestrained, could scatter an entire chopped onion throughout the house, I bared my teeth at her and "mantled" my onion protectively, like an eagle over a toothsome carcass.

Then the telephone rang.

Of course.

I overturned a bowl to hide the onion and dashed off to answer the call. On the other end was a stranger, a mother who commuted fifty miles each way daily to attend the university near us. Her voice still held distress as she related her tale. I listened closely, one eye on Chip who was trying, so far unsuccessfully, to pry up the bowl with her beak.

The woman told how she'd been downtown between classes and found a pigeon on Main Street unable to fly.

"*Adults* were *kicking* it!" she choked, outraged.

She had scooped up the hapless bird and begun searching for someone who could care for it. Her own heavy schedule and lack of knowledge about bird care prevented her from doing it herself, but she was determined that the creature be helped.

One after another, vets and members of the naturalists' society turned her down. A biologist at the university glanced with open contempt at the pigeon in her arms. He denigrated it as an "introduced pest."

Aren't we all?

And just *who* has done the most damage since arriving in this land – humans or pigeons?

And just *who* introduced pigeons?

We're all part of this country now. And from time to time, each one of us needs help.

Discouraged, the woman took the pigeon back home with her later that day. She bedded it down on newspapers in the bathtub – how much kinder than a cage – set out water and wild-bird seeds, and tried to prevent her dog and young child from distressing it.

After hearing all this, somehow I felt no surprise that the career she was preparing for was nursing.

On the advice of a friend, she called me and became almost coherent with relief when I told her we'd be delighted to take on a pigeon. Mack and I don't distinguish between "good" and "bad" birds. They're *all* fish that come to our net – so to speak.

I added directions for finding our house, then returned to the kitchen, just as Chip, who'd pushed the rim of the upside-down bowl closer to the onions, managed to pry up the edge and extract one generous chunk. She shot past my head, clutching her prize, and uttering a short squawk of victory.

I figured she'd earned it.

The woman arrived next morning on her way to class, clutching a cardboard box. When I opened the top, I was astonished.

The small inmate still bore a few wisps of down on his head and breast, and a tail still only half its proper length. The area of skin around the base of his bill and on his throat was still bare of feathers – because squab (baby pigeons) are fed "pigeon milk," a regurgitated, curd-like secretion from the parents' crops. Feathered faces would be repeatedly soiled. Unable to coo, his voice consisted of thin, piping cries interspersed with snuffy honks that reminded me of an adolescent duckling learning to quack.

In other words, despite the evidence of winter before our eyes – snow swirling through a frozen world beyond the windows – this was a *baby* pigeon!

The new arrival whimpered and cringed when I reached in for him, but quieted down once I began cradling him in my hands. The faces of young pigeons are so winsome. Their bills seem far too long because of their bare juvenile faces, and this gives them a long-nosed dignity – almost an hauteur – that is entirely refuted by the whimsical tufts on top of their heads. Their round, solemn eyes can look as sad as a basset hound's.

The rescuer, after shyly mentioning that she'd named the pigeon "Miles," in the hopes that he had still miles to fly, took an affectionate leave of him, having miles to go herself. After she'd gone, Chip bounced down on my shoulder, reeking of onion like the stranger who's always next to you in crowded rooms.

Luckily, she doesn't belch.

She leaned forward, peering curiously at this new arrival.

Miles looked healthy, well fed, and bright-eyed, and I mar-velled that his parents had found enough food in the snow and slush of winter streets to support a family. Miles may not have been an only squab. I found no visible parasites in his clean, beautiful plumage, but dusted him with rotenone powder as a safe deterrent against mites. Then I set him down gently in the indoor garden – where Bashō surprised me.

He who had seen so many wild birds come and go – including pigeons – showed unusual alarm at the large stranger standing mildly before him. Rather than just raising his back feathers defensively, Bashō kept a nervous eye on Miles and scurried behind the plants to safety.

Miles, looking almost disappointed at the abrupt disappearance of one who seemed closer to his own kind than the rest of us, turned away and sought the seclusion of the far side of the garden.

Then I noticed that, although he was weaned to the point where he could pick up food, he lacked discrimination; he swallowed Bashō's tiny, hardened droppings, Beejay's broken pieces of sunflower hulls, and proper seeds with equal enthusiasm. Human toddlers exhibit similar open-mindedness when putting things in their mouths. My own mother, at such an age, was caught pushing a live baby mouse into hers – a piece of personal history she regretted divulging, since I never allowed her to live it down.

I decided therefore to move Miles to a corner of the studio floor where he'd not only have seeds and grit *exclusively* before him, but could learn pigeon ways from watching Molly.

Unfortunately, I didn't consult Molly.

I spread newspapers in a corner near my easel and added food, grit, and water dishes. At an angle to the wall I set a cardboard box on its side to provide privacy when desired. Then I set Miles inside it to create a secure home base for him. For a long while, he remained within, then ventured timidly out and peered in all directions.

From her high shelf on the opposite side of the room, Molly lay in stillness, watching his every move.

Eventually, Miles began to pick up seeds, and preen, and then rest on one foot, tucking up the other like a tired shopper in a mall at Christmas. Finally, he lay down, lolling on one side of his deep keel in that position of repose so characteristic of pigeons.

I left my work nearby, wandered over, and squatted down beside Miles, sometimes holding him, more often just murmuring in tones that I hoped would convey reassurance to one at foot level who eyed human shoes with fear.

Suddenly Molly fluttered down to the floor, her great wings – larger than those of fully grown street pigeons – gusting and scattering seeds. Papers blew off my table and swept along the floor. The tufts on Miles's head swayed like kelp in the tides and his eyes widened. Clearly, he was impressed.

Cheered by the earthly descent of this imposing visitant, Miles perked up and ventured closer, with disarming naïveté. Back at the table, I watched with a scepticism born of long experience. Molly's seemingly friendly eyes could thaw a December snow scene on a country calendar. But I knew she was a shoo-in if lifetime achievement awards were ever offered for being a perfidious cad.

Molly had laid her plans well. As she pattered quietly about, picking up various seeds like any normal pigeon, I reflected on the loss of her considerable talent to the theatrical world.

She was a consummate actress.

The two birds strayed around the floor for half an hour, eating seeds or preening, always maintaining a short distance between them. Whenever Miles approached too near, Molly would shake her wing and warn him off, though her eyes remained warm. Puzzled, accustomed to nurturing adults, Miles would pause uncertainly, and Molly would move on.

I pretended to work on my painting, determined to give at least as good a performance as Molly, but watched covertly. I didn't buy that innocent act.

And a good thing, too.

When Miles's back was turned, and he was fully engrossed in nibbling a row of books, Molly's eyes suddenly hardened. She slid silently and rapidly towards him. At the same moment, I shot off my stool. Luckily, I reached Molly before she could seize her unwary victim. Scooping her up, I tossed her rudely onto her shelf, where she swelled and cooed with anger and frustration. Eventually she cooled down, drank deeply, then lay on her belly once more, watching Miles benignly.

And plotting.

Later, Mack picked up Miles and sat down with him, trying to build up his confidence. And Miles responded. He perched quietly on Mack's hand or shoulder, stretching his wings and preening his new plumage. Already we could see the characteristic pink and green iridescence on his neck.

Then Mack taught him to drink out of his glass of water. He held it in front of Miles, at the same time emitting drinking sounds that, however repelling to anyone else, did incite Miles to lean forward curiously, dip his bill, and take a short drink. He made note of the procedure, too. Next day, Mack had only to hold his glass up to him and Miles drank immediately.

"We're ready to pub crawl," chuckled Mack.

But heights made Miles uneasy. Whenever Mack stood up with the youngster still on his hand or shoulder, Miles peered down at the distant floor, first on one side, then on the other, with owlish eyes of alarm. Finally – encouraged possibly by the instincts of generations of sky-soaring ancestors, all cooing internal instructions at once – he'd rally his energies and jump, gliding down on spread wings to a creditable landing. Then Mack, to reinforce success, would pick him up again, and Miles, emboldened, would jump more readily.

Edna, fortunately, showed no desire to intimidate Miles – but succeeded anyway. She'd hop up to him curiously, with upright interrogative ears and a quickening nose. Miles would freeze in horror, straining to cry out with voiceless, defensive wheezes. Then he'd turn and flee on a blur of pink feet.

Through the next few days, Molly rigidly sustained her utter disapproval of this interloper from the streets. For his part, Miles soon understood that, despite their mutual classification as pigeons, Molly was no ally in this human world. Though I reminded her – meaningly – that *all* "fancy" pigeons were descended from these wild rock doves, or common pigeons, Molly turned a deaf ear.

Instead, she invaded his corner, rummaging through his resting box, eating his seeds, *daring* him to evict her. But Miles, only half her size, stood helplessly in the middle of the floor, crying and shaking his left wing in what was intended to be a menacing manner. Twice she leaped on him, biting and striking him with her wings before I could snatch her off.

But gradually Miles grew more insistent about his rights. Perhaps, too, he sensed our sympathy.

His breathy honks and squeals of protest became more vigorous as Molly's bullying attitude persisted. Whenever she strode menacingly toward him, but caught our threatening gestures and verbal warnings, she'd pause, or veer away. Miles, no doubt convinced that he'd cowed her himself, would puff up accordingly. Soon his self-confidence became almost palpable. The exaggerated action of his left wing – the pigeon equivalent of a clenched fist – now began to remind me of a street thug swinging a bicycle chain with casual belligerence. His defensive attitude developed into one of bravado and challenge, while Molly, hampered by our interference, seethed visibly.

Between rounds, she'd recline in a tempting sunpatch on the floor, while her adversary lay in his reclaimed box, watching her warily.

And I worked frantically at a painting while the lull lasted.

The first night, I had bedded Miles down in his box and covered it with a towel before adding a couple of wide boards to prevent any early-morning raids by Molly. On succeeding nights, he chose his own roost in a set of shelves, beginning with the lowest – which I hastily lined with newspaper.

By the end of a week, Miles had risen, shelf by shelf, a rising tide of newspapers following him until, with evident satisfaction, he claimed the top shelf for his own. Once he was settled for the night, I'd erect a barrier around him, in case Molly rose before I did. Only when I was on hand for a day's work did I dare to let him out.

This hostility between the two birds created difficulties for Bashō as well as us. Leaving Molly and Miles together, whether briefly or for hours, was downright dangerous, given Molly's greater size and irascibility. Thus, whenever we intended to leave the house, we locked Molly in the studio and carried Miles downstairs to the indoor garden.

Chip and Beejay seemed indifferent to the youngster's presence, but the arrangement didn't suit Bashō at all. Though Miles displayed no aggression towards him, Bashō showed obvious distress when near Miles. The pigeon would calmly explore the garden, bathe in the large, communal waterdish, and eat – all peaceful pursuits – but Bashō would remain agitated. Unable to drive the larger bird out, Bashō himself would depart. When we returned, we'd find him hiding in the kitchen, in the laundry room, or even just inside the front door – as though he were planning to leave as soon as it opened.

Though we failed to comprehend Bashō's fear, we had to acknowledge it. Unwilling to distress our diminutive elder, we again restricted Miles to the studio. Before we left the house, however, we'd place a large, bottomless wire cage over Miles, his dishes and his resting box. This protected him from Molly.

Then we draped a towel over part of the cage so they wouldn't even have to *look* at one another.

My theory about the Great Flood is that Noah, far from wanting the dove to *return*, sent it *away* in the hopes of finally establishing peace on the ark.

One night we shrugged off our yoke of avian perplexities and left – not to say *fled* – the house for the saner realm of the woodlands.

A full moon glowed before us, blurred by frail snow flurries that gently tickled our faces until we stepped beyond the trees sheltering the house. There the winds, galloping like wolves across the frozen fields, hurled themselves hungrily on us. The drifting flakes, now equally beset, swept sideways and stung our eyes. Our faces were burning with cold before we finally escaped into the far woods and stillness.

But as we followed the beckoning curves of the tree-lined trail, the magic began.

An eerie brightness, not darkening steadily like dusk, but holding like muted daylight, surrounded us. Snow-laden spruces with bowed shoulders and limp, white fingers mingled with the reaching hardwoods, whose snow-woven branches of light-over-dark faded into grey softness beyond our heads. Springs surfaced in black trickles of open water enclosed by puffy borders of snow, their edges laced with exquisite formations of ice.

The moon followed us like a great eye – now benignly at the peak of a great spruce, like the radiant top of a Christmas tree. Now hovering above a dark jagged branch like a luminous owl. Now quickening its pace and slinking behind the young hardwood grove, paralleling our progress, yet keeping a wary distance.

Like a shape-shifter, it shone suddenly out of still water. Out of clear icicles clinging to branches. Out of our eyes when we looked at one another.

Trees creaked and popped in winds, unfelt by us, that wrenched their tops. Only when the sheltering woods fell away briefly from around us could the icy breath chill our faces. We pressed our ears against slimmer trees, listening in wonder as their trunks relayed the wild activity high above us in humming vibrations, like high-tension wires.

The trail, packed by a neighbour's snowmobile, gave us solid footing – unless we stepped off it. However, the newly fallen snow disguised any boundaries. When I strayed too far in thirsty pursuit of a particularly tempting icicle, I plunged suddenly to my hips and was ignominiously hauled out.

Back home, we sipped cocoa before retiring, and stood in the darkened dining room watching two flying squirrels illuminated by the outside light. They glided down from the trees to the feeder so rapidly that it would be more accurate to say that they appeared instantaneously. There they crouched, nibbling fistfuls of seeds, their great dark eyes ever watchful. Enchanted, we lingered, yawning sleepily but reluctant to leave. Then, just as we began to turn away, the flying squirrels vanished and we paused, curious to see why. After a few moments, the delicate features of a deer caught the light as she emerged from the darkness under the trees.

Then another arrived.

And another.

Soon five deer were close before us with lowered heads, nosing in the fluffy snow for seeds. Their ears, like woolly periscopes, scanned the night for danger, but their eyes remained calm and present. Before long, they discovered the hidden apples that Mack had tossed out for them earlier. Their rich, reddish coats paled rapidly in the thickening snowfall as they stood still, chewing rapturously.

In the early morning, when I rose to write, the sky had cleared. Moonlight irradiated the rippled icicles beyond the windows. White fields and chequered spruce trees glowed with that special light that is created only when the full moon lingers in the western sky while the east is beginning to brighten.

Below the windows lay snow dimpled with deer tracks.

CHAPTER 9

NOT ALWAYS MAN'S BEST FRIEND

M eanwhile, Poe the raven was recuperating well in his aviary. His body had filled out normally once more and, as his energies grew, his restlessness also increased.

The weeks passed, and he began tearing idly at one of the two-by-four uprights in bored frustration, quickly reducing its thickness by half in one area. Mack responded by suspending a great marrow bone in that spot. Poe chewed on that instead, the bone thudding so hard against the wall of the pen that the noise resonated clearly indoors.

During severe cold, Mack would bring Poe's meats inside, thaw them, and return them. Poe, quick to comprehend any of our efforts on his behalf, would tuck in almost immediately – eating, as Mack put it, *raven*ously.

Poe's breathing still remained stabilized, though weather conditions varied drastically. The eight-by-eight-foot aviary was built into an angle of the house, which gave two solid walls on the northeast corner for shelter and two walls and a ceiling of open caging. Poe's favourite perch was, predictably, the highest one, located in the solid-walled corner. A plywood cover added extra protection, and here he waited out winter's vagaries in the shadows, a dark form with gleaming eyes.

He remained a solitary – but dry – witness throughout one capricious day of blowing snow that faded into a night of freezing rain which, in turn, opened on a warm morning of steady dripping. When the other wild birds began to reappear, as bedraggled as though they'd just endured several rinse cycles, Poe surveyed them with great dignity, his own plumage as immaculate as always.

At first light each day, Poe's deep, throaty calls – with astonishing variations – always prefaced the shrill cries of the jays as they swooped down out of the trees for their waiting seeds. Only occasionally did he vocalize in full daylight – a short burst of high-pitched barks – but whether as a call or a response, we never determined.

Throughout his necessary confinement, Poe watched the endless succession of wildlife activities around him. A pair of ravens who had nested nearby for years became frequent visitors, no doubt mesmerized by the wealth of food in Poe's pen, as well as by the inmate. Mack, hoping to encourage their visits for Poe's sake, tossed extra bones and chunks of meat on top of the aviary for them to share, to the delight of the irrepressible jays, who also partook.

Dried weed stalks rose out of the snow beside Poe's pen, and one day I watched juncos shuffling along the curving stalks nibbling seeds, while other juncos below collected the fallen ones.

A passing dog paused by the aviary door one morning, lured more, I'm sure, by the reeking bones than by Poe, who was watching warily from his corner.

A welcome gift of trout from the local hatchery not only added variety to Poe's diet, but excited his visitors – a neighbouring cat hooked at the caging with frustrated claws, and raccoons clambered over ceiling and walls following the tantalizing odour.

The bird feeder beside the aviary stimulated activity day and night. Jays, as blue and white as a sunbright winter's day, perched on the extreme tops of the surrounding spruce trees during their times of sentry duty, while other jays fed eagerly below. But only the great ravens, when they posed motionless at the tops of the dead, jagged trunks, could recreate the original totem poles. Especially when looming out of mist and silence, their gaze all-seeing, did they become gods.

Red squirrels, during milder days, also joined our avian clientele at the feeder, or chased each other in rattling twangs across Poe's aviary. Voles, more wary, gathered seeds hastily and unobtrusively, then fled with their booty.

Night was just as busy as day for Poe. When snow lay too deep in the woods for saw-whet owls to catch mice, the owls would haunt the feeding station – for so did the mice. Appearing as suddenly and silently as a thought, an owl would light on a low branch of the serviceberry tree beside Poe's aviary. He'd study the scattered seeds and debris under the feeder, his head swivelling abruptly whenever he detected other sounds nearby.

Then movements below would attract his attention. As his ears relayed more activity beneath the snow, where mice scurried in their tunnels, his wings would loosen expectantly and his golden gaze intensify like a rapt chess player's. Suddenly he'd drop as soundlessly as a rock, talons extended for their prey.

Barred owls, too, often hunted near the feeder, their plumage of alternating light and dark streaks melding with particular ease into falling night snow.

One evening, I stood for half an hour in the darkened living room, admiring a barred owl near the muted outside bulb. Then I turned away reluctantly, and switched off the light. The hour was late and I was tired. In the indoor garden, Beejay and Chip dozed in their trees beside the window. I climbed the stairs, yawning.

As I undressed drowsily in the bedroom, there was a terrific BANG!

I sprang like a gazelle just as Chip shot past my face into the closet, her eyes like dinner plates. Mack burst out of the closed TV room in a blur of question marks.

"The *owl*!" I gasped.

I dashed to the head of the stairs and galloped down recklessly, followed by Mack. We ran to the window, turned on the outside light, and spotted the barred owl moving around shakily on his branch. His right eye remained shut, while his left eye, half-open, peered out groggily. Our concern mounted until we finally watched his closed eye open once more. A couple of tiny headfeathers remained plastered to the window beside Chip's tree in the indoor garden.

Indoors, Beejay, unable to flee like Chip, still clung to his branch well above the window, his eyes absolutely enormous in the shadowed room.

The owl, so abruptly deprived of a meal, may still be marvelling at that grackle's punch.

We left the outside light on low to mirror some brightness off the glass, and to further darken the interior.

But Chip spent the rest of that night on my bedside lamp.

As winter began to wane, and milder weather predominated, skunks also rummaged for edibles under the feeder beside Poe. One skunk in particular awed us. He was the most beautiful we'd ever seen. His white stripes were more like two cascades rippling down – and almost vanquishing – the black fur, before arching through the nearly pure white tail like a glorious fountain.

Not surprisingly, we called him, "Waterfall," though perhaps, with a little mental effort, we might have risen to more creative heights.

But despite his various visitors, Poe's restlessness increased. He often opened his great wings when leaping between his most distant perches. Or he landed on the caging itself, where he'd cling, flapping briefly. The aviary was too small for flight by such a large bird, so unless we released him, we would never know if he were able to fly. Accordingly, we opened his door one day, but to our surprise Poe refused to leave. Mack finally slipped inside and gently shooed him out.

I waited at a distance as Poe emerged, looking around warily. He immediately headed out into the field, following the bushes along the fenceline. We held back, watching and expecting Poe to take wing, or at least to *try*, but he continued on foot.

We closed in, hoping to compel him to fly, and Poe loped rapidly across the snow, at last making an effort to lift off – unsuccessfully. No wonder he'd been reluctant to leave. Clearly, his left wing was unable to bear him. We darted ahead and shooed him back slowly towards his pen, which he re-entered almost eagerly, leaping up lightly to his usual perch.

The injury was months old before we'd even met Poe. We had serious doubts that he would ever fly again.

"Nevermore," quoth Mack, as we pondered Poe's dilemma.

One aspect of helping wild birds carries with it more than a touch of frustration – dealing with the attitude that creatures must entertain us. Whenever someone brought us a nestling or an injured adult, Chip often swooped down curiously to land on my head. Or Bashō, seeing me feed mealworms to a strange bird, would call out for his share, perhaps tugging my pant leg for emphasis.

At that point would come the question, "How do you train them to do that?"

Train?

Or a child would stare at a bird sitting on my hand. Accustomed primarily to frenetic cartoon birds doing impossible stunts, or plastic bird toys that squawk and gyrate when a button is pushed, the child, clearly unimpressed so far, would ask, "What does it do?"

Do?

Or, as in Poe's case, we were informed – by various sources – that we could train him to talk. Especially – yes – if we *split his tongue.*

I was stunned that such stupidity still persisted.

Somehow, in a culture glutted with artificial entertainment, much of it highly questionable, the marvel of a living bird – its inherent beauty and its natural activities – isn't enough. Birds, as well as other creatures, must be recreated in our own image, often so they can amuse us in degrading, unnatural ways, like circus animals.

Dogs are favourite choices for such practices, and a dog dressed in silly clothes, walking on its hind legs, is, to me, a distressing spectacle. Working dogs, or well-disciplined house dogs, are another matter *entirely* – though even then, nature may have the last word.

Or the last laugh.

I recall, years ago, being one of several hundred people who were watching dog trials at a major fair. Each dog and trainer would enter the ring at one end, and a judge was positioned halfway down, on one side. A dog, when released, was to range throughout the ring, obeying silent directive hand signals from his human partner, who had to remain near the entrance. Silence from the spectators was considered essential.

One young beast did reasonably well until he noticed the judge standing motionless, his hands behind his back. He, too, was under orders – not to move while the dog was being tested.

The dog, tail wagging, veered aside and trotted gaily up to the judge. There, adapting the natural salutations used among dogs, he began sniffing the fly on the judge's trousers.

As his fascination grew, the wagging tail slowed to a preoccupied tremble and his eyes grew somewhat vague. His nose, now fully engrossed in the source of this alluring aroma, began nudging his victim in his enthusiasm. His frantically gesticulating owner had been utterly forgotten, while, around the spotlit ring, thousands of eyes watched in a taut silence which began to crumble into desperately suppressed snickers.

I truly felt sorry for the judge. His face had deepened through every rosy hue to the purple of an overripe raspberry. No doubt he was praying fervently that the brute wouldn't lift its leg next.

After a couple of agonizing minutes, which must have felt like hours to the hapless judge, the dog finally turned away. And *sneezed violently* – the final humiliation.

I don't remember just where the dog finished in the standings. But I can guess how that judge rated him.

On another occasion, I was travelling by subway in a distant city, unfortunately at rush hour. Trains slid in, slid out of echoing stations as passengers funnelled in, funnelled out. Doors wheezed open like sighs of exhaustion, expelling their stale cargo. After another inhalation, they tightened their rubber lips until the next station, the next releasing sigh.

The regulars read newspapers folded like puzzles, turning one small part to expose another, their eyes determinedly avoiding other eyes, their bodies barely swaying as the trains hurtled in and out of black tunnels. Less-experienced riders clutched handholds, lurched, apologized – were ignored.

The train disgorged us and, amid a driving wedge of humanity, I began climbing stairs. Despite the impression of unrestrained confusion, there is an efficient flow at rush hours created by the regulars. They don't have to linger worriedly before signs or subway maps. They stride without hesitation at the quick pace of all city dwellers.

And they *resent* obstructions.

As we gained the top of the stairs, the speed slowed drastically. People bumped up against one another. Tempers flared. Movement became possible only if we all pressed forward along the wall to our right. I peered ahead curiously. Those approaching us were edging along the other wall. So something was amiss in the centre.

Then a distinct reek of urine struck me.

Suddenly, I was at the scene of the crime and I clutched wildly at the laughter that welled up inside. A man and a large dog had also disembarked. But though the exit loomed alluringly ahead, the dog simply *couldn't wait* any more.

She had squatted down in stubborn defence of a dog's right to pee in this crazy concrete cosmos.

And she was peeing *still*.

Her luckless owner, utterly humiliated by this demonstration of nature in the raw, had unwisely drawn his long raincoat around the dog as well as himself. Whether this was to shield her from the vulgar gaze, or to make them both vanish as though he were wearing a magician's cape, wasn't clear. There he remained, red-faced, his eyes struggling to convey a nonchalance that fooled no one. From beneath his coat emerged a long hairy tail and a stream of yellow urine. And probably the canine equivalent of a sigh of relief.

Only a rush-hour crowd could fail to see the humour.

I was hurried past by the pressure behind me, but I glanced back merrily and spotted the dog's face under the curve of the coat.

I swear she was laughing too.

Fortunately, the inventive actions of a dog don't *always* leave emotional scars on everyone else. Mack and I know a dog who stands upright and walks into a lake beside his equally upright master when they both go swimming. Once he's standing belly-deep in the lake, the dog loves to smack the surface with his front feet and snap at the water that suddenly splashes up.

No aquatic toy could match "Riley" for laughs.

But there have been moments when I, too, wished heartily that human discipline could utterly subdue a dog's natural inclinations. I recall putting a friend's dog outside one autumn night to answer nature's call. Hunting season was in full swing, so during the day the dog had been restricted to the house.

When the creature returned a short while later, she padded in past me with the uneasy look of one who has dined too well.

Dined?

Moments later, she disgorged a revolting mass of entrails all over the living-room floor. Evidently, she'd found the remains of a deer that had been eviscerated by hunters.

An unspeakable stench expanded like an enormous hot-air balloon, pushing against the walls and ceiling, pressing tightly to our faces like plastic wrap. Struggling to breathe, I rolled my eyes in one helpless gesture of nausea, and fled.

After all, it was *her* dog.

That particular beast shone on another memorable occasion when we were on a drive together. We stopped finally in a rural setting to enjoy a picnic lunch. The dog trotted into an empty pasture to contribute her mite to the agricultural industry. Then she wandered further, nose to the ground, exploring.

As we ate, we watched her idly, noting that she, too, seemed to be enjoying herself. Even rolling luxuriously. Then our eyes narrowed suspiciously.

Rolling in what?

When she turned back to the car in answer to our calls, the answer became clear long before she arrived at our feet, panting and bright-eyed. She'd found very wet, dark-green cow faeces of a vintage malodorousness that left the deer entrails *nowhere*.

I couldn't believe that one mild cow could exude such fetid slop – and still *live*. And that a dog would want to *roll* in it shook my faith in the instinctual wisdom bequeathed by Mother Nature. I locked myself, gagging, in the car, rudely renouncing all claims of friendship.

The dog, astonished at our sudden change of mood, was dragged unceremoniously to the nearest brook for total immersion, thereby endangering all aquatic life downstream for the next few miles. Not for days did the reek fade from the car.

After that episode, the dog's name deteriorated from the whimsical "Muffin" to the more appropriate "Meadow Muffin."

Perhaps Muffin's eccentricities could be construed as frustrated artistic temperament – though, speaking as an artist myself, I've never been driven to such olfactory consolations. At a local theatrical production, Muffin stole the show.

Her owner was involved offstage in operating special effects, so it fell to me to direct the dog. When the theatre suddenly darkened in preparation for the final act, Muffin and I would tiptoe quickly across the stage and hide in the wings. There, we'd watch the players until the end, when the male lead was left alone. He was playing the role of a man neurotically afraid of dogs. After a brief soliloquy, he'd exit on our side. But only for a few seconds.

This was Muffin's big moment.

The actor would hastily – but silently – provoke her in a familiar game of chase that Muffin had loved for years. She'd begin lunging excitedly – but quietly – at him while I held her collar. Then he'd dash back on stage again, bawling with "fear," just as I released Muffin's collar.

She'd tear after him as naturally as any street dog, barking wildly and pursuing him all around the stage props till he fled finally up the aisle. Then, obeying my muted whistle – although a *train* whistle would have been submerged in the uproarious mirth of the audience – she'd trot offstage, briskly and triumphantly.

She never forgot her lines.

And she *never* failed to bring down the house.

When the show, a howling success – so to speak – played an extra performance in a distant city, Muffin went "on tour." To crass comments long afterward about has-been actresses, we'd retort hotly that Muffin wasn't out of work.

She was merely between jobs.

Muffin was one of those woolly-faced trotting tangles – like an animated hearth rug. The kind of dog you find yourself addressing at one end, only to be answered by a testy bark from the other.

At one time, I was caring for two tiny ducklings, both downy and delightful. From the moment she met the babes, Muffin's dormant maternal nature sprang into life. Warning her to be gentle almost seemed superfluous. She immediately adopted them, and would lie down contentedly with both peeping ducklings "swimming" through the woolly waves on her back. Her owner and I could even slip off briefly to a neighbour's house and leave her babysitting in the yard. Muffin clearly felt uneasy whenever I handled the babes, and watched my every move with anxious attention lest I harm them. Even when the ducks were grown, they loved to root with their bills through her tangles, gabbling excitedly, while she sighed patiently and endured their frenetic probings.

Within those matted mysteries, one could only imagine what their busy bills were finding.

Muffin, however, had been unusually gentle. Untaught, undisciplined dogs can be lethal to poultry and ducks.

My first duck was a large, handsome black and white drake with an iridescent green head – and the saddest brown eyes.

No wonder.

He'd been used to train a young retriever by being tossed into water, grabbed by the dog, then borne back to shore in its jaws, quacking with fright, only to be tossed out again, over and over. His wings had been bound, which deepened his terror, but rendered the job easier for the dog. And, of course, the trainer.

From the viewpoint of the duck it was an unthinkable existence.

I received him in late autumn, anxious to better his life in any way I could. Gradually, with kindness, comfort and – especially – fresh lettuce through the winter, the sadness in those brown eyes faded and was replaced by warmth and contentment.

I dubbed him "Ducklips," a deplorable sobriquet redeemed somewhat by the fact that his closest companion was my goat, a Toggenburg wether (castrated male) named "Goatlips."

His singular name derived from a priceless photo of him reclining luxuriously in sun-warmed hay, his half-open eyes leering at the camera and his "lips" curved into a devastating smile which could be amusingly construed as seductive.

Ducklips and Goatlips grazed together, bedded down together, and, on hot afternoons, lay side by side in the shade near the doorstep. Whenever anyone drove into the yard, Goatlips would come thundering up in great excitement, bleating greetings to all. Following him with equal enthusiasm would be Ducklips, quacking softly and waddling with all the speed his generous girth would allow.

Each night I'd sit in the hay beside both of them before I finally turned out the light. I'd treat Ducklips to fresh lettuce and Goatlips to a sweet ration mix.

Then Ducklips and I would do our duet: I'd whistle "The Blue Danube" waltz and the two double beats at the end of every line would be quacked in place by Ducklips.

When he'd slip his bill under his wing and close his eyes, I'd get up to leave. Just as I was closing the door, one soft double quack would touch the darkness like "goodnight."

His cruel, untimely death from two dogs seeking amusement was heartbreaking.

And bitterly ironic.

CHAPTER 10

THE AWAKENING LAND

Like a slow but persistent tide, spring began to advance. It rolled in briefly, fled, then surged in further and retreated again – but not quite so far. And like the swaying fronds of barnacles, unquestioning, we responded to these inevitable swings between seasons, gleaning what we could out of each ebb and flow.

During more rapid rebounds, we felt as though we were trapped in a revolving door between winter and spring, exposed to both in rapid succession but unable to escape into either.

The first day of spring, teetering on the fulcrum between days and nights of equal lengths, and following a half-and-half moon, seemed appropriately undecided about how to present herself. After trying a little sunshine – *far* too sprightly – and a deadly gloom – too *sombre* – she settled for a white sky whirling with icy sparkles too tiny to be designated as snowflakes.

Mack slipped outdoors to fill the bird feeder, but a moment later reopened the door and called me urgently to come out. When I joined him, he pointed down the hayfield. Six deer had emerged from the woods and were searching the ground for suitable forage. As though in keeping with the see-sawing seasons, five of them bore typically reddish-brown coats, but the sixth was winter white.

Disbelieving, wondering if I were seeing someone's goat instead of a deer, I returned with binoculars. But when all the deer, startled mysteriously by something closer, bounded away, six long tails waved like banners. There were definitely no goats.

The white deer's face was as brown as those of his companions, and on one side of his body he had a few large, dark spots. Later, when I suggested facetiously to someone else, equally smitten, that Frosty the Snowdeer stood before us, she denounced me for my lack of imagination.

"At least call him 'Chocolate Chip,'" she retorted.

And the name stuck.

The white deer delighted us with every sighting, and word spread. Neighbours who spotted him told their friends, and often,

in the evenings, when he was certain to be grazing in the lower hayfield, a strange vehicle would park on our quiet road. The passengers would climb out cautiously, with cameras and binoculars, eager to watch Chocolate Chip. He stood out from the others, as Mack put it, like a light bulb.

We were luckier. We saw him not only every evening but at more spectacular moments. Once, after viewers had come and gone, disappointed when he didn't appear in the lower field, we saw him in the upper one instead. Late sunshine had just burst through the crowding dark clouds, transforming the land into golden richness. Chocolate Chip and a buddy were playing.

While the brown deer was beautified with an edging of light, Chocolate Chip seemed, by the alchemy of sun and clouds, to have been transmuted into pure gold. He danced with the numinous grace of an unearthly being.

One night, under a full moon, Mack and I set off for a walk, but paused when we were partly down the hayfield. Ahead, we could see the shimmering forms of nineteen grazing deer. Then Chocolate Chip wandered into view, his beautiful coat glowing bluish-white under the globe of the great moon above.

A spirit deer.

Two shadowy Canada geese flew through the beauty overhead, with compelling, throaty calls – like the voice of the sky and wind vitalized. On the nearby lake, flanked by pale trees, moonlight glittered, darting across the surface with every breeze, like flocks of tiny migrating spirits.

At dusk, on the last day of March, we watched Chocolate Chip with a brown deer in the distance. The weather had been consistently dark and wet. Clouds of heavy mist still haunted the hilltops and water droplets beaded every branch. Sound was muffled, as though the vapour had plugged our ears with dank, grey fingers.

We both felt that Chocolate Chip looked a little different in some way. Are there *two* white deer? we wondered.

The next morning, I spotted Chocolate Chip through an upstairs window and alerted Mack, who looked for him from a downstairs window. His view was somewhat obscured by the tall chokecherry bushes that defined the fenceline – and this knowledge I wickedly took into account.

Then I called out, "What's that white thing on the other side of Chocolate Chip? Is it a snow patch or the white deer we saw last night?"

"Where?" he cried, and I heard him scrambling for the binoculars and a better view from a different window.

"Just beyond Chips. I can see it better up here. I think it's a *second* white deer facing away with its head down – but of course I don't have binoculars."

I smothered my giggles as I heard him try another window.

"*Oh!* Look at it *now*! HURRY!" I shouted, when I could control my voice to sound convincing.

Mack finally charged for the stairs, knocking over a chair in his haste, and galloped into the bedroom where I stood, staring outside and shading my eyes, an image of concentration. He crowded eagerly up to the window. Only when his binoculars were pressed to his eyes did I step silently back, grinning like the Cheshire Cat.

"I just see Chips," he puffed, scanning the area.

Then the penny dropped – and so did the binoculars.

"Oh you RAT!" he moaned in disgust, as he turned away.

It was April Fools' Day.

"At least you were dressed this time," I snickered.

This was a malicious reference to an earlier April that floated in on heavy rains, with floods in low-lying areas. Mack was still asleep when I called from the window in simulated wild excitement.

"Mack! Look! A SEAL!"

"Wha-a-a-ah?" His eyes struggled to open, but failed.

"Hurry! I can't be*lieve* this. A *seal*, for gawd's sake!"

A professional couldn't have bettered *that* delivery. Mack shot out of bed and flung himself at the window, blinking and clutching the sill with both hands. A cold wind blew in, as merciless as I – Mack was stark naked.

"Where? Where?"

But I was incoherent with laughter.

The tide of spring began to push forward more determinedly each day, washing over the awakening land and leaving flotillas of early migrants clinging to the trees.

The first male grackles joined our winter regulars at the bird feeders, swelling their iridescent black chests to release their characteristic calls, then deflating and feeding, while Chip watched intently from the window.

One fox sparrow appeared in the scattered ground seed, unobtrusive with its streaked, brown-and-white breast and long, fox-red tail. The next day, two more joined the first.

Over a hundred robins swept down out of a south wind and dotted the fields, where a low mist hung like the last breath over each expiring snow patch. They trotted, paused with cocked heads, trotted again, pursuing darting insects and spiders that sought to elude them.

A red-winged blackbird called from a still-dormant marsh, and an early red-bellied snake lifted its small head warily, its dark back blending with last year's rotted, flattened stalks.

We set out for an early-morning walk beneath a clear sky. A flood of light and warmth flowed from east to west, tinting the pallid moon that floated yet, though night had been submerged. Tight buds, buoyed up all winter on branches, began to respond to the tidal pull of spring, as the sap rose higher and higher. They loosened their tight clutch and grew sticky. Slowly, their sails began to swell, warmed by the undefeated sun.

A snowshoe hare, in a pale blur, dashed between alternating plots of frozen snow and thawed ground, like a moving chequer in a game between the two seasons. Nothing physical could have caught that fleeting form – only our eyesight.

Alders lined the steaming brook. Rosy sunlight kindled their frosty branches, while long blue shadows of nearby tree trunks slid like swords through the incandescence, slowly cooling it again. A single crow cleft the early-morning sky that joined night to day. In its bill, it bore a large twig for nesting material – a key to unlock the solitude of winter days and let in the concerns of a busy family life.

The sun lifted higher and higher, its rays resolutely piercing even the most stubborn crystals on the trees, even the coldest hollows. Our faces became sun-warmed on one side but remained night-cool on the other – till we turned for home. Then, like the changing times, the pivoting days and nights, warmth flooded our cool sides, while our warm ones steadily chilled.

High on a maple branch, two pileated woodpeckers mated. Their black and white plumage, like yin and yang incarnate, resolved all opposites, even gender, into one. In the reddish morning light, their striking crimson crests flared like flags.

In keeping with the duality everywhere, the lake also seemed of two minds at once, its frozen centre ringed with open water. Spring meltwaters, with all the enthusiastic energies of youth, sprang down the time-honoured brook path that cut through the sloping land. But their lighthearted calls were silenced suddenly in the staid calm of the lake, quiescent in its ancient hollow.

On the far side, we paused beside a spring that gurgled under a puzzle of mossy tree roots. Where its clear waters rippled into the lake, small clusters of bright-green underwater plants flourished, and fingerlings swam – like a miniature tropical world.

When our shadows loomed over them suddenly, they darted under a protective floating log, its far end still gripped by ice. The knobbly form, smoothed and silvered by decades of lakewater and sunshine, has changed so little in the thirty years that I've admired it that it may have fallen from the shore before I was born.

It may have begun life before my mother did.

It may still grace the lake when I've passed on.

CHAPTER 11

TREE PERSONALITIES AND DWELLINGS

The paths we followed on our walk were ones I'd created many years earlier, beginning in early autumn. My starting point was a tiny, shallow swamp that lay only a short way into the woods. Long ago a birch had fallen into it, and, at equal distances along the trunk, three young birches had risen. The water, rich with aquatic vegetation, had been a favourite with ducks each spring. By summer, the swamp would be drained and filled by luxurious ferns. But the following spring, water would return. And so would the ducks.

I set out one autumn day to begin my trails, passing the swamp in its usual spot. I ventured deeper and deeper into the woods, trimming any branches that threatened my eyes, cutting down only small, dead trees when necessary. Suddenly, inexplicably, I found myself *approaching* the little swamp.

I paused, and got my bearings – but only figuratively, of course. I'd scorned the help – or, in my case, the added confusion – of a compass. Then I set off resolutely in a *new* direction.

Only to find myself *once again* on the brink of the swamp.

This recurring nightmare happened several times, convincing me finally that the restless thing was following me. There couldn't be *that* many swamps with a prone birch bearing three youngsters.

Before I began seriously to consider walking backwards – like Alice – in order to get someplace new, I decided to wait for the first snowfall. One mid-December night obligingly left several inches and the next morning, I began again. But after a long day with little progress, I concluded that, although the swamp now seemed less mobile, several invisible people were also trailing through the woods – each leaving tracks that exactly matched my own. The stiffened leaves of a beech tree, moving in the wind while I rested, bewildered, began to sound suspiciously like muffled laughter.

Only by sheer obstinacy did I complete my meandering trails against such odds. Subtly defined, they flowed uphill and down, seeking out particularly noteworthy trees, areas of deep moss, dells of ferns.

And swamps.

Our woods are thick with hardwoods and softwoods at every stage. Some are especially enormous. They loom up in silence here and there, brooding watchfully among the others like guardians. An ancient beech or maple may look like a standing dead trunk, beaten almost out of any semblance to a tree by decades of extreme weather. Part of its body may even be fallen away and decaying on the ground. But high over our heads, that victorious tree will lift up young branches with sleeping buds, waiting to be roused for another season of renewal.

Many trees have become particular favourites.

One of our trails leads to a pine with such an enormous bole that Mack and I can barely join hands around it. Only eight feet from the ground, unusual in a white pine, its solidity breaks out into great serpentine branches undulating away from the main thrust of the trunk, more in the manner of an oak. The summit of this floating mountain of green and glinting needles rises well above the surrounding spruce, hardwood, and pine offspring.

This would be the ultimate choice for a magnificent tree house – one of the more ingenious kind that refrains from driving nails or bolts into its accommodating host.

Near the Great Pine are two whimsical maples, lone humorists among their straight, staid companions. One maple rises from the ground in the usual way for about six feet. There its indecisiveness becomes apparent as it divides cleanly into an adamant Y form, each half of the tree pursuing its own interests.

Only twenty feet away is a second Y-shaped maple, its two arms flung high and wide in mock horror. Or like a jubilant fan when the home team scores.

Mack has dubbed the two trees "Y?" and "Y-knot?"

Coppice trees, like arboreal bouquets, are scattered among the predominating single and double trunks. There is one magnificent maple specimen with *twenty-two trunks* emerging from a single base. None of the other clusters has attained quite the octopuslike complexity of this one with its healthy, leafy tentacles.

The tiniest trees intrigue me just as much as their elders. In a miniature forest of three-inch-tall maples, each seedling bears two fragile web-footed leaves, as reddish and freshly unfolded as a newborn human baby.

And during one Christmas season, I set aside a gleaming chestnut out of a bowlful bought to be roasted and eaten. I planted it instead. To my delight, the chestnut swelled and cracked, and sent down an exploratory root. Then a green shoot emerged cautiously to bear, in time, two clusters of leafy fingers, like a pair of green gloves spread out to dry. I planted the little tree outdoors in the summer, and it flourished.

Old stumps make great mothers – especially for birch seeds. As a young birch continues to grow, its roots delve hungrily into the rich, damp nutrients of the rotting stump. By the time the stump has finally disintegrated and vanished, the youngster has matured. It has become one of those fascinating, long-legged birch trees that I suspect dances with sprightly abandon on Midsummer's Eve.

Similarly, I've seen large, aging mushrooms with shrivelled, blackened rims and bearing, like old gardeners' hands, a hatch of tiny, white mushrooms cupped gently in their palms.

Exposed roots, often entwined around rocks, are favourite hideaways for small mammals. In winter especially, we see entry holes of various sizes in one great root cluster, with well-worn trails disappearing inside.

We often toss handfuls of seeds inside the doorways.

Sometimes, we'll find an old *cut* stump, holding the memory of a tree whose wood warmed people who are themselves only memories now. Greyed by weather and encroaching lichens, the stump's fallen centre, encircled by a curved, flat-topped rim, creates a cup of concentrated warmth like a miniature walled garden. Varied mosses line the inside, while red-tipped soldier lichens guard the tops of the ramparts.

Within this greenhouse, we'll find spruce seedlings, several only a few inches tall. Or maybe a single youngster eight or nine inches tall, the light-green tips of new growth brightening the ends of the minute branches. Perhaps some of the aged spruces towering over us as we crouch down, peering into this fascinating nursery, began their journeys in similar incubators many decades ago.

Did someone else, taking a breather from responsibilities just as pressing as ours – though in an earlier age – pause as we are doing now, touched by the *sheer marvel* of a walled garden in the wild?

Even in a distant city, we have a favourite tree growing out of a busy sidewalk. Growing out of the tree is a thrusting of wild ferns.

Just above our eye level, fronds arch out in moonlike crescents of waxing and waning curves, renewing themselves each spring, only to decline once again after reaching their fullness.

The quiet persistence of nature amid our mechanized cacophony.

As a child, I suspect I spent as much time in trees as I did on the ground. I revelled in climbing to the tops of the great willows that bordered a nearby brook. Leaning against those swaying limbs on a windy day, floating above the perplexing conflicts of adults and other children, became my lifeline.

Trees played a major role in retaining my sanity – such as it is.

To withdraw myself even further, I lugged armloads of branches up into the trees and wove them into leafy forts. In summer, they were beautifully camouflaged, as was I. But in winter, like birds' nests, they stood out starkly. High in my aerial retreats, I could see the world while remaining hidden. Be *in* it, if not *of* it.

How many times did I leave the house, ostensibly for school, only to climb quickly up one of my favourite trees? I still see my much-tried mother leaving for work far below me while I clung like a burr to the uppermost branches – only slightly hampered by the mandatory dress demanded by my school.

Once the coast was clear, I'd slip back into the house, change to my battered but beloved jeans, and escape for a day of glorious freedom.

Then came the inevitable time of reckoning: the note I'd have to present next day at school explaining my absence.

And how many notes did I forge, developing a dubious skill that in later years would have brought its own retribution? Fortunately – for my mother's peace of mind as well – I directed my energies into legitimate art.

Trees were always my companions, my fellow conspirators, and – obviously – my friends. And they still are.

One evening at dusk, afflicted with intense grief at a recent loss, I wandered across the fields to an old apple tree beside a brook. On impulse, I stopped and leaned heavily against the trunk, one arm curled around a branch, my eyes closed.

To my amazement, I felt the tree breathing with me, breath for breath.

Any illusion that we were separate beings vanished. And with that strengthening sense of unity, of breathing together with the breathing world, I felt a strong surge of renewal. Of restored perspective.

After all, loss is merely change. And each change around us requires a corresponding change in our perceptions.

It is a humbling experience to be reminded – yet again – of what *is*. But then trees can teach us so much. Anything can. If we're open, we can learn, even if the message is non-verbal.

Recently, I was drawing in an interesting area between a salt marsh, vibrant with bird life, and erstwhile pastures, now reclaimed by mixed woodland. As I wandered between drawings, I encountered the imprisoned remains of a tree that had died prematurely. Only a four-foot trunk of spongy wood encircled by peeling bark stood yet, unable to fall as its top had, years earlier. The weapon – steel farm fencing – was still bound around the lifeless bole in the stranglehold that had slowly but relentlessly stifled the tree.

Elsewhere in this "protected area," signs pertinent to its preservation are *nailed* to living trees.

One has to wonder . . .

The discarded tangle of limbs and severed stumps so characteristic of clear-cut practices – or woodland "management" – is equally deplorable. And painful. Such an unforgettable silence prevails when there are *no branches* stirred by winds. And *no songbirds* – just the faint cry of a floating hawk to emphasize the desecration.

It's the silence that prevails when rain falls without the subtle syncopation of drops hitting leaves. Without landing birds releasing a sudden crescendo of drops on other branches. Or on other birds.

There's such a difference between silence.
And SILENCE.

Exposed trees near the ocean shore seem so celebratory of their endless dance with wind and water. Their vigorous partners twist and turn them as tirelessly as they do the shape-shifting clouds that are always moving on, always approaching. A friend of ours calls these ragged silhouettes "flag" trees.

On Newfoundland's west coast, such trees, blasted by gales until forced to creep on their bellies across the rocky land, are called, intriguingly, "tuckamore."

Among our favourites there are many droll trees that bear distinctive facial features – including one that's perpetually chortling over a private joke. Another wears a scattered expression as though reeling from a punch. Or perhaps *just* punch – the liquid

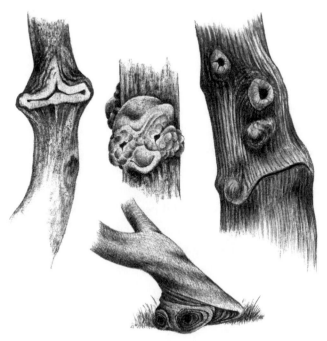

kind. Sly eyes leer out from odd swellings on trunks everywhere, often above gaping or grimacing mouths.

During our walks, we often choose the trail that passes the raccoons' "tree house" in an aged maple. Its great trunk lifts out of the ground only to bend over and grow almost horizontally for about ten feet. Then it twists upright for another ten feet or so before erupting in a fountain spray of energetic branches.

At that last abrupt angle, there is a large hole that leads deep into the hollow, recumbent trunk. Inside, raccoons den up through the winter months, sleeping during bitter cold, and foraging when the weather turns mild.

As we approached one day in early spring, we could see, crossing the chaste snow still surrounding their tree, a long, brown trail of raccoon tracks that began and ended just below the entrance hole. Evidently, they leaped up into their den and descended at the same place.

Mack chuckled. Then he took a couple of apples out of his pocket and tossed them down into the den.

Breakfast in bed for the slumbering raccoons.

The dwellings of wildlings are fascinating. And ingenious.

We once spotted a sapsucker's home drilled into a tall, young spruce tree, long dead. Above the round entry projected a shelf fungus, a perfect roof for protection against rain or sun. Or a predator's eyes.

Recently, a strikingly beautiful nest of dried, woven grasses was given to us. It had been built inside an outbuilding beside the ocean. Created by tree swallows, who mysteriously never returned, the nest contains six minute white eggs dwarfed by a circular froth of large, soft gull feathers, a few of them lightly barred.

While gliding down a river swollen by spring runoff, we canoed past an otter's home, a shadowy tunnel delved into a reedy bank with a few telltale clam shells on the threshold.

Of the more whimsical dwellings I've seen was one created by a tunnel spider. I had planted bright fuchsia flowers in an old black kettle in order to attract hummingbirds. The spider, as delighted by my offering as the hummingbirds, wove a flamboyant gauze funnel all around the spout, anchoring this firmly to nearby plants and other projections. As the funnel narrowed, the gauze grew denser – and escape, less likely. When I peered into the spout I could see the patient architect in his sheltered lair.

Waiting.

One of the prettiest duck nests I've seen was established within the arch of an unusual decaying stump beside a pond. Though nearby traffic never ceased, though crowds of humans passed only ten feet away, the hidden nest remained a secret. The utter stillness of the brooding duck seemed to create an aura of protection that defied the surrounding clatter. Even the drawing I made of it, furtively and hastily, failed to draw anyone's attention – to my infinite relief.

During a warm spring day in the previous year, Mack and I gathered edible fiddleheads near a strong, quick-surging river. We wandered deeper and deeper into the fern belt, following the curled fingers of fronds that beckoned ever before us as we picked half of each cluster only, leaving the other half to mature. At one point, with my mind nearly hypnotized by the murmur of rushing waters in the prevailing silence, I leaned over a log, reaching out for a group of delectable beauties. Suddenly, a flurry of whistling wings exploded in my face, and I leaped back, almost falling.

A ruffed grouse swooped away before me, squeaking urgently, and disappeared into the tangle of undergrowth. When I recovered myself and peered cautiously under the log, I found her nest, artfully concealed, with a mound of eggs cradled in her own plucked feathers – a core of beginnings encircled by symbols of flight.

We instantly fled from her area to collect more distant fiddle-heads, so she would return to her cooling eggs.

Around us rose several dead elms, barkless and silvered, with broken branch stubs. Many of the great trunks were two to three feet in diameter, their massive strength graced by the whorled grain. I glanced admiringly up the torso of one of the silent giants – and laughed aloud.

About ten feet from the ground, we discovered another interesting dwelling. A large hole gaped in the trunk, but it was *crammed* with fur that sagged out in a comfortable curve. Inside, a portly raccoon was snoozing through the daylight hours, his head deep in the darkness of the tree's heart, his woolly back warmed by the strengthening sunlight.

A metric treehouse for an imperial raccoon.

Only our knowledge of the vulnerable ground nest of the ruffed grouse, thirty or forty feet away, tempered our delight in this masked sleeper.

CHAPTER 12

CAUGHT IN THE COILS OF SPRING

The Easter season was upon us, but, far from offering the renewal of growing warmth and unfurling leaves, each day brought skies of unmitigated gloom. Flurries, driven on bitter, bone-chilling winds, needled our faces as we hiked the hilltops. In the swamps, a little water remained open, but the rest froze into thin, wrinkled ice, speckled with snowflakes.

By the south wall of the house stood clusters of drooping crocuses, beaded with water, waiting for a wave of sunlight's wand to transform them into flares of yellow or purple. Behind them, tulips and daffodils, tight-lipped and green, sullenly refused any glimpses of their colourful hearts. Nearby bloodroot shoots, with tightly shut eyes, wrapped their green cloaks around their stems and waited stoically for sunshine.

But in vain.

A morose Easter morning dawned with inches of snow smothering the spring flowers. Large flakes still fell, steadily and silently. In the whitened trees around the feeders, blue jays and grackles gathered, calling hungrily and knocking clods of snow down to the ground; there many of the more determined birds were digging for seeds. As the temperature began to rise, I tossed out scoops of fresh grain for them, but well away from the house to avoid the sudden snowslides that thudded down from the metal roof.

The eaves dripped mournfully as the snow changed to rain.

Indoors, a fragrance of hot cross buns seeped through the house as we gamely ignored the dismal drizzle. In the studio, we solved the question of just what one would give a bunny for Easter by offering Edna a mound of red-clover seedlings that I'd sprouted in a bottle.

It was as good as a sunny morning to watch her chewing them blissfully, ears relaxed, long eyelashes lowered contentedly.

But winter's touch was no longer potent. Spring energies could not be denied in the maple trees as the sap flow persisted. We drove to a distant sugar bush and listened to drops of sap echoing musically in metal buckets. When full, they were emptied into collecting tanks. Then the accumulated sap was piped into the sugar house to be heated and condensed, and we followed eagerly.

We walked out of a cold wind into sudden warmth, sweetened by woodsmoke and heavy with distilled maple mist. One of the workers opened the firebox doors beneath the enormous vat of boiling sap that dwarfed the small building. Intense heat and brilliance reddened our faces as he hurled more great logs into the inferno. Then he slammed the doors, extinguishing the eye-blinking dazzle, and reducing the fire's voracious roar to a muted rumble of satisfaction. Sweat beaded his forehead as he pulled off his protective gloves.

The evaporator was the presiding deity, brooding like a great hen above its busy acolytes. Its hum vibrated the sugar house and pervaded every conversation. Taking temperature and sugar-content readings, draining the golden bounty, adding more sap or more wood, cleaning every apparatus over and over – all were vital rituals in this sacred sacrifice that converted the blood of countless maple trees into sweet wine.

We nibbled at chunks of maple cream, sap that had been boiled past the syrup stage to attain the consistency of creamy fudge. Over fresh snow packed into a deep tray, the owner poured hot syrup, which cooled instantly into a glorious goo – a heavenly concoction that clung affectionately to teeth and fillings, but was worth any mouth-twisting distortions in order to swallow it.

On the wall, in a place of honour, hung a framed photo of Bubble that we'd sent the owner the previous year. Bubble's warm beak and wattles had been coated with melting maple cream when I'd taken his picture, and he'd eaten so much that he was compelled – regretfully – to refuse any more. Below his sticky face, I'd printed, "Maple cream won't rot MY teeth!"

Despite the unavoidable tug of sadness in my heart, it was delightful to see Bubble there. I saluted him with another morsel of his beloved maple cream.

I recall my own efforts to make maple syrup.

Years ago. Before I knew better.

In the mixed woods that lay across the road from my mother's house stood a number of sugar maples. Helped by an experienced friend – who *should* have known better – I drilled holes with a brace and bit into the south sides of the trees and inserted spiles. From them, we hung a motley miscellany of containers, some of which were mere plastic food tubs strung on heavy twine. At the end of each day, as the flow decreased for the night, we'd snowshoe through the woods to each tree, emptying sap into large buckets, which we lugged back to the house.

Our forays quickly packed down the snow surrounding the sugar maples, located, as luck would have it, on short – but steep – hillsides. The sunny warmth of each day, in combination with freezing temperatures at night, soon transformed our quaint sugar bush into a horror of gleaming ice.

We skidded and rebounded from tree to tree, trying to control snowshoes that converted suddenly to sleigh runners on every slope. As though possessed by their own devilment, they spun sideways when we lifted our feet, pitching us into outlandish contortions and leaving us helplessly clutching trees.

If we were lucky enough to have trees handy to clutch.

In their bitter battles with one another, each snowshoe knocked the other askew, so that we lurched off-balance, the foot we needed to lift always being the one pinned down. Our legs were bumped by the buckets so repeatedly that they became dappled with bruises. Even our socks were continually sticky from sap being slopped into our boots.

Exhausted, yet triumphantly bearing any remaining sap, we'd return to my mother, who would be hovering over curls of vapour above the stock pots in her steamy kitchen. Sticky sweat ran down the walls of the cubicle that surrounded the electric stove, and beaded up on her hair and glasses as she patiently tended the boiling sap, day after day. At night, she left the heat on at a simmer and escaped thankfully to bed.

Our final yield was *one quart* of maple syrup – so expensive, so hard-won, that its flavour has never been equalled.

Since that experience, which I refuse to repeat, *any* price for pure maple syrup has always seemed a bargain.

Despite the fitful spring weather, we could feel energies rising everywhere. Each day, for several weeks, we witnessed ravens engrossed in what we concluded was a group ritual related to courtship and solidarity.

Two by two, or occasionally in threes – a yearling with parents? – and with wingtips almost touching, the ravens swooped and glided in graceful arabesques directly above the river. The great birds rarely flapped their wings. Instead, they exploited to the full the air currents that arose as prevailing winds swept across the water and encountered the far slope of spruce and pine wood.

When they rested, the ravens perched in the tops of the pines, preening. Or fluttered to the ground, black forms scattered over whitened fields, searching for food.

Close to these raven dances hung power lines clutched by those huge wooden supports that stride with equal indifference through farmlands or wilderness, over rivers or rocky hills. Here, we invariably spotted our "candlestick" eagles – one on each out-stretched arm of a particular power pole. Silent, unmoving, their white heads like beacons on top of their dark bodies, they regarded their domain and the wheeling ravens through search-light eyes of pale gold.

Against the failing light one evening, we were entertained when an immature eagle landed on the top of a short, dark spruce. As he struggled to gain a solid foothold, beating his huge wings for balance, the silhouetted tree seemed to be flailing its upper branches in an effort to fly.

On one of our spring hikes, we found raven tracks, a twining of random stitches in the sagging sheet of snow that still draped the mossy forest floor. We followed them, noting with keen inter-est that the birds had been examining fallen sticks, picking up but then discarding many, as was evident by the disturbed ground. Other sticks had been removed, leaving an empty gash in the snow where each one had rested all winter. The trailing roots of upended trees had also been rummaged through, and smaller radicles twisted off and taken.

A single croak overhead resonated in the stillness, and we glanced up through the canopy of woven branches. A raven, carrying long rootlets, glided over the heads of the trees and down into a tall, narrow spruce that stood thirty feet from where we watched, motionless. Peering through the crowded trees, we saw him hop closer to the trunk, where dense, lichened branches were tightly clustered. A second raven, probably the female, greeted the first one from their bower.

When we crept closer, we could see the new nest taking shape.

Unfortunately, it was on the edge of Mack's little wood lot, where he'd been felling dead spruce trees for firewood. He'd skilfully dropped each one so as to avoid the young trees pushing up towards the increasing light. Then he'd stripped off branches, cut each trunk into rounds, split the rounds into stove-size chunks, and stacked the chunks into neat rows.

These long, hard hours in his wood lot, with birds and squirrels nearby to contribute to his pleasure, were enjoyable times which he looked forward to each day.

But now, the ravens were busy there.

Mack shrugged. We had enough firewood on hand to warm us until next winter, and nesting season *is* a priority. He would leave the wood lot to the ravens and their young.

One day, we drew near to see how they were progressing. I led the way, stepping cautiously around brittle sticks and over fallen trees, crouching under clutching branches. Mack followed quietly. Both of us kept looking upward, searching the look-alike, scraggy spruce tops for the nest.

Suddenly, Mack tripped heavily over a log, prickly with upright, snagging branches. They cracked and popped like pistol shots as Mack crashed through them to the ground, landing with a violent thud directly behind me. Startled, I squealed shrilly and sprang like a released arrow.

The raven, who'd been brooding peacefully in the privacy of her nest, shot straight up as though she'd been electrically ejected.

With hysterical squawks, she flapped around and around above her tree in turbulent circles.

Her mate, who'd been hunting for food in the nearby hayfield, responded instantly to her cries. We could see him swooping back, a croaking black blur of protective menace, as we hurriedly untangled ourselves and fled.

The alerted forest still rang with their vocal outrage ten minutes later when we closed the house door abashedly behind us.

Back indoors, we found that spring was definitely on the rebound – though we recoiled at our discoveries.

While we were enjoying our hike, Chip had discovered two fresh loaves of Mack's bread cooling under a tea towel in the kitchen. But a more elaborate disguise than that would be needed to fool Chip.

Unhampered by any rebukes of conscience, she twitched off the towel, which landed partially in a greasy frying pan of soapy water. The whole towel quickly became saturated, so that the part trailing out of the pan dripped steadily down the side of the stove into a growing pool on the floor.

Though the bread was too hot to eat, it was cool enough for Chip to create a lunar effect, with craters dug all over the crusts. We now had two moon rocks to slice for breakfast. Beakfuls of bread were scattered over the counter and floor, and more were dissolving in the communal waterdish, where they strangely resembled floating mats of bloated toilet paper.

In our bedroom, Chip had found a package of Mack's chewing gum, which she unwrapped piece by piece. Though lacking the teeth necessary to enjoy gum in the traditional way, she resorted to her usual alternative – and was still pushing the limp sticks through the scum of bread in the waterdish when we arrived home.

Having no immediate use for discarded gum wrappers, Chip had left them crumpled all over the bedroom floor. Though as I remarked – rather pointedly – *anyone* could do that.

Beejay, not to be outdone, had hopped up the stairs to our bedroom to roost – not on the windowsill, as usual, but on top of one of my sculptures. Evidently his artistic leanings were more Expressionistic, where the creative flow is unrestrained – cascades of droppings had slid down the polished stone, with adamant lumps hardening at varying levels for emphasis.

His latest comment, just hot – *and wet* – off the press, was still oozing in a gleaming trickle when we appeared in the doorway.

But then, I've been dealt worse comments by less-qualified critics.

In the studio, Miles, now capable of escaping Molly's aggression by dodging her advances or by leaping up onto a shelf, had attempted to fly. Unfortunately, he landed on my gloxinias and

African violets, which were blooming in a colourful row on a windowsill.

The plants that weren't trampled or broken as he struggled for balance were knocked to the floor and summarily eaten by Edna.

When we opened the door, still reeling from the exploits of the others, we found Miles resting comfortably on the remains of a particularly beautiful violet. Below him, her belly *stuffed* with flowers, lay Edna, stretched out in a postprandial doze. Even her slumbering ears failed to rise at our entrance.

Molly was wedged into Miles's small waterdish trying to bathe, and successfully slopping water onto the floor, if not over herself. She'd already flung his seeds with vindictive finesse over a wide area – and had shat copiously on them. In all directions, droppings from both pigeons were swelling and dissolving in little puddles of water.

There was no need to round up the usual suspects.

We'd caught the culprits.

Red-handed.

Meanwhile Poe, too, was responding to spring's summons. With fully restored health, his restlessness increased, and he hammered in frustration at the aviary structure. Clearly, he needed more room. Especially if he were to develop any flight skills.

His early-morning vocalizations still mingled with those of other birds – guttural croaks of astonishing variety, issued with his throat feathers all pushed out and his great bill pointing sometimes down, sometimes straight up, and everywhere in between.

Once, in the middle of the night, I heard what I thought was Poe croaking. I sat up in alarm, wondering if the aviary was under siege, and readying myself to spring to Poe's rescue.

By waking Mack.

Then I realized that the seemingly distant croaks, coming so strangely at regular intervals, were in reality Mack snoring – and emitting a soft croak over and over.

We had tried to create a more natural diet for Poe by searching for roadkill whenever we were driving. But usually any we spotted had already been claimed by crows. Or if we were obliged to return for one instead of stopping immediately, the carcass had been dragged off by the time we arrived. And after all, the needs of the wildlings were greater – to my private relief.

But *surely* we could offset the stress of Poe's necessary confinement.

Between the veggie garden and the woods stood a tall, triple-trunked spruce tree, with a smaller, single spruce about fifteen feet away. Mack drove cedar posts into the ground, forming a huge oval around these trees, and created a forty-by-twenty-foot corral. Between the bases of the posts, he laid heavy logs. To both posts and logs, he stapled wire-mesh fencing that produced a wall six feet high with a solid bottom. This would not only confine Poe but protect him against burrowing predators.

Next, Mack ran three strands of solar-powered electric wire around the outside of the pen to discourage raccoons from climbing the fence.

Finally, he joined both spruce trees with two long perches made of long, slim tree trunks. He leaned another perch, with crosspieces for steps, against the lowest branch of the triple spruce to give Poe an easy ascent.

Now *real* trees would be his nightly roosts.

After a week of hard work, Mack added the final touches of food and water, then carried Poe triumphantly through the spring sunshine to his "raven haven."

Poe loped around his new domain, exploring everything – the bird bath contrived from a child's wading pool, with rocks forming a stile over the rigid wall; the tempting meats laid out on a scrubbable board; the bird feeder of mixed seeds atop a pole, which lured a steady stream of jays and other birds – company, of sorts. Lifting his head, he could see the large marrow bones situated beside accessible branches.

But even through binoculars from the house, it was obvious that none of our efforts impressed Poe.

His message was clear – he wanted *full freedom*.

At one point, he leaped up onto a tall stump in the middle of his pen. The ground sloped slightly, so that the height of the barrier, though consistent, appeared lower on the side nearer the woods. Strong breezes swayed the branches, and other birds swept in to the feeder and out again on the gusts.

Poe eyed the fence speculatively.

Suddenly, we realized that from *his* vantage point on a two-foot stump, the top of the barrier was only another four feet in height. *Less* actually, because of the sloping ground.

At that moment, as though confirming our calculations, Poe opened his great wings, cleared the mesh, and loped towards the woods. His limited flight skills were just enough for him to go AWOL.

Mack and I shot out of the house and charged after him, one on each side of the escapee. The big spruces had crowded out numerous small ones, which had died – each still standing, each at a different angle. Many had fallen in random heaps like a gigantic game of spillikens. Their stiff, dead branches clawed at us, scratching our flesh through our clothes, while Poe slipped through the maze as fluidly as a fish through swaying seaweed.

A crackling outburst followed almost immediately by a thud, and often a curse, meant that one of his pursuers had tripped or fallen.

Usually me.

Mack's long legs scissored through most of the tangles with enviable headway, whereas I seemed to be struggling in a nightmarish fitness class of compulsory highstepping – *so good for the thighs, my dear* – with my knees in constant danger of striking my chin.

Poe zigzagged on, dodging away first from Mack, then from me, as we gallantly flanked his escape. After only five minutes of this torture, which felt more like an hour, Mack finally cornered him under an impenetrable jumble of fallen trees. He pulled him out gently.

I, having fallen flat on my face, was unable to help. In fact, I needed some of that help myself.

Poe offered no further resistance, and we noted with satisfaction that he hardly puffed; truly, his healed lungs were in good shape. He now shamed the rest of us, who were gasping and blinking away cascades of sweat. We released him inside the pen again, and Mack cut down the stump.

Poe wandered back and forth, back and forth, along the barrier, while we watched uneasily from the house. This behaviour, which he hadn't displayed in the smaller aviary, bothered us. He took no food, only a little water.

As the sun began to slide down into the west, Poe hopped up the crosspieces on the leaning rail into the triple spruce. He roamed out along the great perches connecting the two trees, then continued up nearly to the top of the tree. Tilted rays of sunshine still gilded most of his spruce, though the lowest branches were in shadow – a shadow that slowly rose up the tree for the next half hour. We couldn't actually see Poe, hidden so well by the dense greenery, and we assumed he had settled himself for the night.

How marvellous for him to be roosting in a tree again, we told one another. *Imagine not seeing the sky through caging any more*, we gloated.

But we rejoiced too soon.

Suddenly, the branches camouflaging Poe were agitated. To our astonishment – and dismay – he soared out, gliding on steady wings, riding the last wind before sunset, down, down, into the nearby hayfield. We ran to the edge of the darkening field just in time to see Poe glancing back as he stalked into the woods.

"Quoth the Raven, 'Nevermore!'" murmured Mack.

We let him go.

He'd survived on frozen ground in midwinter for more than two months, much of it with illness and a bare minimum of food. Now, he was well fed, healthy, and with wings that had gained enough strength to support him. Wings that should get even stronger with unlimited room to exercise them. Also, we were on the brink of summer, when natural food would be plentiful for him.

Caging him against his will wasn't an option. We felt we'd given him what we could.

Over the next couple of weeks, we often saw Poe, sometimes walking, sometimes high in a tree. He ranged over a surprisingly large territory – one full of insects and mice.

We could only wish him our best.

Like Poe when he was still in the aviary, Miles, now, was beginning to find the studio too confining. Aided, no doubt, by Molly's aggression, he quickly developed the survival skills he would need upon release. He had progressed steadily from the early stage of being easily intimidated, through that of defiance, to his present attitude of corporate take-over.

His new confidence shone like a spotlight – one that *nothing* could escape. He bathed vigorously each day in a large, flat water-dish, then lay in a sunny spot on the floor, preening himself dry while I mopped up. When Molly descended from her shelf, he chased her until she flew back up.

Mack had helped Miles with his flying until he could spring up readily into flight, with that loud wing-clapping so character-istic of adults. It was Mack who – rather deplorably – dubbed his protégé "Air Miles" as he watched him swooping, banking, and landing with astonishing skill in the limited sky of the studio.

The aging Molly, unable now to dominate this young upstart, remained lying on her shelf, watching with tapping wing and ill-disguised contempt.

But Miles's self-assurance soon became as troublesome as Molly's. One day, when he was in his corner, eating, Edna hopped slowly over, ears erect, sniffing inquisitively. Up to this point, her curiosity had never been satisfied. Miles, so much smaller, had always fled her friendly overtures, first by running, then by flight.

This time, however, he refused to leave his food. He also refused to tolerate her interest. With rudeness that couldn't have been bettered by Molly, he whacked Edna several times across her face with his wing, in that aggressive display so sadly characteristic of the "dove of peace."

Taken aback, Edna hastily withdrew, but unfortunately, her acquiescence reinforced Miles's behaviour. Thereafter, he often sought her out in order to dominate her. Gone were the days when he'd sit on the warm ledge on the front of the woodstove, allowing Edna her whiskery scrutiny. Now, he would even stalk boldly up to her box of hay when she was gathering mouthfuls for nesting, and deliberately strike at her.

But Edna could be pushed only *so far* by this uncouth transient.

One day, Miles not only hit her several times, he lunged at her, snapping with open beak. I had looked up from my painting in time to catch this outrage, but before I could interfere, Edna retaliated. Out of patience at last, she growled and leaped suddenly at her aggressor, jabbing at him with her sharp front claws – those very efficient tools that rabbits use to excavate tunnels.

Surprised, Miles hesitated – but only briefly. Then he went in swinging and snapping, while Edna, with flattened ears, lunged and snarled, over and over.

"MEAT RABBIT EATS PIGEON!" Mack trumpeted from his chair, almost incoherent with laughter.

I flung down my brush and leaped between the two pugilists.

But Miles persisted each day, determined to be boss. Sometimes he won, and Edna fled to her sanctuary behind the stove. Other times, she reacted so vehemently that Miles would hurriedly retreat. Heartened, Edna would quickly follow up her advantage, hopping after her antagonist until he broke into flight.

Fortunately, more benign moments also existed, when Edna allowed Miles to eat the food in her dish – generosity he seemed unable to reciprocate. But when he wasn't provoking his woolly roommate, Miles looked elsewhere for entertainment.

And, to my chagrin, he found plenty.

Though I had removed the remnants of my violets and gloxinias from the studio, my remaining jade plants, so large and tree-like, suggested suitable perches to Miles. He landed on them repeatedly, casually knocking off any fleshy leaves that inconvenienced him.

But his horticultural exploits peaked when he descended onto a luxuriant prayer plant, tipping it off the shelf above my work table. I was crouched before the woodstove, adding fuel, when I heard the flurry of wings, followed by a rustling thud.

I turned my head just in time to see damp earth burst out of the pot all over my half-finished painting and into my jars of brushes and paint water.

Everything needed to be examined by Miles. He toppled an incense burner, sending clouds of soft ash into an open drawer full of drawings. He knocked a photograph of County, a special robin from earlier years, off the wall. And for added measure, he chewed the edge of the frame like a qualified rodent. He tried to destroy County's old nest, which she'd built on top of a cow skull that hung from the wall, obliging me to remove the treasured skull to another room for safekeeping.

The last plant – lodged in a heavy crock, which I'd considered untippable – was skilfully overturned. It landed and rolled, spewing dirt down through several shelves of books and almost filling an old wooden gutter holding an assortment of pencils and pens.

Even Chip couldn't have bettered his style.

One evening, as I was moodily preparing supper while visions of sugarplummed pigeons danced in my head, I heard a stupendous CRASH! from the studio. I hurtled up the stairs and jerked open the door.

An enormous mounted antler from a tundra caribou, knocked off its base, had clanged into the flimsy metal heat-shield surrounding the woodstove. Edna, terrified, had shot out of her sanctum behind the stove and into her litterbox under the work table, where she was sitting bolt upright, eyes bulging like bowls.

Miles, still flapping wildly around the room, landed heavily on top of a whitened cow pelvis placed artistically – but unwisely – on top of the bookcase. Why, oh why, do bones intrigue me? The pelvis spun down, skidded across the floor, and struck the litterbox like a torpedo. Edna, determined to sell her life dearly, sprang out on impact and flattened herself under the stove in the best air-raid tradition.

Miles, circling in frightened confusion that was compounded by my sudden roar, clutched onto a lampshade. It immediately tilted, but at least stayed clamped to the bulb. In his agitation – or, perhaps, relief – he promptly *shat* on it.

Fluidly.

And copiously.

Clearly, young Miles was ready for the outdoor aviary.

Or, put another way, if *he* didn't move out there, *I would*.

CHAPTER 13

SPRING UNSPRUNG

Early the next morning, I moved Miles out to the aviary, where he spent most of that day up on the broadest perch, a pigeon owl-eyed at all the activities of the wild birds at the feeder. I also opened the little doorway into the adjoining shed in case he preferred to roost indoors for the night. And I set out lots of pigeon grains, grit, and his bathing dish.

The rest of the morning I spent restoring the studio so that I could enjoy a quiet afternoon painting.

Without disruption.

Edna, looking decidedly jaded, napped.

After supper, Mack and I celebrated the beauty of that spring evening by kindling a bonfire near the veggie garden. No annoying insects troubled us yet, but they were on their way; we'd already seen mosquito "wrigglers" gyrating up and down in shallow water.

Before us, a waxing gibbous moon glided above the trees, an enormous orb whose golden brilliance paled the black sky and dimmed the insistent glitter of stars. Dark spruce silhouettes enclosed us protectively as we huddled by the crackling flames, watching sparks, those true fireflies, spiral up and blink out. A soft breeze slipped between the rocks of our walled fire pit, prodding any reluctant coals into bright flares.

As we sipped tea and enjoyed our desserts, we heard the usual snarling of raccoons eating – and arguing over – the dry dog food Mack had tossed out earlier for them. Vibrant hootings of barred owls from every direction mingled with the muted monotones of nearby saw-whets.

As the eerie cries persisted, ringing out closer and closer, we heard a sudden outbreak of wing-beating and twanging wire from the aviary.

Were raccoons trying to break through to Miles?

We snatched up the flashlight – which of course had a failing battery – and scrambled awkwardly over the uneven ground, following the faint bobbing light up the slope to the house.

The innocent raccoons were still chewing dog food, their writhing upper lips and bobbing noses reminding me ludicrously of humans with ill-fitting dentures eating toffee. They froze at our approach, then fled, still with full mouths.

At the aviary, we found Miles in a terrified huddle against the caging, though no predator was near. We gently transferred him to the adjoining shed, placing him on a comfortable roost. For added reassurance, we left a low light on.

The calls of hunting owls and squabbling raccoons were evidently too much for our "townie."

Thereafter, Miles voluntarily slipped into the shed every evening at dusk to sleep for the night, emerging only when morning brightness crept over the threshold of the small connecting door. As days passed, he grew acclimatized to wind and rain, fog and sunshine.

And also to minimal human contact, as was essential.

We had decided not to release him back on the main thoroughfare in town, since we were unable to teach him about traffic. Instead, we loaded him into the car one May morning, as soon as the Public Gardens were open for the summer, and drove to Halifax.

After we parked, I slipped on a jacket and tucked a protesting Miles underneath. Then we crossed the street into the Gardens with our stowaway.

Whenever we visit Halifax, we seldom miss stopping in the Public Gardens. The trees alone are worth it. Their great trunks pillar both sides of the outer walkways like guardians. In late spring, the fragrance of the northern catalpa blossoms, in the centre of the park, permeates even the streets.

Trees line the lagoons, casting sun-dappled shade for birds and humans. In summer, certain trees ring continually with the squeaky calls of starlings. Others harbour dozing pigeons. Children hide behind the hanging branches of the weeping mulberry that forms a curtained, circular cave.

The flower gardens bear changing blooms of every colour from May to November. Their fragrance sweetens the inevitable smell of exhaust fumes which taint every city, although Halifax is often cleansed by onshore winds from the ocean.

Everyone loves the Gardens. Wedding parties, sometimes three or four simultaneously, pose boldly or bashfully for photos under the trees, or beside banks of flowers. Wheelchairs slowly cruise the paths, or park in the shade, their occupants reading, feeding the birds, or just watching all the activities. Strolling visitors sink down gratefully on benches, rise again rested, saunter on, settle on other benches.

Sun-worshippers glory in the blistering heat of the open space before the Victorian bandstand. Shade-lovers retire to cool benches under leafy canopies, speckles of muted sunlight wavering over their celadon faces as though they sat in a submarine world.

And *everyone* loves the birds.

Dozens of bags of popcorn, bread, crackers, and birdseed are opened every day in the Gardens. The delight of those feeding is matched only by the delight of the feeders: from elderly people, whose multi-creased faces project dozens of smiles at once, to wide-eyed toddlers being taught *not* to chase the birds, *not* to hurl food in their faces. Some of the more daring pigeons sit on outstretched hands, eating and pushing off all challengers. Starlings catch tidbits in mid-air.

We especially enjoy watching those youngsters who discover suddenly the miracle of a live bird eating food out of their timorous hands – a bird *not* motivated by batteries, or governed by switches. A bird whose vibrant beauty shames shoddy plastic – at least briefly – in their eyes.

Flotillas of ducklings in the shallows bob like irrepressible corks around their watchful mothers, or swarm like woolly beetles over the banks, endlessly curious, endlessly hungry. Predatory gulls monitor them with pale eyes, waiting to seize the more adventuresome ones. Sudden outbursts reveal irate duck mothers excitedly chasing the silent gulls, who merely sweep up, glide out of reach, and land out in the centre of the lagoon.

Often a gull, droll with dignity, will ride the small, gaily painted passenger ship that floats there all summer – dwarfing it ridiculously. Each time, we'll call the bird "Gulliver."

A pigeon passenger, on the other hand, would be – of course – a passenger pigeon.

Occasionally an osprey will haunt the ponds, intent on a fish dinner, and often successful. Or a turtle – a discarded pet? – will haul out on a rock to sun itself. Or a lovely brown rat will slip out from under a bush to forage hastily before hiding again, knowing instinctively that no one would welcome him. Except Mack and I, sympathetically tossing an extra handful of seed under his bush.

Thus, the Public Gardens seemed an ideal launching site for Miles.

By the big lagoon, we sat down on a bench, regarded languidly – and speculatively – by assorted ducks, pigeons, and starlings, all resting or preening around us. With a chuckle of anticipation, Mack took a large bag out of his pocket and scattered a handful of mixed grains.

Instant pandemonium broke out.

The bare walkway was transformed into an ever-shifting kaleidoscope of jostling birds pecking hungrily at the seeds. More birds flew in from the trees. Ducks glided towards shore, hoisted themselves out of the water, and waddled hurriedly over, like plump aldermen anxious to join a banquet. Around us rose a confusion of indignant quacks and threatening coos as the birds shouldered each other aside or nipped insistently at one another's wings and tails.

I opened my jacket slightly and Miles cautiously thrust his head out. Then his ruby-orange eyes widened in wonder, as if to say, *Wow! A lot of them look just like me!* He remained utterly still, utterly absorbed, oblivious of my restraining hands. Then he began to struggle eagerly.

The time had come.

I opened my hands and Miles flew ahead a few feet before landing rather abruptly beside the lagoon. His own kind now surrounded him. Finally.

But he looked vulnerable, and I noticed that he trembled often – not a sign of fear in this instance, but of submission to those of higher rank. Years of living with pigeons have taught me a lot about pigeon body language.

Suddenly, for reasons inscrutable to us, the entire flock took wing over the water, with Miles among them. They circled and circled in the sunshine, above the floating ducks, the single gulls, the painted ship. At last they descended and regrouped on the ground.

All but Miles.

Miles was still up there in his first outdoor flight, still turning in wide, beautiful sweeps through the sunlight. We could almost *hear* his jubilation.

When a passing gull crossed his trajectory, Miles flipped up and swung aside with all the skill of his ancestors.

His *prestigious* ancestors, domesticated – *and prized* – as long ago as 2500 B.C.E.

His ancestors, whose flying finesse had provided the first air-mail deliveries for humans.

Miles finally landed on a branch of a tall shrub beside the water, where he gradually settled, watching the activities around him, and eventually preening – always a good sign. Visitors wandered past, or paused to feed the birds, pigeons included.

No one here was kicking them.

Around the distant perimeter of the Gardens hummed the endless traffic, which other pigeons, as role models, would teach Miles to avoid. Or to negotiate, if necessary. Also, Miles, although accustomed to humans, was far from tame. He would no doubt eat the daily offerings of food, but would scurry away from reaching hands.

We left him there.

With confidence.

CHAPTER 14

RAISING EYEBROWS

Spring was at the fullness of flood tide now. As sunshine saturated each day, its strength seeping deep into roots and seeds, we could almost hear the sun-warmed land purring comfortably. Buds yawned and stretched. Slowly, they shook off their lethargy and began to leaf out.

Mack, unable to resist the lure of the sleeping vegetable garden, started pulling out last year's weeds. To his satisfaction, he found that the frost was out of the ground, and that roots slid out as easily as if they'd been greased. Over the next few days, he cleared out all the weeds and dug over the soil, until the great wings of the robin garden were freed and ready for take-off.

Then he turned his attention to a small bed nearby, shaped like a crescent moon. This enclosed our Everbearing strawberry plants.

Last year, a bumper crop had surged to rosy fruition by early summer, and we began to salivate over dreams of fresh strawberry pies. But when we stepped out one morning to do a picking, we found that the raccoons had left a total eclipse in our moon garden. Lunar craters, ravaged plants, and footprints were all we found.

Except for almost audible burps of satisfaction hovering over the remains.

But Mack rallied after that blow. He covered the entire moon with white mesh, permeable by sun and rain – but *not* by varmints. Around this pale crescent, he strung electric fencing energized by the same solar battery that protected the veggie garden from deer.

And it worked.

In October, we devoured three fresh strawberry pies, one after the other. Almost furtively. Dreading any unexpected company that would compel us to share them.

This year he stretched mesh over the fruit when it was still green and attached the electric barrier, confidently promising quarts of toothsome berries for pies. And to his satisfaction, the raccoons did not respond to his challenge.

But the tiny chipmunks did – in secret.

Later, when Mack peeled back the cover, the few berries that still remained had been sampled, then tossed aside – as though a desired standard of excellence hadn't been fulfilled.

Our visions of pies faded yet again.

Meanwhile, beside the new house, I stood in my own private hell.

The bulldozer last fall had done its job thoroughly, and I looked in discouragement at the rubble around me. My winter dreams of blossoming perennials, surrounding the house with beauty, seemed like sheer lunacy.

But even the longest journey begins with the first step. And for me, the first step was to build the beds.

Decades ago, rocks had been heaped along the fenceline by determined farmers clearing the land for crops. Every spring, as persistently as weeds, more rocks would surface in their fields, only to be doggedly pried out and thrown aside once again.

But their bane was my booty.

Under what felt like a summer – rather than a spring – sun, I hauled back enough mossy, lichened rocks to lay out attractive borders for the flower beds. Since the house stood on a knoll, I had become resigned through the years to the grim reality that full wheelbarrows always had to be pushed uphill, whereas empty ones always hurtled down, tugging playfully at one's tired arms. Such is the price of a room with a view.

As the relentless heat continued, I felt as if I were being sautéed in my own sweat. And, from constant bending over, my hair remained a successful soufflé even when I stood up. But stone borders eventually snaked their way around the house.

Then the indefatigable Mack stepped into the fray and wheeled in load after load of mixed topsoil, horse manure, and peat moss, till plumped beds pressed against their rock edges, and order began to surmount the bulldozed chaos.

We worked hard, day after day, allowing ourselves only brief, exhausted hugs after each triumph – when we lovingly exchanged the swelling globules of sweat that swung persistently from the ends of our noses.

When I finally transplanted the day lilies that I'd shifted hastily to the veggie garden last fall, our new beds began to resemble real gardens. More perennials, lugged home from the enticing displays at the local nursery, completed the transformation.

But as one anxiety was assuaged, a new one emerged. I knew that each flower that delighted me visually would delight another creature delectably. Each blossom was really a salad in disguise. Sometimes I wonder if admiring the impossible photos on the fronts of the seed packs isn't the best time of the gardening season.

Before all the conflicts begin.

What is it about gardening that is so alluring? Especially when setbacks so often outnumber successes. Certainly I've experienced enough discouragement to squelch any interest. My first memorable experience with plants occurred when I was a child. I was struggling to open a window when the sudden upthrust of the sash knocked over a plant. Being endowed with excellent reflexes, I caught it in both hands.

It was a long-spined cactus.

In more recent years, I remember preparing beds carefully with rich soil and manure in early summer. Then I opened a seed package. Visions of flowers to come blossomed in my mind as I crouched, humming contentedly. I covered each seed with a sprinkling of earth, watered it, and moved along. But when I looked back along the row, my daydreams were punctured by bitter reality. Both of my ducks were rubbling happily through the damp earth, devouring flower seeds and bugs with equal enthusiasm.

Next door, my elderly neighbour, who not only had a passion for gardening but enjoyed an enviable success rate as well, was sowing corn.

Or trying to.

She loved counting seeds as she planted them, and had just reached a total of fifty-four when she straightened up and glanced back with pride.

Then outrage.

A large crow had been following quietly in her wake, adroitly hooking up each kernel and swallowing it.

Even when my small vegetable gardens have made it past the seed stage, vandals have laid in wait. In earlier years, my hens always seemed to find that the greening rows of new lettuce or peas exceeded any other spot for dustbathing or scratching up bugs. And if my lettuce survived the hens' attentions and matured, I had only to plan that first fresh salad to guarantee that the ducks would enjoy it instead.

Strangely, only Bubble and Squeak, my two roosters, showed no desire to invade the garden. They preferred to wait beside it while I gathered veggies. Wisely, too, for I always shared ripe tomatoes, cucumbers, and other favourites with them – and donated my entire portion of corn borers.

Perhaps, being male, they simply felt no need to exert themselves when they were bound to be served the best anyway. On the other hand, the hens and both ducks – all females – felt compelled to prepare their own if they were to get any at all.

Wildlings everywhere were busy. Winged ones flew in from distant countries, even other continents, and ate hungrily, with little ceremony, at the feeding stations. Woolly ones birthed in secrecy and seclusion, licking and nourishing their young.

Three nursing raccoons and two smaller yearlings still appeared nightly for food. They boldly wolfed down the dry dog food and fresh water that Mack set out for them at the end of each day. With lips curled back over their teeth, they snarled and snapped ferociously at one another. They also chewed with such bone-crunching gusto that our quiet country evenings sounded like a school cafeteria at the height of lunch hour.

When food ran out, the raccoons would claw their way up our mullioned door and jiggle the latch hopefully. Or they'd bound all over our bedroom balcony, chasing one another away from the fallen seeds below the silo bird feeder. When I stepped out to rescue the feeder, the younger two would scamper towards me for cookies – treats they had learned to expect from Mack. As soon as I fled back inside with my prize, their busy fingers would try to pry open the door.

The mothers usually climbed out on nearby branches when I emerged, preferring a discreet distance, where they'd sit up like begging dogs, even their furry ears expectant. I never ceased to be amazed by their nonchalance – as though the ground were directly under their bottoms instead of fifteen feet below.

Once, when the whole gang was on the ground, growling so hideously that we couldn't sleep, Mack slipped out onto the balcony. He peered over the edge into the shadowy throng and began to scold them good-naturedly.

The raccoons, looking up, spotted their familiar Horn of Plenty – personified. Far from being abashed, they began scrambling eagerly up the support posts in hopes of cookies. Hallowe'en is celebrated every night at our house, with masked callers looking for handouts.

And getting a royal welcome as well.

It's whenever they leave faecal deposits on the balcony, or break bird feeders, or sabotage garbage cans, or crush my flowers, that their appeal wanes drastically.

Then they suddenly become *Mack's* raccoons.

The dominant raccoon in the group was a nursing mother that we dubbed "Momma Eyebrows," for indeed, she possessed two distinctive eyebrows perched inquiringly above her mask. Whenever she escaped her demanding brood but found that no food awaited her, she'd hoist herself up the bird-feeder post – gingerly, because of her protruding teats – and peer rebukingly through the kitchen window. Her suggestive eyebrows clearly conveyed her message.

If we noticed her immediately, she'd inch her way back down, knowing food would appear, well seasoned with Mack's apologies (I should be so lucky). But if we didn't connect, she'd continue up to the bird feeder and clean it out to the last seed.

A shameless blackmailer. But then, bribery is a familiar device among human parents too.

Hot weather incubated the land week after week, hatching our flower and vegetable plants with unheard-of haste. But our masked neighbours in their woolly parkas wilted visibly. Momma

Eyebrows, like the descending side of a see-saw, looked progressively thinner and wearier, while her kits, riding the ascending side, were no doubt swelling into energetic butterballs.

She began to emerge earlier each day from her den under the house, seeking fresh breezes as well as food. Slowly, she'd climb up the Great Mother, a matronly spruce that each day and night shelters birds of all varieties, as well as red squirrels, flying squirrels, raccoons.

And the more adventurous chipmunks.

One of these little striped ground-dwellers actually climbed about fifteen feet up the Great Mother and followed a limb that brushed against the wooden railing of the balcony. Then he proceeded to explore the entire balcony with all the thorough inquisitiveness of an experienced renter planning to upgrade.

Momma Eyebrows would choose an alarmingly narrow branch to recline upon, for reasons that speedily became clear. Stretching out luxuriously, and with perfect balance, she'd let her tail and all four legs hang down limply over both sides of the branch – as well as her heated teats.

"Cooling the dinner table," grinned Mack, as he set out fresh water for her.

From her aerial perch, Momma Eyebrows would monitor our activities upside down with hanging head, her open mouth panting with warmth. Or she'd lay her furry face out along the branch. Or across it, like any human head lying on a pillow.

On the hottest days, we eyed her drowsing form with undisguised envy.

Late one morning, I was transplanting perennials donated by friends, hoping to finish before the worst of the heat. Momma Eyebrows appeared at the entrance to her lair under the house and Mack obligingly scattered dog food for her. Then he returned to his labours in the veggie garden. She immediately sagged down comfortably onto her ample haunches and began to chew, her delicate black fingers always busily selecting the next mouthful. Her

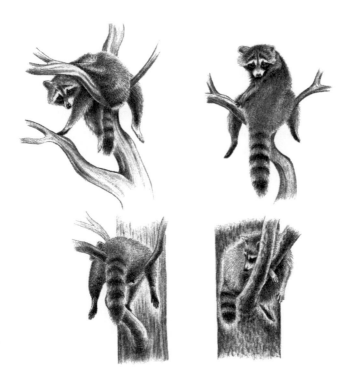

dark eyes peered out of her mask in myopic vacancy, like a preoccupied librarian's.

At that moment, I clumped up, lugging a bucket of manure for my transplants. Directing an aggrieved look over her shoulder, Momma Eyebrows deflated her bulk and squeezed back distrustfully under the house. From her shadowy threshold, she watched me pass before re-emerging to continue her interrupted repast.

But unfortunately for her, I had to make repeated forays past her dinner table, bringing back buckets of water, manure, or potting soil. Or going for more. Though I always passed slowly and murmured reassurances, she invariably retreated and finished chewing in safety. But her eloquent eyebrows conveyed her reproach: hot, tired mothers have right-of-way.

They also have limited patience.

When I passed yet one more time, Momma Eyebrows was lying with her back half still under the house, so she could withdraw with less effort. With her front half out in the sunlight, she rested her chin on her crossed arms and her eyes watched me moodily. Her untouched food – which lay out of reach – was a visible accusation.

I scurried by, now lugging loads of guilt as well.

After I had made another two trips, she turned her head on its side in resignation, rolling her eyes at me despairingly.

We were *both* relieved when I finally finished.

One of the other mother raccoons, "Momma Too," who was shyer and seemed thinner from nursing, also had eyebrows. Hers were perched even higher, as though she were not only in continual surprise at everything around her, but even deeply startled by Momma Eyebrows herself.

When both mothers were side by side, looking up at us with raised brows, I felt an insane impulse to apologize and ask them to repeat their question.

Later in the season, when two or three youngsters began to accompany each mother, our own eyebrows sprang like leaping trout: Momma Too appeared in smug triumph with *four* rolypoly babies.

Who must have resembled their father.

None had her eyebrows.

The woodland around us was flooded now with spring migrants, and the sun rose each morning accompanied by the piercing sweetness of carolling robins. The great serviceberry tree beside the house created a cumulus cloud of white blossoms. From the dining-room windows, we watched downy woodpeckers engaged in courtship on one of the branches.

Warm southerly winds swept down the greening hillsides and

across the hayfields to sway branches of blooms along the fence-line. Then, during one cool day, I looked out with regret at the falling blossoms whirling before the windows – until I realized I was seeing *snowflakes*. In *May*. Fortunately, they dissolved quickly on the frost-free earth.

A week later, I awoke early on a windy morning. I peered out drowsily – then irritably – at *another* freak snow flurry. *More* flakes whizzing past the windows in May.

Till I realized that, this time, they really were blossoms.

Meanwhile, over two hundred miles away, a young couple were driving to work, when they spotted a female robin lying on her back near the centre line of a busy road. At the woman's instigation, her companion pulled onto the narrow shoulder and she ran back. To her relief – and ensuing anxiety – the robin looked undamaged and was still breathing.

But what to do?

They immediately took the bird to a vet, who proved totally unsympathetic and who handled the frightened robin as though she were made of unbreakable plastic. When the couple picked up the bird later, at noon, they found her incarcerated in a small cage without food or water.

Mack and I met the rescuers at a town halfway between their home and ours. Gratefully, they held out a covered box containing a wary robin who'd had enough of humans. But who couldn't fly.

We named her "Jenny," after one of her deliverers.

When we returned, I took her gently out of her box and forcefed her a couple of mealworms, knowing she needed fuel after so much trauma. Jenny refused water when I held a small dish up to her face – but then, even a dish would be so strange to her. So I began dipping my finger and touching the side of her beak so that the water would seep in between her mandibles.

At first, she bit my finger each time it approached – firmly, but certainly not painfully. But as I didn't recoil, and a drop slipped into her mouth each time, she understood my stratagem. Thereafter, she just opened her beak each time, without biting, and swallowed the water with evident satisfaction.

I released Jenny in the indoor garden and she scuttled under an outward curve of driftwood. There she froze in watchful stillness, almost as camouflaged as in the wild. If I looked closely, I could see her white eye-ring in the shadows, like a tiny galaxy in distant space.

From his branch high above, Beejay watched with his crest flared. Chip showed less than her usual interest, being more drawn to the male grackles gleaming at the feeder beyond the garden window; one female robin couldn't hope to compete with their magnetism. Bashō swelled out till he looked like a feathered blowfish and lowered his head defensively, but Jenny never moved. She seemed to be intent on remaining invisible.

I picked up Bashō and cuddled him, hoping the robin would notice him wiggling down cozily and trustfully into my cupped hands. Hoping to ease her fears, even a little.

Then I edged a dish of mealworms, beetles, earthworms, and sowbugs nearer to her, but she retreated even further. Next, I dabbled my finger expressively in a small waterdish, which I pushed over next to the bug dish. Finally, I set Bashō back down in the garden and left them all to sort the situation out.

At this point, the presence of other birds would help Jenny more than I.

Throughout that evening, she moved about a little and I kept my distance. But even watching covertly, I never saw her eat or drink. At dark, I knelt before the garden, reached out and picked up Bashō. He was only a foot and a half away from Jenny, but she never moved.

It's been my experience that, if I can win a bird's confidence, it will respond well to my attempts to help, even if the injury is serious. On the other hand, even a slight injury can prove fatal if the bird feels helpless and threatened. Often, when I've been given a bird with minor damage who's been an unwilling source of entertainment for hours in a noisy family, that bird will compose itself and die as soon as I give it a quiet haven.

This robin had already survived a great deal. In one brief moment on a highway, her life changed direction drastically.

Therefore, I remained kneeling before her, holding Bashō cupped below my chin as an ambassador of goodwill, and talked softly and earnestly to Jenny for about ten minutes. I tried to convey that we meant her no harm. That we would provide her with suitable food, protection, and habitat while she healed. That we hoped to release her back where she'd been living, so that she and her mate could begin another family.

Jenny, motionless, but not rigidly so, faced me throughout my effort, with eyes dark and eloquent.

Robins lay two to three clutches of eggs, sometimes even four, every summer. I knew that Jenny would have been interrupted at some level of her nesting activities. She may have been still incubating. She may have been nurturing youngsters – anywhere from two to four tufty-headed, downy babes.

I also knew that, although a female robin possesses a featherless brooding patch, designed to warm eggs and babes, her mate lacks it. Unless Jenny's babes were already feathered, they stood little chance of survival.

Heartbreaking.

Jenny began to hop about a little, with soft chirps. Then she tried to jump up onto a projection of the driftwood, presumably to seek a higher roosting spot, as would be natural. But the plateau of wood, only ten inches above her, was beyond her strength. She fell back to the ground, where she spent the night.

Watching her closely, I was convinced that she was very sore, perhaps badly bruised, but that nothing was broken. She couldn't fly, but her wings rested in a proper position. And her eyes, those unmistakable communicators, weren't shallow or semi-opaque, as in birds with internal injuries. Her breathing, too, was regular. But the real test would be normal droppings. If they passed as usual, I felt that we could release her in a couple of weeks. And I was certain that, if her mate survived, their bond would still hold.

My earlier experience with County, recounted in my book *Sharing a Robin's Life*, had taught me much about bond loyalty between robins.

Of which I'd been an honorary one.

CHAPTER 15

TAILS OF WONDER, TALES OF WOE

In the morning, Jenny seemed unchanged. Still intensely wary. Although I tossed three mealworms towards her when I was doling out some to Bashō, she ignored them. But this time, when I reached down to pick him up, she leaped successfully onto the driftwood. And from there to the windowsill.

I was delighted. Her droppings, too, looked just as they should, so she had eaten.

Over the next few days, she began eating, though we were sitting at a short distance, watching covertly. But she'd stop if we moved any closer. To replenish her dish, I'd lean slowly over the garden wall from a crouching position, holding out my hand at an angle so she could see her "movable feast" arriving. I'd carefully avoid alarming her by looking at her. Instead, I'd focus on the dish, gently tip my squirming handful into it, and retreat with the same care.

By the time I returned to the kitchen, Jenny would be eating.

It was impossible to leave enough food for her for an entire day. If the dish were left on the ground, Bashō was only too pleased to help her eat her wrigglies. If I set the dish on the windowsill, Beejay was delighted. And Chip could raid it anywhere. I simply had to give her food many times each day until she was able to defend it.

With the gardening season quickening, Mack often brought in special delicacies for the indoor birds – June bugs with a crunch and bulging white grubs. Treats that energized them the way strong coffee fuels drowsy commuters.

Jenny progressed quickly. From the windowsill, she eventually negotiated a padded rail that angled up to Beejay's shelf, where his food dish was kept. Soon, she managed to jump from the shelf to a branch of one of the trees – a day of particular triumph. She bathed regularly, too, in the large communal waterdish, though never if we were near.

I began to develop considerable skill in lurking behind corners and peering through plants in order to monitor her movements.

Once, she tried to fly from one tree to a branch of the other – only a few feet – but fell heavily to the earth below. Luckily, a soft landing. But a week after she arrived, Jenny achieved flight on a downward slant for about five feet – from a branch to the windowsill – using both wings well, and braking normally with spread tailfeathers.

Pleased as we were, we knew that the next threshold was an upward flight.

After so many coy retreats, spring was now in full spate, slipping like water through our clutching fingers. Somehow, each year we mark the gradual transformation from winter, watching leaves unfurl almost one by one. Then we turn our backs briefly to take care of a few chores and, when we next glance around, summer has arrived.

And this year was no exception.

By the time we realized that, once again, we'd missed most of spring, long, dry weeks had lowered water levels everywhere. In the swamps, cattails were standing bare-legged in visible mud, and swollen brooks had dwindled as though someone had turned back a giant tap.

At every window, the beauty of apple blossoms, haunted by bees and birds, brightened the view. Great clouds of blooms glimmered at dusk and by moonlight, capturing even the least light in the delicate cupped hands of their petals. Pine siskins and grosbeaks busied themselves daily on every branch, eating insects, caterpillars, and even the blossoms themselves.

I can't imagine a more aromatic salad. One that really *would* look "too good to eat."

Beneath the Great Mother spruce, a false elder bush lifted cones of intricate white flowers. Nearby – *too* near the veggie garden – a groundhog emerged one morning from the wood stacked beside our fire pit. A few feet away glowed an enormous dandelion, open like the sun. His searching eyes came to rest on this golden delicacy, and even at a distance we could sense his quiver of delight. He lumbered through the silvery, dew-laden weeds, leaving a dark, determined wake behind him, and crouched before his treasure. There he savoured every yellow petal like a gourmet gratified that there was no stint on real butter.

From the balcony one breezy afternoon, Mack and I watched a single dandelion seed passing, upheld on invisible currents like a tiny jellyfish. It rose higher and higher, curving away from us, bearing a spark of life within. In some place that not even our vaunted human ingenuity could discover, that spark, fuelled by earth, rain, and sunshine, would create a beautiful plant. A muchmaligned plant, but one totally edible, and bursting with vitamins. Its early leaves always enhance our salads. Its flowers create wine.

Its roots, dried and ground, produce a nutritious beverage, similar in taste to coffee.

I remember one of my ducks, when she was an energetic black-and-gold duckling, seeking out dandelion flowers – some nearly as big as her own head – and devouring them with bright-eyed enthusiasm.

Watching the little seed float out of sight, I reflected that this was one wanderer that scientists couldn't desecrate with a cumbersome radio collar or ear tag.

↓ ↓

After a second week of R-and-R, Jenny was able to fly well and was ready for release. Accordingly, we caught her as gently as possible one morning – after an anxious scramble between the garden and the kitchen. Then we set her in a small travelling box and laid a towel over the open top, tied down well with string. The box had two screened windows for cross-ventilation, towelling on the bottom for comfort and traction, and a dish of water under one of the windows.

With high hopes, we set off on our two-and-a-half-hour journey to return Jenny to her mate.

We met her rescuers, as planned, and drove to the site on the outskirts of Halifax – an urban area pierced by a busy, winding highway. We all climbed out of the car and invaded an ample lawn surrounded by trees. Then we did an interview with one of the rescuers, Alex Mason, who worked for the CBC, and the original Jenny, about the robin's escape from death and her recuperation.

The finale, though, was the recorded whirring of her wings as she shot out of the box and soared up easily onto the top of a forty-foot pine tree. While Alex spoke his final words into the microphone, we all watched with upturned faces as Jenny oriented herself. Her head turned this way and that, her tail flicked

briskly, and she looked incredibly alert and healthy. After a few characteristic robin "barks," she swooped out and away from the road, and soared out of sight.

We all shook hands jubilantly.

After lunch, Mack and I treated ourselves to another visit to the Public Gardens.

The great trees, like leafy loudspeakers, broadcasted the musical *chr-r-r-r*ings of dozens of fledgling starlings. We paused by one of the small ponds to watch more starlings, youngsters and adults both, bathing and splashing in the shallows. Across the lawns, or in and out of the flower beds, hungry young starlings followed their parents, calling insatiably for more, and still *more*, food. As inescapable as shadows.

In a secret nest, a duck brooded her eggs, with leaves of day lilies and blooming rhododendron arching protectively over her. Other nests, lined with feathers, held only two or three eggs, the beginnings of a clutch – ducks brood their eggs only when the tally is complete.

Drakes, watched by other drakes, were copulating with ducks in ways that made me grateful that I wasn't a duck myself.

Male pigeons, with much bowing, cooing, and circling, courted disinterested females, who clearly preferred to pick up seeds. The behaviour of both genders seemed to me highly reminiscent of their human counterparts – the females busied themselves with meals, while the males ran around in circles with inflated chests.

We picked out two pigeons that might have been Miles before we spotted a third contender – a dark, smallish one searching for, and eating, tidbits of food with ease and seeming contentment. We watched even his slightest move with such fervid interest that casual passersby would have been forgiven for suspecting us of nefarious culinary designs.

But pigeon pie wasn't in our minds.

We were greeting an old friend.

Everywhere in the gardens, perennials and spring bulbs were jostling one another in colourful confusion, and scent-sweetened air exhilarated us. The vibrant green of new leaves on the trees compensated for the grimy grey sky above them. And everywhere, people were feeding the birds.

Including us.

That is, we go there *ostensibly* to feed the birds, grinning and crouching down, while thrusting duck-bills vacuum seeds out of our hands in a few blinks. Or we sit with pigeons on our shoulders, who are anxiously awaiting their turn to replace the other pigeons, who are balancing on our palms and eating with electric speed.

But in reality, the birds feed us; we're always refreshed when we head back out of the city after being with them.

As we drove home, the dreary pall of cloud began to ebb like a tide, leaving a washed sky of pale blue. Bloated thunderheads, tinted rosy and gold in the low sunlight, squatted above the horizon, the endless curves of their tops receding like coral beds in the aerial sea.

A Canada goose posed like a sentinel at the edge of a large pond of pale light. No doubt its mate was warming eggs in a shadowed nest nearby. Clydesdale foals lay in ungainly, white-faced heaps, like collapsible toys, beside their grazing mothers. An eagle lifted ponderously into the air, picking up speed quickly. But not quickly enough to elude the harassment of a single crow, who was defending its nesting territory – where, perhaps, fledged youngsters were being taught. Sprouted vegetable gardens lay like brown blankets with stitchings of green seams in perfect rows.

When we climbed gratefully out of the car at home, the air seemed almost solid with the fragrance of apple, hawthorn, and chokecherry blossoms. Every moment of distilled scent seemed to have remained, accumulating throughout the day, with not the faintest breeze to dispel it. Even the five blooms on our new little lilac bush were enclosed in almost palpable aroma.

We thought back to the happy release of Jenny.

Did she find her mate? Would she begin another family?

Sometimes I visualize spring as a luminous fiddlehead fern, unfurling into its characteristic question mark.

And then pausing. Visibly puzzled.

No wonder.

New life was busy everywhere.

Every morning, on a distant farm, a deer led her new fawn into a herd of grazing cattle and selected a spot for her babe to rest. Then the doe withdrew to the top of a hill, two hundred yards away, to feed. Though coyotes were plentiful, and fawn meat very much to their liking, the strong smell of the herd easily disguised the almost scentless youngster.

As the wily doe knew well.

On another occasion, we watched a snowshoe hare emerging every evening from the woods to eat roadside greenery – opposite a house with a dog. The aging canine was far too ponderous to catch even the slowest hare. But his very presence and frequent barking deterred foxes and coyotes from venturing near.

As the hare knew well.

In the woods, as I sat drawing on a sunny slope, I noticed movement near a mossy pool below me. A branch seemed to be waving in the leafy litter. Then it lowered itself. After a pause, it reappeared. But closer.

Astonished, I realized that I was seeing a garter snake *waving its tail*.

Dogs, yes. Even cats, when annoyed. And, of course, horses – swatting flies.

But *snakes*? Did they even *have* tails? Or were they *all* tail . . .?

This had to be a mating ritual. As if to confirm this, another movement caught my eye. Round the end of the pool glided a second garter snake, enticed no doubt by the tail of the first, cleverly raised like a flag. How else to attract an earthbound mate?

On came the ardent lover, pausing rarely, the tail ever beckoning alluringly, until both snakes lay alongside each other. Soon they were entwined, while I remained watching.

And shamelessly entranced.

I've often used snakes in my artwork as a symbol of unity, like Ouroboros, the mythical cosmic serpent, holding his tail in his mouth and encircling the world protectively. Or as a symbol of renewal, inspired by the snake emerging with new skin out of the sheath of its old. The symbolism is universal and almost endless, with always another bend in it – like Ouroboros himself.

Occasionally, I find those discarded skins, like ghost snakes, complete with intricate, textural designs, as fragile as dragonfly wings. I've found ghost crickets, too. And ghost spiders, the empty legs still clinging naturally to the support last chosen by the living spider within.

Inside one of our dining-room windows, a spider web had grown. Not just a dusty mat in a corner, rousing superior smirks in those more domestically disciplined than I, but a *glorious* web encompassing the whole frame. One evening, while dining, we watched our "web site," fascinated by hundreds of newly hatched spiderlings bustling about everywhere. With their minute bodies catching the lamplight, they starred their little universe like dancing pinpoints of light.

At night in cities, when a streetlight surrounded by heavy mist shines through a leafless tree, I'm reminded of the Great Weaver – a mythological spider image on a cosmic scale. Tangents of bare, wet branches encircling the lamp catch light on their edges, creating a web of brightness around the central spinner of light.

In the woods, Mack cut through an enormous tree, which had lain for years across a walking trail we shared with the deer. When the detached section, at least two feet in diameter, rolled out, the cosmos was revealed.

Spalted patterns rayed out from the centre like the web of the Weaver in the heart of the Tree of Life. A fallen tree, though dead in one sense, is very much alive in another, its great body providing nourishment for myriad life forms.

Truly, this tree was a web of life.

The Great Weaver endlessly forms the entwining patterns of our destinies, creates the visible world, spins out new universes, and connects us all on the invisible web of existence. This links the spider with the snake of renewal.

With the moon waxing and waning.

With time – the passage of change.

꙼ ꙼

Nearby, a barn brimmed over with spring lambs. New arrivals, their fleece still wrinkled from their late confinement in their mothers' wombs, stood in shadowy pens, propping themselves awkwardly on undisciplined legs. Their dark eyes held an inward focus, as they struggled with the mysteries of coordination that thwarted their desire to nurse. At this point, anything without an udder held only secondary interest for them.

Older lambs, veterans of two weeks or more, scampered in gangs, springing buoyantly onto the broad backs of reclining ewes and pushing off all challengers. Like youngsters everywhere, they also fell into sudden, deep sleeps, either heaped together or nestled down on the thick wool of their dozing – but vigilant – mothers.

I held one lamb lightly in my arms, marvelling at the delicate face. And at hooves so minute I could easily cup two in the centre of my palm. An inquisitive muzzle reached up, and warm breath gently traced my face.

In my memory, a dark shadow persisted: my discovery that "Persian lamb," fashioned into coats and collars, was obtained by deliberately aborting lambs, using methods of unthinkable cruelty on their mothers. It's a violation that will always haunt me.

Like lambs, like all domestic – and even wild – animals, much of our material life is controlled by traders in greed and power. Though most of us deplore our decimated natural world, still we are locked into continuing much of the damage, hastened by the few in control. We seem as helpless as lambs to control our collective future.

How great the need for awareness. For change.

And how inspiring the familiar fecundity of spring.

Except, perhaps, the fecundity of mosquitoes.

Outdoors, we worked long hours in our gardens, weeding, digging, and lugging. But as early summer wiggled in comfortably for a long stay, so did the mosquitoes. Despite the window screens, there were always a few waiting in the bedroom when we wearily climbed the stairs and dropped into bed like dead trees in a wind.

Mack speculated that the mosquitoes rode into the house tangled in our bug jackets, but I wasn't interested in theories. After the arduous days we were putting in, I wanted a decent night's rest on a regular basis.

Though I always examined the room before I turned off the light, my closing eyes – like the closing clack of the clapper board for Scene III, Take 12 – became the signal for action to begin. Soon, their familiar, insidious whine would fill my ears, and I'd be flailing wildly. I swell up hideously from their bites, and itch for days. I can't bear even the *possibility* of a mosquito around my eyes when I'm sleeping. If they were bitten, I'd never be able to open them in the morning.

Mack, on the other hand, isn't bothered by their bites. And his imperfect hearing doesn't transmit their approach. He could fall asleep untroubled by a room *full* of mosquitoes. Only when he finds himself pitching about from my gyrations does he realize that we're under siege; I lunge at one mosquito as frenziedly as at dozens.

Left in peace, Mack would sleep like the pure in heart, wake up stung in a dozen places, and never suffer one inconvenient itch.

I tell him he's not even fit to eat.

Desperate for sleep one night, I switched the light back on, and was almost startled to see how small my attackers were. In the dark, they sounded like *mega*-mosquitoes, creatures that would retreat only if I swung an iron mace at them.

But their diminutive size was no bonus after all, since they turned out to be adroit shape-shifters. Even when I caught one between my palms – for *sure* that time! – when I opened my hands, the mosquito flitted away.

Not only unharmed, but seemingly refreshed.

With no chance for sleep myself, it didn't help to hear Mack gently snoring.

During one long night, after I finally *did* doze off – still swinging, but defeated by exhaustion – I evidently struck at the tormentors around my head with greater success. For when I floated groggily into the bathroom in the morning, I found several gory mosquitoes smeared unbecomingly across my face, like one of the more exotic unguents.

As I returned to the bedroom to dress, there was a loud BANG! at the window. I darted outside, still in my nightgown, and scooped up a stunned siskin. The mosquitoes hovering hopefully around the door almost whooped for joy as they charged. Alerted to my peril by the wail of their sirens, I fled inside, still clutching the hapless bird. There, in relative peace, I held her, waiting for her to revive.

Although the gender of siskins can't be determined by sight, Mack and I both involuntarily referred to this one as "she." So we simply heeded our inclinations.

The usual twenty to thirty minutes needed for recovery stretched out to three hours. During that time, I lay back in my studio chair reading, the siskin roosting drowsily on my finger, its body so light as to seem weightless to my duller perceptions. The book lay open on my lap, and with my other hand I rubbed Edna's back over and over, to our mutual enjoyment.

At first, the siskin's eyes widened in alarm when Edna loped over and sat up, ears questioning and nose bobbing at this new arrival. But all trepidation quickly subsided. When she tried a short, though unsuccessful, flight, I rose and began walking towards the door. The siskin, perched again on my finger, peered down with such obvious perplexity at my feet appearing and disappearing one at a time and with such regularity below her that I chuckled aloud. She didn't seem to associate those mysterious appendages with my face and hands at all, as parts of a whole.

Truly, it's illuminating to suddenly see ourselves through the eyes of others. Especially other species.

Two or three times I stepped outdoors, armoured in my bug shirt, but the siskin refused to leave my hand. During the last attempt, as I stood holding her below the Great Mother, a *stone* fell out of the branches above and just missed my head.

Startled, I jumped back, covering the siskin protectively with my free hand. I looked up, but saw nothing unusual. No leprechaun winding up for the pitch.

Then I noticed a squirrel on the ground nearby, turning a large stone over and over with his paws, like a sculptor contemplating the possibility of deathless art from raw material. Finally, he seized it in his mouth and – not without effort – carried it over to the Great Mother and up the trunk. Followed by my wondering eyes, he trotted out along a limb and wedged the stone into the dense greenery, like an apple.

Entranced, if mystified, I watched as two more big stones, almost the size of his head, were "stored" just as quickly. When the apple season was upon us, this squirrel would definitely be in training. But as I glanced up warily, I wondered just how loaded the tree was now.

In a high wind, when those branches were pulled down, then released suddenly, our nurturing Great Mother could become a multiple slingshot.

The siskin stirred abruptly in my hands. Then took flight – but fluttered weakly to the ground, where she sprawled with spread wings, an easy catch for a cat. I wondered if this bird would need two or three days with us before she could manage on her own.

I carried "Sissy" inside, knelt before the indoor garden, and set her gently on the arching stem of a large leaf. Bashō, no doubt relieved whenever a new arrival was smaller than he, accepted her easily. But Sissy, somewhat perturbed by a bird not only much larger, but of an unfamiliar species, regarded him with wary eyes.

I rippled the water in the communal dish, and trickled drops into the side of her beak. She swallowed quite readily. Shortly after, I noticed her sitting on the edge of the waterdish, unalarmed, while Bashō drank beside her. Soon they were eating mixed canary and niger seeds, side by side, out of another dish – as well as finch seeds that I'd scattered near them. She even searched out hulled sunflower seeds to enjoy.

A few hours later, even Beejay, in direct contrast to the "greedy" reputations of blue jays in general, dozed peacefully in his tree, languidly watching Sissy sitting in his own dish, sampling his particular seed selection.

Siskins are remarkably calm around humans – something I've never achieved myself – and Sissy often ate seeds in one of my hands, while I cuddled Bashō under my chin with the other. In Mack's enormous palm, she looked little bigger than a grasshopper.

I recall one morning when Mack sidled out to the silo feeder, wearing his trickster grin. Around his wide-brimmed hat, he'd strewn seeds, and he held out both palms with more. The eager siskins, who would probably eat niger seeds off our tongues even if our teeth were pointed, clustered all over his hat and hands like a swarm of bees. Despite their size – which makes chickadees look big – they're feisty. They won't hesitate to drive one another off, and in this instance some of the more stubborn ones retreated till they were hanging upside down from the brim.

Sissy healed quickly from her impact with the glass, and when I began to retrieve her from odd places – like the kitchen sink, which she somehow flew into, yet couldn't fly out of – I knew she'd be ready soon. Surprisingly, only a day and a half after she came, she flew into the kitchen where I was working, landed beside me on the counter and looked very speakingly at me.

The time had come.

Accordingly, I carried her out onto the balcony and stood by the rail. The veggie garden in its small clearing lay before us. The silo feeder with its continual bustle of siskins hung, swaying, on our right, and mixed woodland surrounded us beyond the gardens.

I laid my face against Sissy's softness, wishing her well. Slowly I raised my head, and watched her bright eyes peering this way and that.

Then she flew – beautifully.

She swooped out over the clearing and swung to the left, heading towards a large, shaggy spruce. As she approached it, another siskin flew out of a neighbouring spruce and followed her in. They remained near each other on the same branch, mates undoubtedly. And reunited at last.

What fun it would have been to have heard what she had to tell him.

The window that caused Sissy's downfall – so fortunately short-lived – is covered with a tight barrier of black garden netting. Normally, this prevents any injury. Even ruffed grouse, striking it at high speed, have rebounded and gone their way, unharmed. But when we examined it, we found that one side had worked loose, allowing the netting to be pressed easily against the glass.

Mack restretched and fastened the netting to produce the desired "vertical trampoline" effect, and all was well after that.

As the hot weather intensified, I worked at extending our bed of lemon balm beside the house. We gather great bunches of this to dry for our tea, supplementing it with wild mint that grows near a beaver dam. When I was ready to add new earth, Mack shovelled topsoil from our roadside pile into the wheelbarrow. Then he pushed each load up one slope, down the other side, around our square asparagus garden, and uphill again to me.

Nothing is ever easy when a house stands on the highest ground.

The last slope was generously booby-trapped with jutting roots and rocks that countered any uphill momentum he could muster better than official speed bumps. From where I was digging the last load in, I'd see Mack coming at a run, his eyes ferocious with determination.

I'd leap partway downhill, grab the front of the wheelbarrow, and pull at a backwards run *uphill* while Mack pushed. When my heels struck a root, down I'd go like a dropped egg, frantic lest the load topple onto me. Or often the wheel would strike an immovable lump, stop dead, and nearly jolt the arms off Mack. Together we'd wrestle the recalcitrant load up the last few feet to the waiting garden.

After one such catastrophe, when the twisting barrow seemed determined to dump the dirt everywhere but in the garden, we collapsed in the shade for a rest. Ruefully, we reflected that we'd be too old to do this if we were half the age we were. Beads of sweat sprang out of our scorched faces and dripped alluringly off our noses and chins.

Our bug jackets, while warding off the stinging hordes that never seemed too tired to haunt us, stifled us like woollen blankets. Our wet hair and clothes clung to us with cloying persistence.

We wondered, idly, if we were simply masochistic and hadn't realized it.

Anyone else would just *buy* herbal tea.

In the morning, I plugged in the kettle. Then I stepped out in the early freshness to admire our labours from the previous day.

And *howled!*

The enlarged tea garden had been thoroughly ransacked. Pale roots lay like exposed nerves. Log borders had been rolled down the slope. And moist excrement gleamed in mounds on top of our wilting leaves of lemon balm.

When I looked away, sickened, I wished I hadn't.

My raised planters, set out so attractively with petunias and geraniums, had also been looted. Soil and upended plants were dumped everywhere. The short wire fencing "protecting" my flower beds leaned at crazed angles – or was utterly flattened. The budding stalks of many of my perennials were bent, or severed entirely. Even many of the rocks creating the borders were dislodged and rolled aside.

There was no doubt in my mind who the culprits were. Unable – before breakfast – to acknowledge that all that work had to be done again, I returned to the kitchen.

Steaming.

Memories of those raccoon tails tied so deplorably to car antennae in the 1950s were only mildly offensive compared to what I had in mind at that moment – and I would incorporate more than just the tails.

Regardless of beguiling eyebrows.

CHAPTER 16

LORD OF THE RINGS

Under many of the trees and along the fenceline lay a final sprinkling of "snow" from the last of the white spring blossoms. Our wooden boardwalk was strewn with a confetti of round petals. Like fading elders in a quickening world, blooms yielded passively to every thrust from the ever-youthful winds, and fluttered to the ground to shrivel.

Perched in a great elm, after a wild night of driving rain, eleven bald eagles hung out their broad wings to dry. They reminded me of communities of cormorants, always with wet wings hanging out, like the ubiquitous sheets drying in urban backyards.

Nodding trilliums dozed beside a singing brook. I found their upside-down flowers, tucked coyly beneath their leaves, by holding my own head topsy-turvy.

On a busy highway, among whizzing cars, a robin lay dead on

her back. Her breast of glowing embers should have been warming eggs. Kindling renewal.

Soon her beauty had vanished, crushed into an unidentifiable smear on the road. Rain fell, cleansing and erasing the smear. And still, the relentless traffic hurried past, indifferent, while her eggs died.

Later, an enormous double rainbow, haunted by a fainter, third rainbow, arched with such vibrancy over the highway that the wet pavement glowed in response.

Transfigured as though in tribute.

In the restored sunlight, a neighbour arrived to tell us about a baby raccoon alone in his yard.

Remembering our violated gardens, I repressed – with difficulty – a caustic retort that involved raccoon burgers. Mack's eyes, too, flickered ominously. But as we approached the area and heard piercing cries of acute desperation, we were overwhelmed, instead, with concern.

Something was definitely wrong.

Splayed against the trunk of a tree was a tiny raccoon, about a month old. He was bundled in thick fur that was immaculately clean from his mother's care, and his diminutive ringed tail hung as limp as a bookmark. His eyes showed that slight opacity of young eyes that cannot see far. Only when we drew up beside him did those eyes grow alarmed.

The neighbour offered thick gloves for protection, but Mack boldly plucked the babe off the tree with one hand. Snarls of surprising conviction burst out, and I jumped. But, on reflection, I realized that I had implements in the kitchen more threatening than those minute teeth. Undaunted, Mack stuck the tip of his finger between them.

And the little creature instantly began to suck.

Hunger dissolved not only his fears, but all pretence of defence.

The neighbour warmed a little milk and we eased some down the raccoon's throat with an eyedropper. Hungry as he was, he struggled against our efforts, taking in only a little before falling asleep, exhausted, in my arms.

Where was his mother?

This youngster could stagger slightly, but not walk. His den had to be near. If the mother had been killed, probably other siblings would be in need.

The neighbour tipped a tall ladder against the tree where the babe had clung. Then he climbed up, looking for a nest hole – but to no avail. He tried nearby trees, still without success. We investigated a wide area around the first tree, peering under twisty roots and into hollow logs, checking even the most unreasonable locations, just in case.

Nothing. This raccoon kit seemed to have been dropped by the gods.

Mack and I looked at each other in despair. We lived with birds, both permanent and transient ones – and birds are always a favourite on raccoons menus. I had lost several beloved ducks and hens to raccoons over the years. We had both repaired and replaced enough bird feeders broken by the rascals to want to spend our minimal free time in more entertaining ways.

Chafing memories of gardens and roadside garbage cans plundered messily made us speculate on the household havoc a tame raccoon could wreak – a raccoon that would need nurturing and teaching for a *whole year*, as wild ones do. Birds, even at their most creative, would seem as harmless as houseplants in comparison.

We shuddered.

We did *not* want to become raccoon parents.

Then we glanced down at the woolly face, which was waking now, and whimpering. Wondering about these strange creatures surrounding him. Wanting only to be reunited with his mother.

He, too, had become embroiled innocently and unwillingly in this situation, where the boundless security of maternal warmth and nourishment had been abruptly transformed into frightening solitude and hunger.

How long had he clung to the tree, awaiting her return?

How long had he cried, never hearing an answer?

How many hours had passed since she'd washed and fed him?

Most of all, *what had happened to her?*

All questions we could never answer.

Meanwhile, "Ringo" needed proper nourishment – and quickly. I tucked him into my shirt and tried to comfort him while we returned home to consult our dog-eared books on animal care. As we drove to town for the necessary supplies, Ringo wriggled in under my armpit, where he finally cried himself to sleep.

We bought Esbilac puppy formula at the vet's, and Infantol vitamin drops for human babies at the drugstore. We also purchased a glass bottle of pop – for the bottle – and a latex teat. Then, after considering those pointed teeth, we added several spare teats. Back home again, we warmed two-thirds of a cup of formula, sixteen drops of vitamins, and two cups of water in a saucepan. Then we poured the mixture into the bottle and presented it hopefully to the babe.

Ringo sniffed the teat suspiciously, approved it, and began to suck ecstatically. In his enthusiasm, he clutched the neck of the bottle, trying to "knead it" as he would his mother's teat, while we struggled to keep the bottom of the bottle uppermost. It pitched and rocked like a dory in a storm.

He suckled and spluttered until we finally pried the empty teat out of his grip. Then he sneezed dramatically, splattering Mack's shirt while I chuckled heartlessly.

I wiped the milky muzzle – Ringo's that is – and Mack turned the rounded belly over his shoulder in order to pat Ringo's back. Ringo responded by belching contentedly, and coughing a dribble of milk down Mack's back.

I washed the bottle and indulged in the superior humour of one whose shirt is still clean.

An unwise move.

The final step to each feeding was to set Ringo down on his bottom, hold up his front feet to straighten his body, and then pat his penis repeatedly with a wet paper towel until he began to pee, a procedure better performed by his mother's tongue. May I *never* be a mother raccoon. When the urine emerged, she would simply absorb it in an act of selfless devotion at which both Mack and I drew the line.

Not surprisingly, raccoon kits and their dens are always clean.

For reasons inscrutable to me, Ringo seemed to respond more readily to *my* touch than to Mack's. Thus this unusual ritual became part of my daily routine – though not without a good deal of unrepeatable humour from Mack at my expense. If I didn't initiate his peeing, Ringo would become as fretful as any human in dire need, and look around just as anxiously.

But as soon as I wielded my magic towel and pee began to dribble, Ringo purred – the raccoon equivalent of a sigh of relief.

Often he'd "nurse" at the same time, and would fasten himself like a lamprey eel to my neck or my chin as I bent over him, trying to "go with the flow." I definitely got the desired results. But the red splotches he'd leave on me in return no doubt created speculations in the minds of strangers that were better left unpoken.

Thus it was always Mack, in another clean shirt, who had the last laugh.

For the first couple of days, though Ringo was fed, drained, and cuddled regularly, he grieved for his mother. He'd peer about yearningly, lamenting in shrill, tremulous cries.

These were cries very different from those of hunger. Cries of bewilderment and longing that we could never assuage or satisfy. We could only cuddle and rock him inside our shirts until he finally fell asleep, wearied and disheartened.

Twice we carried him back to the woods in the hope that his calls would somehow reach her ears. But without success.

We even presented Ringo to a mother raccoon named "Pretty-face," whose dark mask surrounded by distinctive silvery fur gave her a rare beauty. But when she emerged from her den at dusk, leaving her young family asleep and safe, she froze at the sight of yet *another* hungry babe.

"Please take him," we breathed, watching from the window.
She fled.

"And some have motherhood thrust upon them," I murmured.
Reason told us that his mother was dead.
But we never found her. Nor any dead babies.

At night, Ringo slept snuggled among sweaters in a little box, his arms wrapped tightly around a teddy bear that we kept for visiting human youngsters. But just before dawn, when foraging mother raccoons usually return to nurse their young, he'd waken and begin to whimper.

Mack would descend the stairs and shamelessly prattle baby talk. Soon the cries would cease, and I'd drift back to sleep. When morning gradually brightened the room, the light revealed a tiny raccoon, weighing only a pound – like a box of chocolates – curled up contentedly under Mack's ear, close to the reassuring pulse in his neck.

Both of them sound asleep.

After a few days, outward signs of Ringo's grieving faded and he began to bond with his strange new parents. His once *reluctant* parents, who by now were utterly enamoured with their woolly youngest. Between Mack and Ringo, especially, began a solid rapport that strengthened daily.

Now after feedings, when his belly was round and replete, Ringo would haul it up Mack's arm to his shoulder and fall asleep beside his neck, purring happily. Or he'd continue across Mack's shoulders and slide down the other arm, only to drop into a coma of satisfaction in the curl of Mack's elbow.

Though Ringo had lost his mom, he'd gained a whopper of a dad.

In time, he'd nurse to satiety, but resist his usual postprandial torpor. Instead, he'd roll onto his back and play with his toes. Or with one of Chip's toys, his delicate fingers exploring all the inter-locking shapes that create wind-up ducks, rubber lizards, squeaky tarantulas, and the like.

Chip, whose interest could be aroused instantly if one brazenly filched the same toys she'd been ignoring for weeks, would swoop to our shoulders to watch this interloper. If a toy escaped Ringo's waving paws and rolled away, Chip occasionally darted down, snatched it up, and flew away. Later, we'd find it floating in her waterdish.

Ringo's paws were as smooth as any baby's skin. Touching his palms was like touching flour. His fur, though, was surprisingly coarse. Every visitor was fascinated by his soft hands and dexter-ity. And especially by his expression.

Complacency soon became habitual with "His Woolliness." And he wore the bland, perpetual smile so characteristic of a monarch before his subjects. He lolled with regal languor in the laps of admirers, twinkling benignly, as if to proclaim – "Life is good, my people. But hold it with both hands."

His perception changed too, and he began to take more notice. Though Mack fed him, I was the one who prepared the bottles. Ringo, scrambling around in Mack's arms, restless with hunger, would smell the formula heating and spot me in the kitchen. Immediately, he'd struggle to get down, ignoring all efforts to placate him. If Mack finally set him on the floor, Ringo would come romping over to me, all on one side. His front feet would trot individually, but his hind feet, loping as one big unit, would overtake his front end, driving him sideways. Usually, he'd just crash into me – a guaranteed method of stopping himself, as though he'd misplaced his operator's manual with that important passage about brakes. To say nothing of steering.

But when it came to climbing, Ringo was already an expert. He clambered up my leg as if it were a tree trunk.

Once up on my shoulder, he seemed to transform into a furry octopus. Though I peeled one paw after another off the handle of the saucepan, Ringo continually sprouted more paws than I could manage. I didn't even *try* to pour the liquid into the bottle while he was with me.

Sometimes, to distract Ringo at mealtimes, Mack would sit in the sunshine on the doorstep. Ringo, lying on his back in Mack's sun-warmed lap, would fiercely "attack" Mack's fingers while grinning happily. When I arrived, even if Ringo's eyes were shut, I had only to waft his bottle near his face to send him into a wild scramble as he tried to follow the irresistible aroma.

"The way to a man's heart," I'd remark innocently, handing Mack the bottle.

The indoor birds tolerated this furry nestling much as they did the more usual feathered variety. But Ringo, like any other young mammal, needed a lot of physical contact – which took hours out of each day. Upstairs, Edna too demanded her daily quota, and would mope reproachfully if it were withheld. Bashō, unlike the other birds, also enjoyed being held regularly – and used his seniority to pull rank. At his established time each evening, he'd wait at the edge of the garden with almost visible insistence.

Often I'd be cuddling Bashō and cooking supper simultaneously, while Mack cuddled Ringo, and Edna resignedly awaited her turn.

We seemed to have little time left to cuddle each other.

Sometimes I'd be holding Bashō, while sitting beside Mack and Ringo. Then Bashō's trust in me would be obvious to the most obtuse viewer. Ringo would crawl closer to me and sniff curiously at Bashō. But Bashō, looking tinier than ever, would snuggle deeper into my hands, and close his eyes. He had absolute confidence in my protection.

Chip, ever intrigued, would pry herself away from watching the male grackles at the feeders and swoop at this masked rider on Mack's shoulder instead. When Ringo sucked and clutched at his bottle, Chip often perched on our heads, question marks hovering over her own as she peered down at his Bacchanalian ecstasy.

Beejay calmly ignored him, sensing his lack of awareness, perhaps – and his babyhood, which precluded preying on birds yet.

Edna, possessing the high-strung timidity typical of rabbits, was – for her own sake – never introduced. Her lair in the upstairs studio effactually isolated her.

One afternoon, at rather short notice, we were invited to a spiritual drumming session at the Motherhouse of the Sisters of St. Martha in town. In a former chapel, still graced with tall windows and rich panelling, sat various Sisters in a circle. The more traditionally minded eyed the carved hand-drums sceptically, while others sat with an eager air, ready for anything. They graciously made room for us and we joined their circle, feeling unavoidably awkward and invasive.

Mack, in particular, looked as congruous as a horse in a henhouse. But at least he wasn't already beaded with sweat.

The leader, a vigorous, enthusiastic woman, who had made the drums herself, "wakened" one of them, releasing its rich tones. She moved around our circle, sounding the drum slowly and rhythmically. Holding it over every head as well as on either side of our bodies, she purified each of us in turn with its pulsing resonance. I furtively wiped my brow when she drew near.

Then I held my breath during my turn as the throbbing enveloped me, but all was well with Ringo – so far. She moved on to the next person.

When she returned to the centre of the circle, and swung into wild, exuberant drumming that thundered through the chapel, my shirt began to heave oddly. My lingering hope that Ringo would remain asleep vanished. Beneath my chin, a woolly masked face peered out sleepily. And curiously.

The Sisters were electrified.

Eyes widened, all heads turned, and a new stubble of sweat rose on my brow. Decidedly unspiritual giggles broke out, amid gasps of trepidation from the more timid, as tiny Ringo, intrigued, climbed out onto my shoulder. He peered about myopically, his busy nose probably transmitting more questions than answers in his unique surroundings. Then the leader, smiling broadly, broke into more mesmerizing rhythms on her drums, and the session continued.

Throughout the rest of it, Ringo remained on my shoulder, admired, tolerated, or deplored.

But unanimously interesting to all.

Ringo grew quickly, gaining weight like a chronic dieter. And we began to include soft food in his daily fare, such as bananas, which he loved. He utterly rejected the more solid bottled baby foods. And after I smelled them, I didn't blame him.

When we dipped a little of Mack's bread into the formula, Ringo chewed the soggy offering with great enthusiasm – until he'd extracted all the milk. Then, puzzled, he'd wait for us to remove the remaining wad from his mouth. Though he didn't actually eat it, he did gain practice in chewing.

As new teeth began to emerge, his gums became too sore to nurse. He'd grab the teat, drop it, grab it again almost angrily, drop it once more. Hungry and irritable, he'd cry his frustration. Then we'd smear honey on the nipple, an irresistible flavour that helped to override his physical discomfort.

At the end of one trying day, wearied by his fractiousness, we shamelessly added chocolate powder to his formula. He guzzled it down in record time.

All parents get desperate sometimes.

Ringo's coordination continued to improve – by leaps and bounds, one might say. He adored riding on our shoulders as we busied ourselves at various tasks. Our hair fascinated him, since it was as close as we could come to fur. As we worked, he'd run his fingers happily through our hair over and over, giving us not just erect hairdos that suggested perpetual surprise, but delightful head massages as well.

When discipline was needed, we tried to implement it in raccoon terms, snarling loudly and suddenly if Ringo nipped too hard, or bit our faces even slightly. He'd instantly lower his ears and crouch down submissively, his eyes avoiding ours. If we were particularly emphatic, he'd turn away. After a few minutes, he'd reach up tentatively and lick our faces.

Lesson learned. Lesson over.

Play was resumed.

Ringo's needs and our busy lifestyle – combined with the general shortage of raccoon sitters – guaranteed him experiences of which few raccoons could boast. Whenever our absence coincided with feedings, we loaded Ringo's warmed formula into a Thermos, gathered a few toys and a roll of paper towels, and took him with us. His Woolliness was an excellent traveller – provided he was continually cuddled and amused.

A three-hour journey through summer traffic would deliver:

An energized Ringo, fresh for new admirers and adventurers.

Mack the driver, ready for a nap or a coffee, whichever came first.

And me, the babysitter, wilted with weariness and incapable of faking even one final flicker of interest in squeaky rubber hedgehogs, little wire balls containing repulsive inmates with lolling eyes, or bunches of mixed keys – all of which had continually entranced Ringo as he lay in my lap. Or perhaps he was more entertained by me groping around the floor for them after he tossed them away each time.

Wherever we went locally, Ringo rode inside our shirts or on our shoulders, like a woolly burr, while heads turned like weathercocks. He was always the subject of solicitous inquiries, from the natural-foods store to the garden nursery, from the art gallery to the gas station. Suspicions seemed to be afloat that Ringo's slightest wish might not be fulfilled.

Bottle feedings drew all eyes wherever they occurred, and often cameras as well. Tourists jostled one another trying to get close enough to pat Ringo, and intersections became hazardous as other drivers stared – unbelieving – at a raccoon driving by, his face at the window.

At least two children who became ardent Ringo fans were bought toy raccoons as pacifiers by harassed parents.

One day, a friend arrived with several people from Australia who were eager to see Ringo. Raccoons are not indigenous to their country, but when he rolled up, grinning, they squealed with rapture, smitten immediately. For the next half hour, they videotaped and photographed each other with Ringo – who now accepted all adulations as his natural due.

And all admirers as fair game.

He climbed them like trees, tousled their hair, pulled off glasses and earrings, chewed watch straps. He rolled on his back, laughing, while they tickled his belly and dangled keys. Like all devotees, they loved the soft feel of his paws and the dexterity of his fingers.

But when he'd reduced them to the flushed, dishevelled state in which we normally functioned, we pried him off and took them indoors to meet the birds. There, Bashō received the supreme compliment of his life.

"Good heavens, he's so *big*!" boomed one of the women, since Australian quail were even tinier.

No one had *ever* described Bashō as big.

Swelling out his plumage with immense dignity, he raised his few inches up on tiptoe and delivered a triumphant peal that would do credit to a peacock.

CHAPTER 17

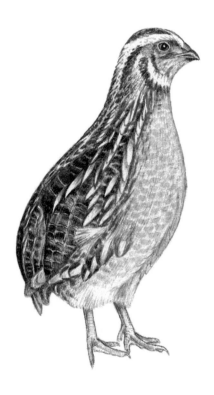

FAMILY FEELINGS

Nesting season, with all its triumphs and traumas, its struggle for renewal against desperate odds, was evolving in a multitude of daily dramas.

Wherever we walked, we heard the harsh cry of sharp-shinned hawks. Sometimes they were being harassed by parent birds that were defending their territories, or mobbed near feeders by vigilante blue jays. Even passing trespassers as large as ravens were being dogged determinedly by pursuers as tiny as starlings.

At the feed store, a man told us his latest adventure. He'd just stepped out his back door to fill the feeder when a grackle, holding a beakful of insects, landed on the eaves near his head. The grackle seemed agitated, flicking its long tail repeatedly and crying over and over with obvious distress.

After glancing up, startled, the man looked around the yard, convinced that the grackle was trying to communicate with him.

He soon spotted the problem: a neighbouring cat lurking beside the hedge. He threw a rock, the marauder fled, and the bird, evidently relieved, flew quietly to its nest in the bushes nearby.

The next day, though the man was indoors, the bird, once more carrying food for its young, landed at the window, upset and calling out shrilly. Answering the summons, the man emerged from the house and looked around the yard, the agitated grackle remaining near him as before.

There was the cat – but further away, on the edge of his property.

Again, he chased it away.

And again, the relieved parent bird slipped into its secret nest to feed its babes.

In the woods near our house, we heard a ruffed grouse drumming, its wings snapping out distinct, low-pitched beats that were amplified by the hollow, moss-covered log on which it was poised. The thumps began very slowly, but quickened rapidly into a drum roll, the whistling wings a blur.

We crept nearer.

Then nearer.

When he paused, so did we. When he continued, so did we – until we were crouched in excruciating rigidity, watching, only twenty feet away. My excited heart was pounding so loudly that I was almost surprised the grouse didn't turn his head towards this beat from "a different drummer."

We have heard ruffed grouse often, dozens of times each year. Usually, they share our feeding stations with the other wildlings, picking up scattered seeds. They balance with exquisite precision on tiny, swaying branches near our windows, twisting off buds and eating them.

But in the woods they are such wary birds – because of hunters – that this was the first time either Mack or I had actually witnessed the drumming ritual.

Above the veggie garden, an eagle circled low, its white head and tail glinting in the sunlight, and a red-tailed hawk wheeled even lower. One of the nesting ravens darted up out of the woods and checked the raptors guardedly, but retired without fussing, unfortunately violating the territory established by two grackles. One disturbed grackle then swooped after the departing raven, upsetting in turn a pair of robins, who lifted out of the trees, barking shrilly at the passing grackle.

Nesting tensions were running high.

I lifted several pots of wildflowers out of a cardboard box. Then tipped out a handful of dried dirt, and what I took to be a dried, beige-coloured leaf – till it righted itself and hopped away.

Over the bank of sweet rocket flowers that were distilling their potent fragrance, several hummingbird hawk-moths hovered. They moved methodically and efficiently from blossom to blossom, omitting none. Their whirring wings spread the flowery aroma whenever the breeze grew still.

In contrast, tiger swallowtail butterflies, fluttering erratically among the plants, seemed to land by mere whim on various blossoms. Or by chance.

But their colourful wing patterns transformed them into exotic mobile flowers, totally eclipsing the hawk-moths in their homely browns.

In the rain barrels, we have inserted long "ladders" of wire mesh, as well as floating blocks of wood, so that creatures tumbling in by accident are able to save themselves. Sometimes, a wet deer mouse, with dark eyes enormous from alarm, will be marooned on the wood. Others who swim to the mesh can climb out on their own. One morning, nine enormous beetles were clinging to the wood and the mesh, and were easily rescued.

Chipmunks, too, are drawn to the barrels for a drink. One day, before we'd installed our mesh ladders, I glanced into a half-full barrel in passing – then dropped what I was carrying and seized the rim. Inside, a trapped chipmunk was swimming round and around at a desperate speed. I pushed over the barrel and the frantic victim surfed out on a tidal wave for several feet before his paddling feet touched solid ground and he was able to dash away.

Thereafter, I set out a low dish of drinking water for the chipmunks, while Mack cut ladders out of wire mesh for the barrels.

Black-and-white bobolinks, with their buff heads, added height to fenceposts that became favourite perches. They clung to tall, swaying grasses, or fluttered over the thrusting new hay now greening the fields, gliding with their characteristic wings-down posture, and rippling out one of the sweetest birdsongs of the summer. The immense length of their migration, beginning in southern South America, never fails to awe me. The *hazards* – mostly man-made – between there and here present staggering odds for survival. And yet they face that trek twice a year.

Crows patrolled the roadside ditches, probing through what passing motorists would consider repulsive green muck, but is actually an intricate world of aquatic life, rich and nutritious. On quiet, spring-fed ponds, wild ducks glided through the bright-green veneer, leaving wakes of dark water. Though they might seem to be floating in iridescent slime, in reality the ducks were swimming through a salad of duckweed – tiny, floating leaves with a generous sprinkling of aquatic insects on a bed of clean water, and flanked by side orders of small frogs.

In the studio, Edna munched steadily through a gigantic heap of dandelion, clover, and vetch leaves, with the concentration of a confirmed gourmet. Only her ears were visible, like a moose eating underwater plants.

In effect, Edna's ears are a second pair of eyes. If she's dozing near me, with her ears and long lashes lowered, and Mack enters the room, one ear will rise and swivel questioningly in his direction, like a furry periscope. Her eyes will remain closed, and her other ear at rest.

Through our round window, I watched dandelion seeds migrating, now in flocks. They were following the single harbinger that we'd seen from the balcony, and seeking their own nesting grounds. Earlier, I'd seen wafts of white hawthorn blossoms whirling by. The circular frame around the glass, the circular petals, the circle of spokes bearing dandelion seeds, all affirmed this eternal round of renewal and fulfillment.

As did one of my most luxuriant violets.

I had rescued one rounded violet leaf from a slushy parking lot just over a year ago. I'd taken it home and planted it, wondering if it would live. If it would blossom. Now it had grown into a triple-centred plant, overflowing its container, and bearing double white blooms with rippled edges.

Reminiscent of the trampled snow in which it had lain.

Chip, with all the attractions of wild grackles around the house, had long lost interest in her toys. Rounded eggs and circular nests, with their own message of renewal, held more appeal for her these days.

I used to cram her various toys into an old ginger jar and plug it with a cork. Chip's delight was to work the cork loose, pull out all the toys, and toss them aside for me to pick up and replace in the jar to begin the game again. Often, I'd hide a peanut at the bottom for a treat.

Sometimes, *she'd* drop the toys inside, and I recall one instance when she was perched in the lip of the jar. Suddenly, she parted her feathers and defecated inside. Then – unbelievably – she turned around, removed the dropping, and began to fill the jar with toys.

But now, other things were on her mind.

She danced by the hour on the windowsills, ogling the male grackles and fluttering her wings as beguilingly as a coy woman might flutter her eyelashes. One day, I heard Chip emitting high-pitched whimpers. I leaned around a handhewn beam and peered curiously into the indoor garden.

She was perched on the edge of the board that fenced the garden. Her tail was raised alluringly, she was trembling her wings and looking coquettishly – not to say beseechingly – over her shoulder at Beejay, who was on the rim of the waterdish directly behind her.

If nothing else, this seemed a strong indication that Beejay was, indeed, male. Only we humans seem unable to distinguish between genders of blue jays. Fortunately, the birds themselves have no difficulty.

Though Beejay blatantly refused Chip's invitation, she began nest-building in a tall plant over our bed, using odd materials that she gathered from around the house. Soon an untidy collection of tissues, bookmarks, and candy wrappers were assembled to create a nest that even the most indulgent critic would have to describe as eccentric.

Though heredity initiated it, environment definitely gave it individuality.

Chip's desire for a family deepened, as did her evident dissatisfaction with indoor life, and we considered releasing her. Though I'd tried several times to do this during her first year, her latent lung weakness had always reappeared, forcing her to return voluntarily for treatment with Panmycin. But she hadn't suffered from that pulmonary congestion for at least two and a half years.

Could she manage an outdoor life now?

Then a stranger called to say he'd found a baby grackle on its own. He'd seen no sign of parents. Would we take it?

This seemed too good to be true. So often baby robins turn out to be starlings. And in my experience grackles, starlings, and redwings are all loosely termed blackbirds.

What would this nestling really be?

The man soon arrived with the youngster cuddled into a towel in a box, and a jar of worms which he held out. "I brought some formula too," he quipped.

As it happened, the babe was indeed a young grackle. And we were jubilant – but too soon. Chip reached over and nibbled reflectively at the new feathers opening out on the young, tufty head. Then she jabbed out suddenly, almost angrily, driving the babe away.

She wanted *her own.*

And she became increasingly anxious and frustrated each day, creating such continual havoc indoors that soon we were all equally frustrated.

One morning when I was bleary-eyed with fatigue, she snatched one of my vitamin pills and zoomed away, initiating an early-morning chase that destroyed any interest I had in being up at all. Later, she drove Mack equally mad by puncturing bags of thawing soup, which consequently oozed over the counter and dribbled to the floor in red pools – gory decor that seemed to inspire Mack in an ominous way when he glared at her. Consoling himself with well-rounded epithets, he set the dripping bags in a bowl, and mopped up the mess.

Then – unwisely – he sought refuge outdoors, but neglected to cover the bowl.

Chip returned to the kitchen and hammered larger holes in the softening bags. Then she pulled out chunks of vegetables, eating some, shredding more, and scattering the rest around the house. Carrots, potatoes, onions, beans – all landed in our mugs and boots, or bloomed on houseplants. Veggies skidded underfoot, or floated in the waterdish. Bits stuck to the wall of the indoor garden.

For added emphasis, she shat in the bowl.

Twice.

By noon, she'd left more droppings in unusual places – places guaranteed to fuel our frustration. Splatters appeared in unappetizing patterns on the breadboard, the stove, and inside the hanging pots and pans. One copious contribution hardened unnoticed inside the toaster, and at breakfast time the next morning, it created a reek beyond my powers to describe.

She subjected Bashō and Beejay to intense teasing, pulling their tails, tweaking Bashō's toes, and screaming perfect imitations of blue-jay alarm calls in Beejay's very face. The state of their seed dishes resembled the aftermath of a hurricane.

In the studio, where I was sanding a sculpture, Chip persistently stole pieces of sandpaper and destroyed their usefulness by soaking them in Edna's waterdish. Or she'd splash in Molly's dish until both her and Molly's feathers were saturated, before shaking excess water all over my books. Or she'd shred plants behind my back – much to Edna's delight, as salad fixings rained down for her delectation.

But Chip showed none of her usual enjoyment in this devilry. None of her gleaming-eyed high spirits.

She seemed thwarted. Unhappy. And evidently determined to reduce the rest of us to the same state.

Chip was a special member of the family, as the more mischievous children often are. But to us, her happiness was paramount.

Accordingly, one morning we opened the window. During the

next half hour, she flew often to the windowsill, stepped to the outside edge, peered in all directions, then flew back in again. We stayed well back, watching with mixed feelings – concerned for her health, yet concerned more for her peace of mind.

Just as we glanced away, Chip slipped out – characteristically sly to the last.

Over the next two weeks, we often saw her with other grackles, and spoke to her. She'd fly to a branch near us, listening intently, the pale nictitating membrane of her eyes moving very slowly, as was usual whenever she shared intense, intimate moments with us. But she didn't volunteer any closer contact.

Neither did we. We just wanted to convey that we were there if she needed us.

She looked bright-eyed and energetic. Happy at last. Then, one day, I noticed that she was breathing with her mouth open, as was usual when she became ill.

She still preferred to stay out, so we could only wish the best for her.

We never saw Chip again.

But we never again looked at grackles without our hearts kindling.

Instead, the slightest gestures of wild grackles, the least of their calls, held our attention with their painful familiarity. With smiling nostalgia.

"Remember when Chip . . .?"

"Remember when Chip . . .?"

Our irrepressible personal trickster remained as timeless as the universal one.

The young grackle, meanwhile, flourished in the indoor garden, tolerated and taught – indirectly – by Bashō and Beejay. Eventually, he was transferred to the outside aviary, then to complete freedom with supplementary feedings until he achieved independence. A gentle release.

But when a female purple finch, with her right wing drooping from a cat bite, was brought to us and set down in the garden, Bashō – surprisingly – objected.

Raising his feathers to swell his natural size, he stalked her with all the menacing intimidation of one who has finally encountered someone smaller than himself. Though his actions went no further, the finch understandably found his attitude disturbing.

No doubt her rapid recovery was due in part to Bashō's lack of hospitality.

A starling fledgling was also brought to us at this time, rescued from death by dehydration and starvation when he was found trapped – mysteriously – inside a dryer vent. Since he was already suspicious of humans, and able to forage for himself, only a few days in the aviary were necessary to help him on his way. Sometimes so little can make such a difference to a creature.

Everywhere, we saw birds struggling to survive.

A sparrow, newly fledged, crossed the road one day in front of our car. The little creature was beating its new wings as hard as possible, and its body was strangely upright, lacking the proper balance that wind under its tail would provide – once a tail had been grown. A parent bird was escorting the youngster, flying below in a similarly upright posture, as though holding up the babe by sheer will. The parent's excited cries of encouragement were clearly audible in our car while we watched, entranced. To our immense relief, he crash-landed triumphantly in a roadside bush.

From the kitchen window, I caught sight of a mother grackle flying up to a feeder. She abruptly chased out a young grackle, filled her bill with seeds, and swooped down to the veggie garden. Her own youngster emerged cautiously from under the lush bean plants when she clucked. Then he hopped over eagerly to be fed.

I was lucky to have seen this encounter. The yellow eyes of grackles are like great searchlights. No matter how furtively I skulked about indoors, trying to resemble a chair or a lamp, in order to see if Chip were among the wild grackles, those golden beams spotted me every time. Then the alarm would ring out and ten grackles lift off as one bird.

Other creatures, too, were busy with their young.

Not twenty-five feet from the window, we watched a spotted fawn in the hayfield at dusk. We couldn't see the doe, but when Mack stepped outside quietly, the unseen mother turned her own version of a searchlight on him, then gave a loud WHUFF! of alarm.

Across the field they fled, bounding lightly over the clutching, tangled grasses, flaunting white tails like impudent banners. And the fawn was leading the way.

The adventures of yet another family became entwined with our lives about this time, with the opening chapter taking place in the yard of the local high school.

School.

The very word, for me, conjures up the arch enemy of creativity: conformity. Yet here I was, facing the prospect of painting a mural in the regional high school.

From initially rejecting the proposal, I had gradually begun to welcome the challenge of creating something meaningful, despite being restricted to using household enamel paint over bland, concrete blocks. Something of lasting significance was needed for young, energetic students incarcerated year after year in a windowless, almost airless, institutional building of unspeakable dreariness. In my artwork, I have often incorporated brick patterning to suggest the stifling impact of rigid conformity. Thus, it was with a meditative eye that I pondered the two-storey end wall looming over the stairs.

How could I prevent the inflexible layout of the blocks from undermining my message of creative freedom?

In a sudden flash, I decided to adopt the principle of aikido: instead of expending my energies to fight the monotony of the blocks, I would defeat them by using their own tedious pattern as my weapon.

The completed image would be the full height of the wall, so Jeff, my agent and a seasoned friend, undertook the task with me. He assembled several units of metal construction staging and added a few heavy planks for us to stand or sit on while we painted. These could be inserted at different levels as needed.

The whole structure – though theoretically sound – wobbled unnervingly when I climbed up the side and crept out tentatively on top, trying to clutch a flat wall that seemed to persistently sway out of reach. I felt as if I were standing on a two-storey card table during an earthquake. From the vicinity of the ceiling, I could look down between the two planks to the cement floor – at least half a mile below.

We both wore hideous vapour masks that might flatter extra-terrestrial beings but did nothing for our appearance – beyond giving us reason to laugh heartily at one another. At least they muffled any profanity escaping at stressful moments, since we had to shout to be heard.

Hoping to complete the project over one rigorous weekend, we worked almost around the clock, and pooled our abilities: I was better at drawing; Jeff had a better head for heights. Between us, the mural emerged, with me continually correcting Jeff's work, and he continually encouraging me to climb out on a shaky tower, thereby risking my neck.

There were moments when I suspected that he wanted me up there in hopes of putting an untimely end to my perpetual criticism.

Working across the lowest regions and leaving the interstices white, I painted each brick black. Upon this foundation of relentless conformity, I finally blackened even the interstices to produce a smog-ridden city skyline of endless buildings and spewing chimneys. Up each side of the wall, I continued blacking the bricks. But as they approached the centre, they were texturized, dissolving under the surging power of a gigantic spiritbird rising up the middle of the wall.

Unfurling above the city skyline, this spiral of creative energy opens its wings upward and outward.

Within the bird's breast is a rising "school" of fish – restrained, like pupils, by currents beyond their control or comprehension. But the fish grow in size as they rise, paralleling the evolving spirit, and culminate in two crossed fish of power that see in all directions.

Above them, a winged soul. Above it, a soulboat on the sea of life.

Most of the mural was rendered in black and white – the rigid "right" or "wrong" characteristic of our limited schooling system.

However, around the expanding power of the spirit, I added energized auras of red, the colour of pain, of sacrifice.

And, conversely, of full-blooded vitality.

Within the spiritbird's breast, the images of fish and soulboat are golden. As is the seed of promise, of potential, painted like the sun and held in the huge, open beak.

Golden, too, was the enthusiastic response from the students – and *most* of the teachers – which brought an exhausting job to a satisfying close.

But one element of the mural's completion was not visible in the final image: the maternal aspirations of a country deer mouse.

·🐾· ·🐾·

On the final morning of the project, I pulled up to the school and began unpacking my painting supplies. Suddenly, a very pretty – but *pregnant* – deer mouse scurried worriedly past me inside the van. She vanished almost immediately.

Concerned about her "multiple" destiny, I reparked the vehicle beside a meadow of tangled grasses and small bushes that bordered the schoolyard. A brook lined with alders skirted the meadow, and could provide drinking water for her. Then I left the door ajar as a hint. Surely she'd relinquish such a noisy, lurching nursery for something with a more natural setting.

When I finally left for home, I saw no sign of her, and assumed she'd upgraded her abode.

However, a few days later, when I had been driving for about an hour, I caught a movement out of the corner of my eye. To my amazement, the long-forgotten mouse – now disturbingly slim – scuttled past my feet.

With my eyes on the mouse instead of the road, I swerved towards the centre line, suddenly remembered the road, and looked up again. An elderly cyclist, pedalling sedately towards me, jerked as though electrified. He twisted his bike away to avoid my van but caught his wheel on the rough edge of the shoulder. Lurching back across the road, I looked hastily in all directions for the mouse.

But all I saw was the cyclist framed in the rear-view mirror – now stopped, and shaking his fist at me.

At that moment, the mouse trotted past again, this time bearing a tiny baby in her mouth.

One after another, she carried her precious cargo from one hidden nest to another that was equally hidden, while I veered down the highway trying to watch out both for her and the oncoming traffic.

I counted *nine* babies.

I was impressed by the interesting parallel between the mouse and the high-school students, as they all dealt with the limitations of an unnatural environment. The mother mouse perceived the van as a network of hidden paths, in and out of the walls. No doubt many of the students, too, had evolved escape routes for survival within the academic structure – inner paths that served them well.

For those who dare, doors open.

That evening, I placed mixed seeds, peanut butter on a slice of bread, and a dish of water in the van. And avoided driving it. When the food finally remained untouched after a couple of days, I was certain that the deer mouse had shifted her family once again – this time, hopefully, to a quieter nest in the surrounding woodland.

A mobile home is no place to raise a large family.

CHAPTER 18

THE RINGLEADER

Ringo, meanwhile, was flourishing. His coat was thick and shiny. His energy enviably high. His eyes bright with interest.

He could also urinate without assistance from me.

We now fed him a wide variety of our own foods that included bread or crackers with peanut butter, bananas, cooked egg, dried cranberries, whole-grain cereal with raisins, cooked pasta and grains, pancakes, thawed berries, and cornbread. And a daily bowl of puppy formula.

For a special treat, he was given a Fig Newton.

As Ringo doubled in size, his beloved Fig Newtons seemed to shrink, so he soon cajoled us into allowing him *two* a day instead of one. They remained such a particular delight that, if he were given one in passing, he would lope after us clutching the cookie in his mouth until we stopped. Then he'd cling pleadingly to our legs until we finally sat down and allowed him to clamber into our laps to eat his prize.

Only there was he convinced that he could dine in perfect safety – that we would protect him against any lurking cookie thieves. However, to Ringo's continual despair, those moments of blissful chewing would come all too quickly to an end. Soon, he would be reduced to mournfully picking up stray crumbs with his delicate fingers.

Not for lack of effort did he fail to convince us that Newton's law really read, "More is better."

Mack, accustomed to being ostracized by the rest of us vegetarians when eating fish, offered the skin one evening to Ringo, who became an instant convert. He licked his fishy fingers over and over with his fishy tongue, and then searched Mack's pockets in the hopes of finding more.

I found it wiser to be upwind of the pair of them after fish suppers.

Thereafter, whenever Mack felt a yearning for fish, he bought enough for the two of them. He also bought meat solely for Ringo, freezing it in small quantities for daily use, lest our vegetarian lifestyle hamper natural raccoon development.

Ringo's coordination and awareness progressed rapidly, and he became fascinated with the indoor garden. He could now dart into it so quickly that we hesitated to bring him into the house. The birds, not being releasable, were too vulnerable. Yet he needed a safe place when we weren't home.

So we converted the shed adjoining the aviary into a raccoon den.

We took a wooden box and nailed it to the wall near the ceiling with the open side of the box facing upward. A sloping log down to the floor gave him a ladder. Then we lined the box with a blanket – our version of a cozy tree-hole. His food and water dishes were placed in a corner of the floor, which was already covered with vinyl for easy cleaning. A sturdy tree stood in one corner, a reminder of a saw-whet owl we'd cared for and released successfully, and now this tree would give Ringo climbing experience.

From the centre of the ceiling, we suspended Ringo's teddy bear on a short elastic cord. This rig provided great amusement for Ringo, who'd hurl himself with grins and growls onto the bear. It would swing out and back, up and down, with Ringo still clinging to it and chewing. But as soon as he let go, the bear would spring up and away, and Ringo would leap at it again, bringing it down like a linebacker nailing a quarterback.

A small door connected his shed to the open-air aviary – which was empty, for once – and we intended to leave this door ajar all night. The aviary itself, walled with wire mesh, was impregnable even to a mouse. But with wild raccoons foraging nightly on the other side of the pen, we hoped that Ringo would be attracted to them, and would learn appropriate raccoon behaviour from his own kind. These were lessons we couldn't provide.

Mack, who volunteered to cope with the unenviable task of cleaning up Ringo's droppings on the vinyl floor, also nourished a secret hope that Ringo would make his deposits outside, and that the rains would disperse them. But the one dropping left out there responded to a brief shower by growing a head of mould three inches deep – much to Mack's chagrin. Instead, Ringo's human upbringing won out.

Like the rest of us, when nature's call came, he trotted indoors.

Unfortunately, his human upbringing also resulted in the wide eyes and clinging arms with which he ardently greeted us after his first night in the outdoor pen. He almost seemed to be shouting, "You can't leave me out here all night. There are wild animals *everywhere!*"

Eventually he grew accustomed to his nightly visitors, much to our relief, and we dared to hope that he would eventually be assimilated into his natural world without too great a handicap from our influence.

Within such a peaceable kingdom, His Woolliness graciously reigned, demanding contact and cuddles as his daily due. All visiting children worshipped him, and one lucky little girl who stayed with us for several days carried Ringo everywhere. He, in turn, seemed mysteriously intrigued by her ears, and fingered them so frequently that we were afraid they'd still resemble scarlet flags when she went home – hopefully without meeting any bulls.

One hot afternoon, two youngsters accompanied us into the "throne room." Squeals of delight burst from both children when Ringo's furry ears rose out of his box above their heads. He blinked and yawned lazily, and sat up. When I placed my face close to his, he licked it amiably. Then I wafted a Fig Newton past his nose and he instantly became alert.

His passion for them had already dubbed him "Pig Newton."

While the kids watched, enchanted, he clutched the cookie tightly in his hands and bit off a mouthful, sitting back on his haunches and chewing blissfully with half-closed eyes. Bite by bite, the cookie disappeared. Then he left us all weak with laughter by earnestly prying a wad of sticky fig filling off the roof of his mouth with his fingers – much as a human child will struggle with peanut butter on moist white bread.

If he had finished his treat with a thorough flossing, I doubt if any of us would have been surprised.

One fresh morning, summer beckoned, luring us away from our tasks to enjoy the generosity of her short season. To revel in her warmth and fragrance. Her transience.

We needed little persuasion.

Already meadows everywhere were ringing with the strident piping of crickets, melodious door-wardens to autumn. Taking the hint, we scooped up Ringo and followed the path to the lake.

Ringo rode on our shoulders, his nose twitching continually, his head turning this way, then that. His eyesight seemed decidedly inferior to his hearing and sense of smell, as is usual for nocturnal creatures. Often his grip tightened from his awareness of what lay beyond our perceptions. Sometimes he scrambled to get down, so that he might follow at our heels instead, nose to the ground in rapt fascination.

At places of irresistible attraction – a rotting stump, bones from a fading carcass, or water in any form – he stopped, both hands busily exploring, his nose conveying more elusive knowledge, his gaze as abstracted as a philosopher's. Occasionally, he vanished into the undergrowth.

Whenever his lingering, or disappearance, was prolonged, I called out a high-pitched *oo-oo! oo-oo!*, each cry twisting up higher at the end, a call I've heard wild baby raccoons use.

Ringo never failed to respond.

Immediately abandoning his find, or backing down a tree, or climbing out of a brook, he would quickly materialize beside us. Then we'd cuddle him to reinforce his prompt response, and continue our walk.

Near the lakeside, I swung Ringo back up on my shoulder. Then Mack and I lifted his battered aluminum canoe, each dent a souvenir of his fishing expeditions in Newfoundland's rocky waterways, and carried it to the water's edge. Ringo clung to my head, question marks hovering over his own as the strange form bumped and scraped noisily into the water. Mack climbed in first, and made his way to the stern, where he settled himself. Still onshore, I pushed the canoe farther into the water and scrambled over the bow, Ringo nervously clutching my ears with both paws and making my head feel like a two-handled jug.

Then all clatter ceased as we slid silently out onto the still waters of the lake.

On the other side, two young boys, under the watchful eye of their mother on shore, were curving through the water like seals.

Soon their playtime squeals were disrupted by excited shouts – they had spotted Ringo, sliding down my back into the canoe, only to reappear on the bow. There, he posed like a woolly figurehead, peering myopically in the direction of the splashing boys, while his curious paws cautiously fingered the canoe's structure.

Mack steered us closer to the beckoning boys. Soon they were swimming around the canoe in delighted circles, calling Ringo's name and rocking us on their waves. Startled by the sudden confusion, Ringo left the pitching bow and scrambled back up onto my shoulder for comfort. Taking the hint, Mack waved goodbye to the boys and steered us away into quieter reaches.

Trees arched over our heads as we drifted lazily over the sun-dapples. Shoals of minnows darted, first this way, then that. Water spiders twitched away from our approaching bow. Pollen dusted the surface of the water, creating a solid golden floor.

I eased my paddle under a small butterfly, and lifted it out of the water, where it had been struggling to free itself. It perched on the paddle's tip long enough to set its flying gear in order, then fluttered away to resume its short, mysterious life.

Ringo's confidence quickly returned in such peaceful surroundings. Lured by the damp, heady aromas that teased his senses, he was soon hanging over the edge of the canoe, his hind feet hooked securely onto the gunwale, his front paws scrabbling in the water. Several old hardwood trees have floated in the lake for untold years, sculpted and smoothed through the seasons by the persistent lapping of water and scraping of ice. Each has been slowly transformed into a floating garden, bearing clusters of young spruce and birch, wild rhododendron, and brilliant mosses. Tucked among these are the intriguing carnivorous sundews, fatally attracting tiny insects in order to digest them.

Dragonflies darted over the floating gardens, also devouring insects, but with a haste reminiscent of city drivers wolfing down fast-food horrors as they dodge through tangles of traffic.

Mack guided the canoe over to one of the logs so that it loomed up right before Ringo. Following his whiffling nose and curious paws, Ringo eased down onto the log, feeling through the greenery and fingering the slippery sides of the log as far under the water as he could reach. His eyes gazed vaguely into space, as though his vision were directed through his paws at various hidden discoveries, instead of out of his head at curiosities visible to the rest of us.

He reminded me of Goatlips, one of my goats. He would lie beside me in the woods as I sat soaking up the beauty of a vale of ferns in brilliant autumn golds. Contentedly chewing his cud, Goatlips processed messages received by his sensitive hearing, his eyes looking outward at levels of forest life well beyond my own – more limited – perception.

Then suddenly he'd swallow. His gaze would change.

Instead of outward, he'd stare inward, as he concentrated on organizing his next cud out of the hastily swallowed foods stored in his rumen. Soon, the bulge of a new cud would rise up his throat into his mouth, the steady rhythm of chewing begin again, and Goatlips's gaze would once more be directed outward.

I've also noticed that inward gaze with pregnant goats, when a kid stirs inside a doe. Her attention is immediately directed into her womb, while her outer watchfulness dissolves into blankness.

I'm told my own expression is similar when I'm seeing a painting idea with my inner eyes – an interpretation I find preferable to less-flattering alternatives.

Ringo, scrabbling with eyes in his paws along the log, had that same intent-but-vague look that belied his submarine concentration. He became so engrossed in his findings that he failed to notice Mack wickedly backing the canoe away, despite my protests.

Soon, the vacuity in Ringo's eyes changed to horror as he realized he was alone. His ears scanned the lake, zeroing in on the canoe as he heard me remonstrate again on his behalf. Whimpering and squinting at us anxiously, he hurried along the log, pushing hastily through clumps of bushy growth that had so fascinated him earlier. The end of his log lay gently nudging another, which angled slightly out of the water. He scrambled onto this one, which pointed towards us, and trotted down to where it submerged.

Though by this time we were paddling towards him, Ringo cautiously felt his way down the slippery, sloping log under the lapping waters until he suddenly found himself afloat. With ears folded, eyes wide with alarm, and his head flat on the water like a beaver, he swam earnestly towards us, all four feet pumping below.

At the bow, I leaned over with welcoming cries and swung one sodden, clinging raccoon out of the water and set him down behind me. Bursting with relief, he shook himself vigorously, almost disappearing in a blinding spray that left us all equally wet.

In a canoe, we had no chance of escaping our dues.

Then he galloped down to the stern and slithered up Mack's back, splaying his wet, cold fur against Mack's warmth, and affectionately chewing his ears. Mack writhed, and I chuckled heartlessly.

"Serves you right!" I chortled. Which was a big mistake.

Hearing my voice, Ringo stopped abruptly, peering at me with his mischievous, beady eyes. Then he tumbled down Mack's front – thereby wetting any areas that might have escaped – loped back up the canoe, and threw himself rapturously on *my* cringing back.

The effect on such a warm day was like being hit with a shovelful of snow.

I howled and shuddered. Then reached back and pulled Ringo over my head like a sweater. Clinging to my hands with his cold paws, Ringo sprawled on his back in my saturated lap, laughing shamelessly with open mouth, while Mack snickered behind me.

Though he became the wettest of us all, Ringo dried the quickest, and when we finally arrived home, Mack and I were the ones who looked as if we'd been swimming. Smug Ringo rode on our shoulders, warm and dry, leading us to reconsider the existence of justice after all.

We canoed often with Ringo during those summer days, and his confidence rose rapidly as the lake world became familiar. The floating logs, with their living gardens, never lost their fascination. Often he'd prowl the shoreline too, feeling curiously through the rich silt and probing under protruding roots of overhanging trees. Frogs, one of the natural foods of raccoons, sprang unheeded past his absorbed gaze and disappeared safely beneath the water.

Mack and I shook our heads. As parents, we had a lot of teaching ahead of us.

One evening we drove to a coastal cove where a wide, deep brook tumbled out of a fold in the hills and glided musically into the ocean. Driftwood, seaweeds, dead jellyfish, crisp crab carapaces, and seabird bones littered the shore – all equally intriguing to Ringo.

Though perhaps the dead jellyfish, with its singular reek, held greatest appeal.

Strange rock formations erupted out of the pebbled beach, with bright leaves of salt-hardy plants peeping from upper crevices, while barnacles clung below. Great twists of silvered trees arched across the ground, like visible ghosts from long-vanished forests. Ringo busied himself constantly, climbing and feeling everything with his searching fingers, his nose and ears ceaselessly questioning, his gaze as vacant as an empty box. His energized curiosity seemed boundless.

Until we finally headed home. Then, instead of scrambling around in my lap playing with toys, Ringo lay in the curve of my arm, sound asleep.

CHAPTER 19

BUTTING IN

One morning, when coolness in the air held that chilling hint of autumn's approach, I rooted energetically through my sculpture supplies: chunks of stone and planks of aged wood all stored in the old goatshed. As I paused for a few moments' deliberation, caught between two carving ideas of equal appeal, and wondering which one to start, my eyes fell on a worn salt lick almost hidden by hay in a corner.

Suddenly, goats were looking at me.

Goats lolling back in fragrant, hay-filled stalls, their eyes half-closed as they chewed blissfully. Goats with vivid personalities, each one different from the next. Goats that left a legacy of bizarre experiences that are fixed – or is it seared? – in my memory.

And, no doubt, in the memories of others.

Goats are a potent blend of the lovable and the exasperating. I could be teary-eyed with affection for them one moment and thirsting for their blood the next. No other creatures I've known could reduce me to such accelerated Jekyll-and-Hyde hysteria.

Except art curators.

One afternoon, years ago, I sat quietly in the autumn woods admiring a tree. Then I lifted my sketchbook, dug in my jacket pocket for a stub of charcoal, and began drawing.

Or tried to draw. But no marks emerged on the paper.

Then I realized I was holding a dried goat dropping – and laughed.

Goatlips, one of my closest buddies, lay cuddled companionably against me, chewing his cud. I stroked his warm fur, still chuckling. Then I rubbed his head between his massive horns, sending him into a blissful trance that even halted his ruminating – temporarily. At that moment, it was difficult to believe how furious I'd been with him earlier that day.

Unbeknownst to me, he'd let himself out of the pasture *yet again* – like an irrepressible Houdini. Ignoring the acres of meadow grasses and laden wild-apple trees that surrounded him, he'd chosen instead to vault into the vegetable garden and devour the only fresh greens still remaining for my supper.

Every leaf of Swiss chard.

As in the continual round of moves and countermoves of an endless game of chess, Goatlips and I pitted our wits against one another.

He'd crack the code of my latest latch on the pasture gate, and gorge smugly in the flower garden, until I'd spot him and explode. When I'd regained some measure of composure, I'd drag him back to the pasture and fabricate an entirely new method of latching the gate, by using a crossbar.

He'd destroy my brief illusion of victory by breaking through a weak area in the fencing instead. Then he'd chew putty off the mullioned windows of the house while I was in town. When I'd return, he'd welcome me as I climbed out of the car, tear the

oil-change sticker off the door – again – and eat it. I'd retaliate by
mending the fence and pushing him back into the pasture – only
to be joined by him at the house door.

He'd gone *under* the fence.

Standard gate hinges, too, made of thick, tempered steel,
worked well for two-thousand-pound horses – but failed to restrain
a hundred and fifty pounds of persistent goat. As part of his daily
entertainment, Goatlips would butt the gate over and over until
both hinges burst asunder and most of the screws popped out.
Even when I used *several* hinges, and attached them with four-inch
nails, this merely slowed him down.

I resorted, finally, to carving large patches out of an old car
tire, cutting myself repeatedly in the process and cursing steadily.
Then I hammered the patches in place as hinges, using half a pound
of nails as well as a handful of two-inch screws. The flexibility
and thickness of the new hinges lent them a shock-absorbency and
strength that rendered them more durable than steel.

At last – I had the final word.

But only on hinges.

When Goatlips was about a year old, a second goat joined the
family as company for him when I wasn't available. "Noa" arrived
as an exquisite three-week-old French Alpine kid. He was one of a
demanding set of triplets, so perhaps his mother felt a little relief
along with her natural regret at losing him.

Since he was still nursing, I fed Noa bottles of warm milk,
and he tugged greedily at the teat, draining the entire contents in
moments. As I watched him jerking and gnawing on his substitute mother, or butting it with rapacious joy, I'd discover that,
quite unwittingly, I'd folded my free arm protectively across my
own bosom.

Nanny goats must develop either benumbed udders or an abnormally high tolerance for pain.

When Noa grew bigger, he demanded more than one bottleful at a time, and I'd warm up extra milk. Often, though, his eyes were bigger than his multiple stomachs. He'd leap and prance and wiggle his tail in great excitement as I approached with the second bottle's worth, and hurl himself onto the battered teat, sucking instantly. Then, after two or three swallows, he'd stop short with wide, vacant eyes as though realizing suddenly that he had already been fed.

Abruptly dropping the teat, he'd shake his head firmly and stalk off, for all the world like a dieter who cannot be tempted by a favourite dessert.

Where Goatlips excelled in demolishing hinges and unhooking my various makeshift latches, Noa shone in manipulating door-knobs. From his stall just inside the goatshed door, he'd take the doorknob in his mouth, turn it, push the door open, and peer outside, all in one smooth motion. Sometimes, if the open door was still within reach, he'd grasp the doorknob and close the door again.

Then I took in two young ducks, Ernest and Edward. Who, when they matured, were renamed Ernest and Emily. They were lovely, white dark-eyed ducks – but with one crucial failing.

They teased goats.

As Goatlips and Noa grazed, the ducks would stand by their faces, gabbling and jabbing at them, and biting their ears – sometimes actually notching them. When the goats ran out of patience, they'd simply tuck in their heads, thrust their horns under their tormenters, and toss the ducks easily over their backs. Then resume eating.

Time and again, I looked out the window to see two flightless ducks soaring through the air. If only I could tether *them* instead of the goats, I'd muse, darkly.

Finally, I came to the conclusion that the ducks were getting not just what they deserved, but what they wanted. Like children returning over and over to a favourite midway ride – one with just the right illusion of danger to be thrilling – so Ernest and Emily hounded the goats. Those ducks *loved* being thrown like footballs.

For their safety, and my own peace of mind, I gave them away to a good home. But a boring one, probably.

The people had no goats.

Eventually both Noa and Goatlips, being males, developed enormous horns, unlike the smaller ones characteristic of does.

Goatlips's horns, nearly two feet long, curved directly back and slightly outwards. They were several inches thick at the base and warm with life. The tips were only half an inch wide.

Noa's horns were more flamboyant. Easily two and a half feet long, they began curving backwards from his head, then veered straight out on either side with the tips finally turned forward. Nearly three feet of space separated the ends from each other. If he suddenly turned his head away while I was standing beside his neck, one horn would hook into my body and hoist me off my feet. Walking with him in the woods was like being with someone who had a stepladder strapped across his back. To pass between two trees, Noa had to turn his head sideways.

Fortunately, both goats, though they looked formidable, were gentle creatures. Extremely friendly and curious.

Though not everyone had that impression of them.

Once, the three of us were strolling companionably along one of the back roads on a beautiful winter's day. Six inches of sparkling fluff lay untouched as yet by the plough, while around us, snow-laden trees glittered in silent beauty. Only the swish of our footsteps disturbed the silence. Or defined it. As we rounded a curve in the road, two cross-country skiers hove into sight before us.

Noa and Goatlips immediately perked up at this unusual apparition and broke into an eager trot. I was near enough to catch the sudden switch from pleasure to horror on the faces of the approaching skiers. Unable to pick up their heels and run, they froze helplessly in their tracks as two large goats, bearing enormous horns, halted before them, and began sniffing their clothing.

Intrigued, Goatlips started nibbling on their skis and poles. Noa sampled their expensive jackets and gloves. A disagreement between them as to which goat was entitled to the tantalizing tassel dangling from one of the hats led to both goats suddenly rearing up and dancing toward each other on their hind legs. Then they rammed horns in a resounding crash, only inches away from the skiers.

This was the goats' usual way of settling disputes, and never involved anyone else. But the horrified skiers had no way of knowing that. By the third collision, they were clutching each other for protection, while the goats whirled around them, charging and rebounding, and bawling irritably.

I arrived on the scene finally, choking back laughter and assuring them that both goats were as gentle as kittens. Unfortunately, Noa and Goatlips had locked horns by then and were squealing and wrestling vigorously, forcing me to leap aside frequently in order to avoid being accidentally gored.

Understandably, my words of comfort lacked credibility.

Directly their path lay clear, both skiers fled, poling their way to freedom with flailing arms and long, desperate strides.

I suspect their impression of the goats matched that of a stranger who drove into the yard one day. He was halfway between his car and the porch when he spotted both goats thundering towards him, bleating shrilly. No doubt his fear magnified their already impressive horns in his eyes. Cut off from his vehicle and not realizing he was being welcomed, he bolted towards the house – only to discover that the porch door was locked.

A precaution to keep the goats out.

He instantly sprang onto the windowsill, clawed his way up the wall, and pulled himself onto the roof, an astonishing feat he couldn't have achieved under normal conditions. He was *not* a young man. Wide-eyed and breathless, there he doggedly remained, to the great disappointment of the goats circling below. They both enjoyed visitors and no doubt felt that there were great possibilities in one with such similar agility and originality – despite his lack of horns.

Unfortunately for that same person, he was obliged to make a return call. Though no goats appeared the second time, he adamantly refused to leave his car. There he remained, honking repeatedly until someone went out to him.

When he asked about the goats' whereabouts, he was told casually that they'd both gone for a drive to the beach, an answer that struck him speechless.

He left, a beaten man.

Both goats loved being hugged and rubbed – indeed, Noa would sink into a trance of ecstasy while I brushed him. Only when I was halfway back to the house would he become aware that I'd finished, and I'd hear his regretful call begging me to return.

But Goatlips and Noa thoroughly disliked having their horns held – even by me. Their horns were their primary instruments of defence.

A friend who hadn't seen the goats for years dropped by one day. He was impressed by their horns, but sceptical about my stories of the physical strength of animals less than half his own height. To prove my words, I suggested that he try to hold back Goatlips while I ran out of sight. The friend, a tall, burly fellow, agreed – only slightly contemptuously. He seized Goatlips by his collar and one horn, and I dashed away, around the corner of the goatshed, calling.

There was a sudden "HEY!" from the visitor.

Then Goatlips appeared at a gallop.

Alone.

My visitor followed, ruefully rubbing his hands.

"Wow," was his only comment. He'd forgotten to allow for the strength of love and loyalty.

Noa and Goatlips were notorious for devising escapes from the monotony of the pasture and seeking entertainment elsewhere. One afternoon, unaware that they were loose, I received a terse phone call from a neighbour to "*Come git yer goats!*" Mystified, I bolted out of the house and up the road.

In the farmyard stood a half-ton truck with the tailgate down. Inside the box, piled against the front, lay a huge mound of fresh turnips hauled from the vegetable garden in the lower field. Crouched on top of the turnips – and too frightened to move – was a visiting relative of the farmer, a small woman, whose bulging eyes of horror rivalled the turnips for size.

Directly in front of her, Noa and Goatlips stumbled awkwardly among the turnips, tearing out succulent mouthfuls with unbridled greed. Inevitably, in true goat fashion, they discovered simultaneously that only one turnip was really worth eating. Immediately tempers flared. Within seconds, turnips were rebounding like ping-pong balls off the plank walls of the truck box, the woman was screaming, and both goats were squealing furiously and crashing horns.

At this point, I arrived utterly breathless, having helplessly watched the situation unfolding as I ran. I sprang among the rolling turnips, bellowing and slapping rumps, and chased the culprits out.

Unwilling to confront the grim faces of my neighbours, and their nearly hysterical relative, who was still squatting among the turnips, I flung cheery apologies over my shoulder. Then I hauled two protesting goats back down the road.

Several times a week, the goats and I hiked together through surrounding meadows and woodlands, both Noa and Goatlips highly alert, and often responding with cocked ears to sounds or scents I failed to perceive.

These walks were great opportunities for them to "dine out" as well. They continually snatched mouthfuls of various greens, stored them in their rumens, then enjoyed chewing their cuds for hours after we'd returned home.

An enviable version of fast-food take-outs.

The only wild green that ever disagreed with them was wild rhododendron, locally called "lambkill" because it can be fatal for sheep. After one such meal, Noa and Goatlips threw up for three days, tossing their heads with every upheaval and spraying vomit everywhere. It left an unbelievable stench that lingered for weeks in the goatshed.

And for years in my memory.

Yet despite that experience, each time we passed lambkill on our walks, I had to force the goats away from it. They couldn't resist it. In some strange way, their instincts seemed to let them down with lambkill, though they always knew which wild mushrooms to eat and which to reject.

Both goats adored eating berries, so that it was difficult to leave them at home when strawberries, raspberries, chokecherries, or blueberries were ripe.

But including them was even harder.

I had to repress any excited murmurs at particularly succulent clusters, or they'd catch my enthusiasm and "horn in." As it was, we were all as fiercely competitive as pigs at a full trough.

Most importantly, I had to keep my wits about me.

Just reaching too far would leave my bucket vulnerable. As my fingers closed around the desired berries, Goatlips would suddenly plunge his head into the bucket and begin wolfing down the contents. I'd howl and grab his collar, but he'd brace himself so rigidly that I'd need all my strength to haul his head up – a procedure that would choke anyone but a goat.

Just as his head – still chewing – would finally rise, Noa would push into the bucket. Goatlips, outraged, would break free from me and both goats would burst out fighting, bucket and berries flying like birds.

They were incorrigible.

And insatiable. Only once do I recall Goatlips being so gorged on berries that, when I offered him one last handful on the way home, he actually refused.

It was a gesture that I felt deserved national recognition.

One afternoon, when we were all picking raspberries, I stumbled into a hidden wasps' nest. I let out a screech that nearly paralysed my mother, who was picking twenty feet away, and instantly electrified the goats. In an explosive scramble, goats, bucket, berries, and I all lit out in different directions, pursued by angry wasps.

My mother, totally imperturbable, deplored the wasted berries.

I deplored her lack of sympathy as I bought raspberry jam later that day at a local bazaar.

Goats aren't the only creatures I've included on berry-picking expeditions. A friend stopped in one day, bringing an offering of thick cream, and we set out to pick wild strawberries, taking with us "Rubble," my adolescent duckling.

That year, berries were particularly large and plentiful. We each chose promising patches about ten feet apart, and crouched over them with the concentration of dedicated chess players.

But Rubble was the queen, and could move in any direction.

She adored strawberries, and she sought them in my container as it began to fill. But whereas I, like another queen, had been well schooled by the goats in protecting my berries, my companion was only a pawn. He was accustomed to picking with humans – a pastime that develops no defensive skills whatsoever.

And Rubble, I swear, soon realized this.

Despite being inseparable from me, she deserted me – an unheard-of event – and attached herself to him. To his despair. Again and again, I could hear his muttered imprecations as he struggled not only to keep her from thrusting her busy bill into his container, but to pick strawberries faster than she could. Unlike mere humans, Rubbie could see-and-snatch simultaneously, her advantage clearly being that she and her own internal container were closer to the berries to begin with.

When we finally returned to the house, I could actually see my friend's face fall as Rubbie, despite her bulging crop, trotted briskly indoors in front of us.

But he needn't have worried. At the table, Rubble soon fell into a sound sleep in my lap, with berry stains still on her beak.

Across from me, my guest stared ruefully at his berries, now enhanced with brown sugar and a generous cascade of cream. I sensed, somehow, that the same amount of picking time usually netted him a bigger bowlful.

I like to think that images of duck *aux fraises* were *not* hovering in his mind.

Besides berries, Noa and Goatlips also adored apples. Wild trees grew everywhere, each one producing fruit with a different flavour.

I'd gather an armful, watched intently by both goats from inside the pasture. Each one was anxious to be first in the receiving line, and they'd jostle and hook at each other impatiently, their eyes no doubt picking more apples than my hands. Mindful of Noa's propensity, as the larger goat, to get the lion's share, I'd pitch the apples, one at a time, over the fence into every part of the pasture.

Apples bounded here, bounded there, like gigantic ping-pong balls, and I laughed myself into helplessness watching the goats. They darted everywhere, chasing every apple in motion, and almost running into each other in their desire to catch or corner even the smallest. Each goat, of course, wanted them *all*. They'd snatch up one apple, crush it hastily while running for the next, and swallow great chunks to be chewed later.

Only a goat could eat like a pig and not end up as sick as a dog.

Their feeding frenzy reminded me of voracious kids going from door-to-door at Hallowe'en, chewing steadily and stickily.

On our walks, the goats sampled apples from every tree – much as my ducks of yore sampled every puddle – each one tasting different, no doubt. And, like the ducks, the goats had their favourites. One tree bore flawless apples of such a size that it was known locally as the "sixteen-ounce tree"; most of the apples actually weighed a pound each. When Mack and I were collecting some recently for pies, he, too, was awed. "We only need six of these to make a dozen," he gloated.

Thus, whenever the goats and I turned in the direction of this special tree, they'd both begin to trot. Then *run* – even if their destination were a hundred yards away. By the time I caught up, they'd still be chewing and fighting over the windfalls.

After I had watched deer daintily eating apples, goats – at least mine – resembled deprived barbarians on a binge.

My walks with the goats sometimes took us along quiet dirt roads, where a passing car was a rarity – something that, alas, is no longer the case in this frenzied world. And one day, on a straight stretch of plain road, we all spotted a strange sight: a large, dark object smack in the middle.

As we drew near, both Noa and Goatlips began to step very hesitantly, poking their heads well forward, then jerking them back again and pushing them forward once more, over and over – mannerisms of extreme wariness. Their noses told them no more than their eyes, since we were upwind.

What on earth *was* this?

Not a rock. Not anything recognizable. Just a solid mysterious lump, like an asteroid fallen from the sky.

Both goats had by now separated, one to each side, spooked by this apparition, their ears like flags, their tails straight up and stiff. I ventured close to the thing – then burst out laughing.

It was the biggest, most compact cow dropping I'd ever seen.

Both goats immediately expressed their relief in their usual way. They peed. And the sound affected me as it always did when we were out together.

With a sigh of resignation, I joined them.

Unlike dogs, the presence of goats, with their deerlike characteristics, never alarmed any wildlife we encountered. Even when, for the duration of hunting season, I insisted that they each wear a plastic vest of strident hunter orange, for protection.

My species, however, was invariably suspect. After all, *we* were the ones who came to the woods with guns and traps instead of humble wonder.

Down at the lake, wild beavers would float nearer, intrigued. The goats on the shore, with equal curiosity, would lean closer with lifted ears. Though I'd remain motionless, as soon as the beavers caught sight of me, *whack!* They'd suddenly disappear in bubbly swirls.

The goats would be quite taken aback. They'd watch the watery ripples for several moments with puzzled eyes before continuing our hike.

No doubt their perplexity was augmented by their innate dislike of wetting their feet.

On our walks, I soon discovered that no puddle lying in their path was too small to avoid. If a swampy area confronted us, both goats would either step carefully from tussock to tussock, or range aside seeking a drier detour.

My stubborn effort one day to pull Noa through a wide, shallow brook was justly disastrous. As soon as his feet were wet, he sprang for the other side, knocking me down into the water with a vindictive splash.

On only one other occasion did I insist that Noa step into water. Arriving at the goatshed early that morning to do my usual chores, I discovered that Noa wouldn't, or couldn't, get up on his feet.

Horrified, I examined him closely.

Except for his insistence upon lying down, he looked his usual bright-eyed self. I finally pulled him up and found that he was very reluctant to put any weight on his feet. They seemed exceedingly tender. For the next twenty minutes, I tugged and coaxed Noa to the roadside and up into the truck, a distance he should have been able to walk in ten seconds.

A visit to the vet determined that Noa was suffering from laminitis, an inflammation of his hooves from too much rich ration. This was a puzzler, since the quantities I'd been distributing to each goat were correct.

By hiding and peeking in later days, I discovered that every morning, as soon as my back was turned, Noa, being larger, would instantly appropriate the rest of Goatlips's ration before finishing his own.

Noa's greed had caught up with him.

After he'd received an anti-inflammatory injection, I brought Noa back home with instructions to soak his feet in cool water. Since the very idea of forcing a goat to stand with each leg in a bucket of water was utterly unfeasible, I had to devise an alternative solution. To my lasting relief, I live on a dead-end dirt road seldom used by strangers, otherwise what transpired would have drawn crowds.

In the middle of a huge puddle spanning the road, on a rainy day, I sat in a wooden chair, my legs crossed nonchalantly. On my feet were tall rubber boots, the elevated one dripping muddy water. On my chilled hands I wore mittens. Looped twice around my neck was a scarf. Because of the steady drizzle, I held an opened umbrella in one hand. In my lap lay a book, and, in my other hand, I held a mug of steaming tea.

Beside me, with all four inflamed feet cooling in the puddle, stood a dejected goat, who had been too sore to protest about getting them wet. A rope from his collar was lashed tightly to the chair. Tied onto his back with string lay green plastic garbage bags to protect him from the rain. Both our heads were hidden under the umbrella. But two enormous horns protruded on either side.

I cling to the hope that most reputations for eccentricity are derived from such logical solutions to unusual problems.

It was this fastidious attitude towards being wet that revealed to others Goatlips's bond with me. One summer afternoon, I had driven with Goatlips and two human friends to the beach. We'd packed a succulent supper for later, and had taken a canoe for exploring the salt-water inlet.

We all strolled the sands with pleasure, examining interesting pieces of driftwood and shells, though Goatlips showed a little disappointment in the lack of edible curiosities.

Sun-hardened seaweed and rubbery stalks of kelp weren't his favourite fare.

Then I and one of the other picnickers launched the canoe and paddled out onto the placid beauty of the inlet, sending bright ripples through the mirrored reflections of rocks and trees. A great blue heron took wing from a nearby island. Over our heads glided sunlit gulls. I assumed that Goatlips would be content on shore, helping the other person build a fire and set up supper.

But not so.

As soon as we pulled away from the shore, he began bleating anxiously. I called out words of reassurance from the canoe, but he responded with cries that grew louder and louder. Soon he was tearing up and down the beach seeking a dry pathway to us, his eyes fixed on our diminishing forms.

Then, unbelievably, the goat who loathed wetting his feet suddenly leaped into the ocean and began swimming after the canoe, crying shrilly over and over, his imploring eyes never leaving us. We immediately spun around, paddled swiftly back to shore, and climbed out of the canoe, amazed and contrite. Goatlips, still crying, turned around at the same time as we did and headed for land. He hauled himself out of the detested water, puffing, and gave himself a vigorous shake. Then I rubbed him down with a beach towel and hugged him remorsefully.

He never left my side for the rest of the evening.

The fastidious nature of Noa and Goatlips emerged in other unusual ways. Despite their passion for apples, if I took a bite out of one and offered it to them, they'd reach out eagerly for it, suddenly sniff it with grave suspicion, and utterly reject it.

However, if, during one of our roadside walks, we discovered an alluring mound of smelly cigarette butts dumped from an automobile ashtray, they'd devour every one. They'd even quarrel with clashing horns over their revolting treasure.

I recall trying to grow mushrooms in the manure pile one year. I scattered a package of spawn, but nothing grew, and I abandoned the idea, thinking that perhaps horse manure was needed instead of goat.

But the *following* summer, gorgeous mushrooms rose like fat, white umbrellas all over the manure pile. Each day, I gathered a bowlful – watched with distaste by the more finicky goats, who wouldn't dream of rummaging in manure.

Until they realized I was gathering gourmet food.

One morning, as I was leaving the pasture with my booty – gloating – Goatlips caught up with me at the gate and sniffed the mushrooms curiously. Then he snatched a bite before I could stop him.

The jig was up.

Thereafter, I had to rise earlier every morning in order to beat the goats to the newest arrivals.

And often, I didn't make it.

Both goats loved travelling in vehicles, but Goatlips, possessing horns less likely to accidentally maim his admirers, was the one who usually came with me on house visits. He'd lie on the car seat, chewing his cud and curiously watching the traffic untangling around him, as we inched our way down the town streets. On such family outings, all we lacked was a triangular sign on the back window reading, "Goat on Board."

In houses, Goatlips would recline with great dignity on a rug, watching his thralls scuttle to and fro to ply him with offerings from the kitchen. Cookies, candies, squares, homemade bread, pretzels, chips – all was fish that came to his gourmet's net. High on his list was a touch of sherry or wine, after which he'd lick his lips greedily, his eyes bright with pleasure. Alcohol always sent his tongue darting in and out like a frenetic snake's with its other end plugged into a strobe current. Though an unusual performance, it was his highest accolade.

One favourite food was fresh cherries. He'd eat them one a time, chewing solemnly and pursing his lips to contain the juices. Then, with devastating hauteur, he'd casually spit out the pit.

Cleaned.

One afternoon, I noticed a mountie standing at the edge of a street in town. Cars passed continually in front of his disdainful eyes, an unbroken stream of passengers, each much like the last, coming and going before him. His feet stood casually apart. His hands were clasped loosely behind his back. He was unquestionably bored.

And a ripe candidate for the unexpected.

I was driving a tiny Volkswagen at the time, and the cramped back seat overflowed with Goatlips. He lay on the seat, steadily chewing his cud, his bearded face with its distinctive white markings filling the side window as he watched the passing world. As we drew opposite the bored mountie, there was a brief moment when he and Goatlips were face-to-face. Then we moved on.

I glanced back curiously.

The mountie still lounged with spread feet on the curb, his hands behind his back, his hauteur challenging the world to take him by surprise.

But his dulled eyes were electrified with disbelief.

Yet another stalwart mountie was destined to be embroiled in caprine confusion. One spring afternoon, I threaded my shaky Volkswagen carefully around heaving asphalt and bottomless craters thinly disguised as a road. I was returning home with two delightful doe goats to round out the family.

As cars passed me with almost predictable regularity, I suddenly heard a siren behind me. I glanced up into a rear-view mirror full of flashing lights, and pulled off the road. Since I certainly hadn't been speeding, I assumed I was being spot-checked for possible licence or permit violations. While the mountie climbed out of his car, I rummaged for my papers and rolled down the window.

My back-seat passengers, who had been dozing, immediately stood up, heads turning curiously. Just as the mountie leaned down casually to my window, a goat thrust out her head from behind mine and nuzzled his face affectionately.

The man sprang back as though he'd been bitten.

Saucer-eyed and speechless, he stared helplessly as a second muzzle wormed out beside the first.

Choking back my laughter, I assured the man that both does were merely friendly and inquisitive. Reassembling his dignity, he frowned professionally, peered closely at me, then into the interior of the car through the windows.

"Would you like us all to get out?" I asked politely.

"No, no!" he answered hastily, "That won't be necessary."

Unable to fathom his actions, I asked why I'd been stopped.

"Why were you driving so slowly?" he countered. A light dawned. He thought I'd been drinking!

"Because of the babies," I replied sharply.

"Babies?" He looked at the goats. "You mean them?"

"They're pregnant. The road's so bad I was afraid of bumping the babies inside them." I was gesturing with my vehicle papers as I spoke, and, at that moment, one of the goats reached over and snatched them hungrily out of my hand.

"HEY!" I bellowed, and clutched wildly at the culprit.

A frenzied scramble followed as I squirmed halfway into the rear of the car, accidently blasting the horn with my behind and scaring both goats into a plunging panic.

Finally I slid back down behind the wheel, flushed and breathless, but triumphantly gripping the sodden papers. I looked out the window.

The mountie had fled.

CHAPTER 20

BUTTING OUT

Those two little doe goats contributed to a few hectic years of milking schedules, and produced delightful, mischievous kids that would spring into my arms whenever I entered the pasture.

Unless, of course, they had escaped. Which they did regularly.

The first doe that I brought home in the Volkswagen had been Alice, a beautiful white Saanan. Like all goats I've known, she was an impeccable passenger. We arrived late in the evening, after such a long drive that only Alice climbed out with alacrity. I struggled out as if learning to walk. After stretching luxuriously, I led Alice over to the goatshed, opened the door, and switched on the light.

As we stepped inside, Goatlips, Noa, and a transient male named Pat all scrambled to their feet, blinking in the sudden brightness. I led Alice over to meet each of the others, before bedding her down in the stall reserved for her.

As we approached Pat, the homeliest of the three boys, Alice gave him a brief once-over – and instantly dismissed him. Next in line was the handsome Noa. Alice's ears twitched forward with sudden interest, and she nuzzled his face speculatively. Then I led her, lagging reluctantly, on to meet Goatlips. As soon as she caught sight of his distinguished face, her interest rose again, and she pondered him thoughtfully.

Then she dragged me back decisively to Noa.

Within seconds, she was flirting with him, lifting her tail coyly and trying to lick his face. Alice had given her heart.

But alas, her love was unrequited.

Noa, after according her the brief interest due to any new-comer, became indifferent to her romantic overtures, and began to eat instead. Though being a wether had cooled his potential ardour, being a male, he was always hungry.

I pulled a disappointed Alice away to her own stall. Like all women, she would have to learn that food comes first.

Goatlips, however, whether jealous of Noa's easy conquest, or stung by Alice's consummate rejection, soon developed a surly belligerence toward her. He frequently threatened her with his horns, though she was never within reach. The irrepressible Alice retaliated by tossing her head saucily, with her tongue darting in and out, as though she were blowing kisses. Goatlips would bleat angrily and bang his stall, but Alice would continue to mock him – and gaze adoringly at Noa at every opportunity.

A second doe, called Kamala, soon joined Alice. Kamala was a fastidious Nubian, who took particular enjoyment in her pendulous ears, a characteristic of that breed. Whenever she trotted or frisked (she was too ladylike to *romp*), she'd artfully toss her aristocratic, aquiline nose, obviously mindful of the swing of her long, beautiful ears. Like Noa and Goatlips, the dainty Kamala loved visiting indoors, and often accompanied me on short walks to a neighbour's house. When her kids were born, she was an affectionate mother.

And particularly attentive to their ears.

Poppy, a striking French Alpine, arrived next, a brash tomboy with a bossy streak. She immediately dominated the other two does. I had wondered vaguely why a grey goat appeared to have been named after a red flower. When I turned her out of the goatshed on the first morning after her arrival, I found out why.

Poppy romped briefly around the pasture, then stopped in front of the roadside fence. Carefully eyeing the three strands of barbed wire above the fencing, she backed away a few paces, waggled her tail, and sprang with fluid ease right over the top. In a twinkling, she had plunged into the dewy sweetness of the hayfield on the other side of the road.

Thereafter, until she was heavily pregnant and bore a large udder, Poppy's passion was to "pop" over any fence she encountered. Evidently she'd been named after a verb, not a flower.

How I wished that her previous owner, with less wittiness, had called her after a ground cover, like Creeping Jenny.

Molly, a black Nubian with frosty ears, was the fourth, and last, doe. She was a sad goat with a withdrawn personality and a timid nature. She lacked the initiative to leap over fences like Poppy and, unlike Kamala, seemed indifferent to her pendulous ears. Apparently, she'd had miscarriages, and I watched with concern as her pregnancy developed.

When her twins were born, she instantly rejected them, kicking the little creatures away whenever they tried to approach. I had begun to despair that Molly would ever accept them, when suddenly her chronic melancholy was transformed. She began sniffing her kids, licked them tentatively, then welcomed them into her heart.

As a mother, Molly blossomed.

Eventually, though, I ceased keeping does and kids. Their personalities were just as intriguing as Goatlips's and Noa's, but far more demanding overall.

Lactating goats require a lot of water, which in those days I had to haul by bucket from a spring in the woods, winter and summer. Milking schedules had to be maintained, breeding bucks located and borrowed at specific times, larger quantities of hay and rations bought and stored.

The smaller size of the does allowed them to push easily through gaps in or under the same fencing, which only tantalized the larger Noa and Goatlips, laden as they were with enormous horns.

Also, one small pasture meant that the does, being hornless, had to rotate with Noa and Goatlips, lest any tempers flare – particularly between Alice and Goatlips. Poppy, too, liked to be boss and would challenge anyone, whether they had horns or not.

As well, it was impossible to find homes for buck kids. Anyone wanting a goat wanted a doe.

With a mixture of regret and relief, therefore, all were sold except Noa and Goatlips, and we quietly resumed our simpler routines and woodland walks together.

One memorable evening, I took Goatlips to a Christmas party for the library staff at the local university. The gathering was in full swing when, suddenly, the arrival of Santa Claus was announced. One of the female staff members was dressed as Santa, in the characteristic red costume and long white beard. The usual sack of goodies was flung over her shoulder. She burst through the doorway and circled the party room with ringing "ho-ho-ho's," followed closely by Goatlips as one of Santa's reindeer, wearing a fancy red blanket hung with jingle bells and bows.

An uproar of astonishment and merriment nearly lifted the library from its foundations. All the staff members, laughing and joking, crowded around the pair in disbelief. Then followed half an hour of pure bliss for Goatlips, as everyone petted him and inundated him with an endless variety of party snacks and fancy sandwiches.

Never did a reindeer have it so good.

One Christmas custom which both goats enjoyed was that of bringing home the tree. If the snow were particularly deep, I'd strap on snowshoes. Then we'd set off, both goats trudging in my wake, to hunt for the perfect Christmas tree – one that was not too dense, not too tall.

And one which bore enough excess greenery so that some resemblance to a tree would still remain to be decorated after the goats had pruned it all the way back.

As we walked, my only Christmas present to them – colourful sleigh bells that attached to their collars – rang out musically with every step. I loved their cheery chiming, but the goats never seemed to reflect my enthusiasm.

I delighted in plodding through the deep fluff underfoot, but the goats, with their small hooves, plunged to their knees and hocks at every step. The second goat would always step carefully in the footsteps of the first goat, who would follow the trail of the snowshoes.

I quickly learned not to stop.

Whenever I did, Noa and Goatlips would climb gratefully onto the backs of the snowshoes to escape the deep snow.

Immovable as rocks, they'd bring up their cuds and chew stolidly, while I struggled helplessly to lift my feet.

I couldn't step forward with their added weight and, since they were behind me, I couldn't push them off.

Sometimes, if I were walking too slowly, the lead goat would step onto the back of a snowshoe just as I was striding, and I'd be thrown down into the snow. Before I could untangle myself, both goats would be stuck like barnacles on top of the snowshoes, ruminating blandly. I found it easier to consider a tree's potential by circling it hurriedly rather than by pausing with a speculative eye.

Once the tree had been chosen, I'd cut just the upper few feet, leaving the lower part to branch out and continue growing. Then I'd drag the treasure home, with Noa and Goatlips nibbling at it as steadily as if it were a travelling salad bar.

At the end of the Christmas season, I'd haul the dry tree out of the house, while it shed needles merrily, and tip it into the pasture. There both goats would munch, absorbed, on the bristly branches, and strip off the bark till only solid wood remained. The remains would be cut up and added to the kindling supply.

I'd marvel that such soft muzzles could even touch hardened needles that so easily pierced my thick mitts. Much less *eat* them.

One New Year's Eve in the early days, when friends had gathered at my tiny house to celebrate, I slipped out just before midnight – ostensibly to use the outhouse.

But at the stroke of twelve, I returned, leading in Goatlips dressed as the infant New Year. He wore hastily contrived diapers with gigantic safety pins, and a banner across his chest proclaiming the year. It was youthful garb, strangely at variance with his mature beard.

And his dignity.

After such public humiliation – especially from the diapers – he was ready for his share of party favours.

The *edible* ones.

Both goats really enjoyed being included in special gatherings of people, whether on firelit beaches, with portable music or on communal hikes, where they'd hook away anyone who dared to walk beside me.

They even loved joining ice-skating parties. If a long cold spell set in without a snowfall, neighbours would gather at the frozen lake, and I'd walk over to join them, my skates draped over one of the goats.

When we emerged from the woods, we'd see a laughing medley of skaters of all ages whirling over the glassy surface. Around the edge of the frozen lake, snow-laden trees would create a silent ring of beauty.

I'd make my way over to one of the logs wedged in the ice. There I'd sit down, fasten on my skates, tie my boots together, and drape them over the nearest goat. Then would follow the pure joy of gliding over the ice in the crisp winter air with the others, sometimes speeding so swiftly that wind tears would creep down my cheeks.

Unable to manage ice, both goats would remain on the snowy shore, chewing their cuds and watching my every move. However, if an inch or two of snow covered the treacherous surface, they'd follow me out onto the lake, and trot behind me while I skated.

If I stopped to talk, Goatlips would place his horns gently against my rear. Then he'd start to propel me across the ice, rapidly picking up speed till we were overtaking other skaters, Noa lumbering along behind us.

One little neophyte skater, three years of age, had the thrill of her short lifetime when Goatlips gave her a ride on his back. The goats were definitely "party animals."

Just as the goats were attracted to people, so many people were intrigued by the goats. I remember watching a snowplough push its way steadily up the road, clearing away the latest major snowfall. Suddenly the massive machine ground to a halt, a tiny door in the cab opened, and the driver emerged. He remained poised on the step, focussed a camera on the goatshed, took several photos, then continued ploughing the road.

Mystified, I turned to another window and found that the goats had climbed up the manure pile onto the roof of the goatshed. There they were frolicking happily, and pushing one another off the roof into the deep snow on the ground.

The following summer, I phoned a main office of the provincial telephone company. As I described my rural address, in order to assist a repairman in locating me, the woman on the other end of the line broke in suddenly: "Oh! Are you the person with the goats?"

I was floored. The office I'd phoned was forty miles away.

When Noa had come to me as a three-week-old kid, I was assured that his potential buckhood had been, as it were, emasculated. When he was tiny, it was pure delight to hold him nestled in my lap, an endearing armful. When he grew too big to hold, he'd kneel in my lap while his hindquarters still stood nonchalantly beside my chair. But as he grew even bigger, and sported monstrous horns, I was forced to discourage this delightful habit.

Unfortunately, his developing hormonal system caused him to erupt angrily whenever he was thwarted. And with such lethal horns, Noa could be dangerous.

Also, he tended to get sexually aroused, and would frequently spray innocent admirers with semen, an embarrassing display that was difficult to disregard – and was particularly fascinating to children.

Clearly, his juvenile emasculation procedure had failed. Noa, like Goatlips earlier, would need to be castrated.

Accordingly, I loaded him into the truck and drove to the veterinarian's office, where I strolled in casually, leading a reluctant

Noa. His natural timidity at entering a strange building, with peculiar scents and muffled cries of distant animals, was soon dissolved by the admiring attentions of other clients.

One dignified woman, a lady of established reputation in town, stepped up, furred and bejewelled. She cooed lavishly over Noa. Pulling off her white gloves and laying them on the counter, she patted him daintily as she spoke. Wafts of expensive perfume tantalized Noa as he adoringly nuzzled this furry vision.

To my sudden horror, I realized that Noa was getting aroused.

Before I could turn him, he loosed an enthusiastic spray that caught the unsuspecting woman all over her full-length furs. In the shocked moment that followed, I have no idea whether she or I blushed more hotly with embarrassment. But at least she could flee.

And did. Leaving her gloves behind.

Years of unforgettable experiences with goats never resulted in recognizable caprine imagery in my artwork.

But they left their mark in my tendency to butt my head stubbornly against difficult paintings – and exasperating curators – long after anyone else would have given up.

Perhaps, too, my inclination to escape the rigid confines of social norms was honed by my reluctant admiration of the goats' innate defiance of fences.

CHAPTER 21

Faux Paws

N, not a retreating wave sucking back rounded beach rocks with a clatter.

Nor the rhythmic throbs of a great horned owl at dusk.

Not even the soft hiss of wind through pine needles.

Nor the ecstatic peals of Handel's "Hallelujah" chorus.

Nothing surpasses the sound of rain on the roof after weeks of pitiless dry weather, when plant tongues trail to the ground, and the beaming blue sky has acquired a tinge of malice.

How we *longed* to hear that rain.

But each morning, the radio announcer jovially predicted another sunny day – to the delight of beach lovers, who aren't surrounded by snap-dry kindling posing as trees. And who don't have anxious eyes on gasping gardens.

Clouds rolled in – and we grew hopeful.

Clouds rolled out – and we despaired.

Evidently, the rumour about clouds being saturated sponges longing to squeeze out their excess moisture was unfounded. They seemed more akin to wads of lint from a gigantic dryer.

I stuck exploratory fingers deep into my new flower beds and was disturbed to feel dust. Earthworms were following their traditional ploy for survival and had macraméd themselves into intricate knots to conserve body moisture. Fortunately, Mack's veggie garden was holding up better under its protective mulch of seaweed.

Then one night I awoke and padded resignedly downstairs for that familiar reason that unites so many of us who would rather be sleeping. From the open bathroom window came the mournful keening of wind through spruce needles. Stronger gusts plucked demandingly at the branches. The trees began to rock on their toes.

When I lay down again, I heard it: a restless rippling of rain across the skylight above me. A rippling that grew stronger and louder while I listened with every ear I possessed. Like a distant band marching closer, the rhythmic drumming, entwined with tremolos of wind, swelled till it dominated my hearing.

I wouldn't wake Mack yet. It would be cruel if this were just another teasing sprinkle of two minutes' duration.

But soon I felt surprised that the rain itself didn't rouse him. Big drops like billiard balls were scattered by thrusting cues of wind and rolled across the skylight, jostling one another down the corner drainpipes into the empty rain barrels.

As exhilarating syncopations thudded overhead, I was reminded of a particularly heavy rainstorm that overtook me one muggy summer day when I was driving on a distant highway. Traffic slowed and snailed in both directions. Headlights peered shortsightedly through the gloom.

In startling contrast to the dreamlike languor that suddenly prevailed, windshield wipers jerked frenziedly, though still not fast enough to yield more than a split second's clear view. And spasmodic yellow flashers stacattoed the murk.

I switched off radio music muffled by the metallic clamour of rain pelleting on the roof. Then I eased the car over to the shoulder of the road, joining and joined by other cautious drivers. Bolder drivers passed, slashing the quivering surface into fleeting furrows that quickly refilled. Lunging waves clawed at the sides of the parked cars with every passage.

Suddenly, a door opened in the vehicle ahead of me, and a figure climbed nimbly out. He wore the briefest of bathing suits, and carried a bar of soap and a washcloth. With the disarming lightheartedness of someone capering in the privacy of his own shower, he sudsed and scoured himself from plastered hair to bare feet. Then turned his body accommodatingly for a final rinse of purest rainwater.

Though his long, pale limbs see-sawed and scissored before my streaming windshield like a galvanic ghost puppet, I found the raindancer far from ridiculous.

Within the stifling sauna of my vehicle, smothered in steaming clothes, I watched him enviously.

I awoke with a start, and realized that I'd dozed off after my ruminations. Raindrops still clattered on the skylight with all the enthusiasm of clog dancers getting well into their stride. And gusts of rain sprayed the windows in sudden rattling crescendos. But now a watery grey light had seeped into the room, creating an underwater glimmer. Rain had been falling for hours.

I wakened Mack to rejoice with me in this celebratory downpour. But our mutual joy was abruptly divided as Mack remembered the rain barrels and leaped out of bed. The bang of the outside door resounded as I was still descending the stairs. I peered out a window – then laughed heartily.

Like the bather in front of my car, Mack was vigorously bobbing up and down, his bare legs like spindles connecting his streaming jacket to his gumboots. He rapidly transferred buckets of precious water from overflowing barrels under downspouts into empty tubs waiting nearby.

When they were filled, he ran to the goatshed and returned with more containers and a watering can. Then he began soaking the flower beds beside the house wall, where the soil still remained fairly dry. Rain sluicing down the metal roof sloshed away in gutters to the barrels instead of falling on gardens below, so that these beds were frequently in need of water – especially the arching ferns on the north side.

As I plugged in the kettle and began to assemble breakfast, I glanced out the kitchen window at Mack barrel-racing without the usual assistance of a quarter horse. He galloped down to the veggie garden to thrust a hose into yet one more barrel. Then spun around very impressively on his hind legs and dashed back in record form to another overflowing barrel by the house, where he hastily activated the siphon. Finally, he appeared with the wheel-barrow and placed it under a steady drip from the woodshed roof. Next to that, under a weaker drip, he set a plastic juice jug that had never found its way back to the kitchen.

Since he was obviously determined to fill every container we possessed or die in the attempt, I gave serious thought to hiding my own gumboots – till I remembered, with relief, that they leaked.

It rained. And it rained. Thundering down in a steady roar, so that the great belly of the house purred with comforting reassurance. I could almost *hear* the reviving woodland swallowing and smacking its lips. In my mind's eye, earthworms untied themselves and stretched gratefully.

And although the deluge slowed finally, it didn't stop.

When breakfast was ready, not only was every vessel full, or refilling rapidly, but all the gardens were soaked and smiling.

As was Mack.

The late summer days now were noticeably shorter. Shorn hay-fields were half-grown again, and greener after the renewing rain. Starlings swept in tight gusts, whirling on common impulse, restless to become wind and be gone.

I carried my carving tools outside to the back deck and set up a chunk of pipestone that had kindled a challenging idea. Mack passed me, lugging an armload of two-by-sixes to begin a second woodshed, one small one being inadequate. Around his sweating neck clung a five-pound woolly scarf with a masked face and eyes glinting with good humour.

Ringo's male nature had begun to assert itself in territorial displays. Which is a polite way of stating that his urine again became prominent in our lives. Our first intimation came when Mack passed the den of the wild raccoons under the house.

Ringo, rolling along in Mack's wake, like a sailor on leave after months in the North Atlantic, stopped short. Sniffing intently, he followed his nose to the mouth of the den, into which he peered – cautiously.

Then he peed, cautiously, right on the doorstep – and in several other spots for added emphasis. There was to be no misunderstanding about just *whose* territory this was.

As though that experience opened the floodgates – so to speak – Ringo began marking his claims everywhere.

While Mack laboured on the woodshed, Ringo "helped" by peeing on the hammer just before Mack's fingers closed on it. Or by peeing all over the handsaw, just as it was set down. Mack wiped his hands on his workpants so often that Ringo evidently felt no need to pee directly on him.

A small mercy, for which Mack felt profoundly grateful.

Despite Mack's irritable snarls, Ringo also persisted in grabbing half-driven nails with his delicate hands just as the hammer was descending. Or he'd climb up Mack's back and out along his arm, reaching for the slimed handle of the saw as it was cutting. Spilling the nails in a glittering arc over the floorboards yielded more possibilities for creative urination – an opportunity that Ringo exploited to the full.

My mistake lay in laughing with the heartlessness of one whose work is progressing well. And whose clothes don't stink.

Yet.

But as I bent over my stone, chiselling out the form that haunted my imagination, Mack retaliated by draping Ringo across my shoulders to impede my project. Then he returned to his own with the buoyancy of one freed of a ball and chain.

Though I continued to carve, smiting vigorously with a hardwood mallet, or churning up dense dust as I burrowed into the stone with an electric rotary tool, Ringo adhered to my shirt like chewed gum. I peered between two black hands clutching my goggles from behind. I submitted reluctantly to having my head massaged and both ears nibbled, while clutching at my fleeing concentration. Fortunately, my respirator escaped Ringo's ingenious efforts to pry it off my head entirely, although at one point, curious fingers felt their way underneath it to the corner of my mouth. He also shamelessly explored under my shirt, tickling me into capers that were dangerous while wielding whirling cutters.

Finally, to my unbounded relief, he fell asleep across my shoulders, with trailing legs and tail. I worked on, wearing my mask, and Ringo, exhausted from supervising, slept the sleep of the just – wearing his own mask. Dust and fragments of rosy pipestone continually coated his fur, so that when he awoke, he looked like a raccoon carving coming to life.

I soon learned *not* to lay out my chisels on the deck floor after Ringo – regrettably – discovered them there, and launched the entire set on a sea of urine. And I unplugged the electrical carving device whenever I worked manually, lest Ringo pee on the foot pedal with its frayed connection and recharge us both.

Mack found himself in his own private hell when he began to attach the rafters of the woodshed. Ringo, with an enviable head for heights, trotted easily along them, dutifully dribbling urine which the breezes sprayed into Mack's upturned face.

Farmers for miles were probably wondering just whose bull was bellowing in outrage that day.

But it must have been clear to every raccoon downwind that Mack was Ringo's property.

When both Mack and I had coerced our individual projects to completion *despite* Ringo's assistance, we decided to build a greenhouse. Northern Nova Scotia has a short growing season, and early summer dawdles on its reluctant return to our latitude. By June, we're usually still salivating for fresh lettuce – organically grown, *not* the sprayed produce available in supermarkets, which is hosed down with sulphites and probably glows in the dark.

A friend told me once of a biologist he knew, who was raising insects for research. Having run out of garden lettuce, he substituted bought lettuce – and the insects all died.

One has to wonder about the food we eat.

So, with leafy visions to lead us onward, we assembled a complex collection of windows – some of wood, others of aluminum; several that opened, more that didn't; windows with mullions, and windows without. We also gathered together used lumber in varied widths, and wire mesh for the floor to foil burrowing chipmunks.

His Woolliness, of course, presided.

He climbed all over the structure as it grew, and all over us at any time. We worked with him lying across our shoulders, gripping easily with his hind feet while running his hands through our hair or gently chewing our ears. When we finally pulled him off over our heads like a scarf, he'd loll on his back in our arms laughing, and daring us to be annoyed.

He became obsessed with chewing the measuring tape, running off with it in his mouth after pulling it out of our pockets. He broke off the tab, so that the entire tape retreated out of reach into its case. Then he ruined the retracting mechanism, so that we worked with yards of twisted metal tape underfoot, snagging around boards and tripping us at crucial moments.

For precise measurement, nothing is more exasperating than using a tangle of metal tape, sticky with repeated urinations, which collapses instantly when held out – or is suddenly jerked away just before the pertinent numbers come into focus.

Replacing the tape proved futile as well as costly. The new tape soon became indistinguishable from the old.

As Mack and I struggled to complete the greenhouse, His Leakiness peed territorial messages all over hammers, saws, and even the electric saw, electrifying us emotionally if not physically. He chewed our pencils. He clawed his way up the backs of our legs while we were balancing on ladders. Or sat coyly one rung below, so we couldn't descend.

He knocked over every container of screws and nails so often that, if we were to tally up just how long we'd taken to build the

greenhouse, we'd have to halve the figure to eliminate all the hours spent retrieving hardware from the soft soil.

He also had a genius for sitting immovably just where he'd be most in the way, digging up worms and eating them. In the now-drizzly weather, his paws became very muddy, especially when he'd begin his food-hunting by retrieving drowned spiders and moths in the rain barrel before digging in the soil.

We soon became covered with muddy paw prints. Mud streaked our hair, smeared our ears, and coated the insides of our pockets. The handles of our tools became slimy with mud and urine in equal quantities.

We looked like apparitions from a primeval swamp.

And smelled worse.

Whenever we sat wearily down, Ringo would climb jubilantly into our laps, gently patting our already filthy faces. His busy fingers would search our pockets for the hundredth time, in case he'd overlooked a cookie, and he'd reinforce the hint by playfully chewing our fingers. He was still so young that affectionate contact was necessary for his well-being.

Or so we said, as we slipped him another cookie just to watch his ecstatic response.

Once we stopped, our frustration at our slow progress vanished and we played wholeheartedly with our furry trickster, aware of how quickly he was growing towards adulthood and a natural life with other raccoons – or so we hoped.

Often Ringo would fall asleep in our arms at this point, prolonging our break even further. Then we'd become more aware of our fatigue and hunger. Soon lunch would be suggested, and when we finally resumed work on the greenhouse, we did so with renewed vigour. Visions of fresh lettuce during the snowy months spurred us on in spite of Ringo's equally renewed vigour – His Liveliness being the only one lucky enough to have napped.

Before long, we were back in the throes, struggling not only to create a functional greenhouse out of a muddle of odds and ends – a feat in itself – but to meet this challenge while impeded at every turn by at least a dozen baby raccoons disguised as one. It was a relief when we progressed so far that we were able to shut Ringo out while we worked inside – a short-lived moment of triumph that he quickly countered by chewing the vinyl sweep off the bottom of the door and tearing one of the screens by climbing up it.

We definitely could have worked more efficiently without Ringo. But with him we had twice the fun.

One evening, we swung His Snoopiness to our shoulders and set out for a short walk before dark. We headed for a little swamp that should have provided interest for Ringo's curious nose and hands, but the water was so low that mostly mud remained. So we crossed the fields to a brook, with better results.

Ringo, scenting it, began to scramble restlessly long before Mack and I became aware of the rippling murmur of running water – although with Mack's hearing, I wasn't surprised.

As soon as I heard the brook, I remarked, "Good. There's lots of water for him." Mack made no comment.

Until we could *see* the brook. "Good!" He turned to me. "There's lots of water for him."

"Wonderful," I replied. With just the right touch of surprise.

Only the week before, I'd brought in a generous heap of clover, dandelion, and grape leaves for Edna before Mack and I set out for a walk. As I hastened downstairs again to where he was waiting by the door, I justified my delay: "I got Edna some nice fresh greens."

"I don't think they'll be ready." Mack replied, gazing out the window at a feeding sparrow.

"What?" I asked, perplexed.

"The beans."

"What beans?"

"The ones you want," he replied, testily.

I left it at that. If we tried to unravel that one, we'd have had no time left for our walk. I also consoled myself with the reflection that some day, if I resorted to talking to myself, I would at least be assured of a sensible response.

Ringo slithered down Mack's legs, loped over to the brook, and waded in without a pause. His busy fingers felt under the curved banks of moss and tree roots. He dislodged stones to discover their secrets. He chewed mysterious morsels that he popped too quickly into his mouth for us to identify. And he drank. Though his paws became wet, his thick fur seemed waterproof. Only when we had difficulty in distinguishing him under the dusky trees lining the brook did I give my special call to reel him in. He came obediently, but tugged by reluctance.

By tantalizing odours.

By intriguing sounds.

On our way back home, Ringo preferred to roll along at our heels, his nose working unceasingly, and his hands pausing to examine anything that seemed irresistibly fascinating. At the door of Ringo's shed, Mack shut him in, with the bribe of a Fig Newton to quell all protests. Ringo's nocturnal nature seemed to be waking, and his territorial nature was all we could manage at this point.

Not until nearly midnight did Mack, looking out a window at the stars, realize that he'd left the big door open into the aviary – which, in turn, opened into Ringo's shed. Horrified that Ringo might have long ago wandered off – to the delight of roving coyotes – he thundered upstairs and shook me awake to come outside and do my raccoon call.

I blinked up at him, uncomprehendingly. Then I struggled out of bed as Mack tore back downstairs in what sounded like two bounds. With greater caution, I felt my way down, step by step, my hair like charged hay, my gummy eyes still at half-mast, and feeling no remorse whatsoever at my appearance. Anyone who wakes me out of solid sleep to stand in the dark and yodel like a raccoon deserves to see such a sight.

Forever.

While Mack darted about with a flashlight, searching the bushes and treetops, I stood beside the open cage door, roused my vocal chords, and ululated shrilly, trying to project over the fields if necessary. And feeling grateful that our nearest neighbours weren't any nearer.

After only a minute, I heard shuffling behind me and alerted Mack. He swung the beam of light into the empty aviary just as a sleepy-eyed raccoon poked his head out of his shed, blinking.

I glared at Mack. "Didn't you check his sleeping box *first*?"

But Mack, like any other relieved father, was already cuddling Ringo, and offering His Sleepiness a cookie.

Her Grumpiness went back to bed.

As autumn advanced, so did Ringo's appetite – an already voracious one that I insisted he got from his dad. The marginal difference between them lay not in quantity but in quality. Mack at least closed his mouth when he chewed. Ringo, eating with rubbery facial contortions and a bobbing nose, seemed to be always struggling with loose fillings.

All sorts of strange goodies found their way into Ringo's food dish, including parts of our own meals. I watched His Greediness one morning in a see-saw of indecision. He grabbed a chunk of pancake first, dropped it in favour of a hard-boiled egg, dropped that for a square of whole-foods fudge, and abandoned *that* finally to begin his day with a well-balanced, single serving of Fig Newton.

Both Mack and Ringo shared that satisfaction that emanates from a dinner plate heaped like a burial mound. However, when Mack not only polishes that quantity off with ease, but returns for seconds and *still* has room for dessert – all in twice the speed I need to manage a third of the amount – then I predict that he'll die with a perfect set of teeth that have never been used.

Unless, of course, he simply swallows everything whole in order to chew it all later, like a goat.

Though an easy man to feed, he's a hard man to fill.

I remember his commiserating words as he watched a pregnant raccoon vacuuming food like a Hoover on high. Though her jaws never paused, she was still able to snarl at the other diners – a deplorable technique that I was grateful Mack hadn't acquired.

"She's so hungry, she must have *three* babies in there," he murmured.

I glanced at his mounded supper plate, supplemented with a sandwich and double dessert. All the evidence before me suggested that he had at least a dozen stashed somewhere himself.

As wild apples swelled on the trees beside the house, Ringo lolled on his haunches among the windfalls, chewing the softer ones ecstatically. If we were working outside, he'd carry an apple over beside us and settle down companionably to feast. On our rambles together, the three of us would roam from apple tree to apple tree, along the fencelines and through the woods, sampling all the different flavours created by apples red and apples yellow.

One of my favourite trees produced tart, white apples, with the skin matching the flesh. Scattered over the darkened ground at dusk, the white apples resembled a cosmic nebula.

Heightened by moonlight, they hung from their dark branches like stars.

CHAPTER 22

TRANSIENCE AND THRESHOLDS

W̵e lifted our heads above the whirlwind of our busyness and discovered that summer had long flitted over the southern hills.

Early each morning, a crisp tang in the air announced autumn's presence like a resonating gong. The last vibrations of chilliness would mellow into summery silence only by noon. But as the sun slid down the sky again, coolness rose quickly out of the ground. Rising shadows gripped our ankles, and then our legs, till at dusk we fled to the woodstove.

Whenever rain fell, it peppered the skylights with hail. And when the rain stopped, saturated leaves were clutched by the beaded glass until fingers of wind pried them loose to fly again.

Night frosts routed the protective warmth of the robin garden. Rows of green plumage faded, shrivelled, and moulted, leaving leafless shafts. The floating banners of squash leaves blackened to wet rags. They hung in dreary tatters from bright stems that had migrated far beyond the wings of the garden, creating a trail of plump progeny.

Ripening tomatoes lined our windowsills, and packages of sliced green peppers lined our freezer door. Pumpkins and winter squash lolled on shelves in the hospice – which now doubled as a cool storage room. Mack hung plastic sheeting over the grape leaves to preserve them as long as possible for Edna, who adored eating them.

Migrating birds, windriders on ancient aeolian steeds, swooped down from the trees in gusts, like blowing leaves. And like leaves, they often sprang up suddenly, perhaps to sweep onward, perhaps only to resettle lightly before the next flight.

The eyes of thrushes followed us as they flitted furtively through the woods. Robins, grey-backed like tree trunks, orange-breasted like autumn leaves, haunted the wild apple trees hidden among scattered spruce.

At dusk, our eyes clung to angles of ducks arrowing swiftly through the sky only to hover, fluttering, over the southern hills before fading from sight.

At night, we sat on the roof deck under a sky netted with stars, hearing only occasional calls of migrants passing overhead, stragglers in the stellar wake of greater flocks long gone.

Mornings, bereft now of birdsong, glided silently out of the east with such a prevailing sense of desertion that we welcomed the strident cries of blue jays arriving at the feeders – followed though they were by the harsh cries of sharp-shinned hawks in pursuit.

Transience permeated our lives, a departing flow of the familiar, like a known leaf falling into a brook before our eyes and being whirled away to an unknown end.

Inside, Bashō was completing a moult, and the garden lay strewn with beauty that paralleled the fallen leaves outside. Curved feathers, intricately patterned with autumn colours of brown, gold, and cream, lay everywhere, some upturned like smiles.

While his moult was at its height, Bashō, with new feather points piercing his skin, had felt too tender to be cuddled. And he'd seemed slightly nervous around Edna, perhaps feeling vulnerable in his prickly state. He'd also ceased crowing each morning, as if uneasy at delivering territorial challenges in such an assailable condition.

But finally, his plumage gained fullness again, and his stentorian calls once more rang out from the dusky domain of the garden at dawn.

With cooler nights now, and comfortable feathers that no longer prodded him with spikes, Bashō revelled in being cuddled. As I sat before the studio fire, he'd cozy down in one hand while I read and rubbed Edna's back with my other hand. Winds would swirl around the three outside walls of our sanctuary, and rains splatter the windows and skylight, as though we journeyed through darkness in a glowing ship. On quieter nights, the restless wanderings of hunting owls punctured the surrounding mystery like tolling buoys or the throaty calls of foghorns, warning of shoals.

Often, I'd set Bashō down, and he'd immediately patter over to Edna's dish of rolled oats and rabbit pellets, searching for quail-sized bites – or for the bonus of an unlucky earwig, a delicacy of which he was inordinately fond. A half-dozen earwigs brought in from the veggie garden could send Bashō into blissful repletion.

Edna would hop over slowly, with interrogating ears. But only when her whiskers tickled his back gently would Bashō ruffle with indignation and trot off. Occasionally, he'd swell up and crow at a volume out of all proportion to his tiny size, halting Edna in her tracks, her expressive ears now switching to startled. Or he'd take wing in the sudden lift characteristic of quails, as though their rocket boosters have suddenly kicked in. And Edna's ears, changing from startled, would register astonishment instead, as Bashō hurtled to the far end of the studio. Seemingly refreshed from his flight, he'd reset his feathers with a brisk shake and return for more cuddles.

I usually kept a glass of water beside me for Bashō. Whenever I offered it to him, he always swallowed two or three times, as though to rev up his throat muscles. Only after this preliminary ritual would he bite at the water in the abrupt drinking manner so typical of his species, taking several swallows before settling back in my hand with closed eyes of contentment.

One evening, he noticed my shirt buttons. They were dark and concave, but within, they held a curve of light like water. Bashō rehearsed a couple of swallows, dipped his bill in the light held in one of my buttons – then again, with greater determination – before sitting back in puzzled surprise, while I chuckled delightedly.

Birds always teach me new ways to view the familiar.

But for me, this autumn had added unrest in the form of media encounters to promote my book, *For the Birds*. We had come to the brink of a week in which several such hair-raising functions were scheduled, and the next morning would bring a film crew to the house.

Suddenly seeing our familiar cobwebs and accumulated dust through the eyes of strangers galvanized me, and after breakfast I began cleaning upstairs. The studio in particular, with its spewn ashes around the mouth of the woodstove and tumbleweeds of rabbit fur that could stuff several cushions, seemed in danger of being formally condemned. By early afternoon, I was vacuuming downstairs when I noticed an earwig in the bathroom – further proof of my domestic sloth.

I shut off the machine and carried the scrambling treasure over to Bashō. He'd been listless for a couple of days, so such a treat would be sure to please him.

But as I approached the garden, I noticed that he was standing huddled over, as though in a doze. He paid no attention to me, which was unusual, since he invariably anticipated my arrival on such occasions – which I prefer to consider a mysterious form of telepathy. Otherwise, I have to admit to being programmed to deliver.

But as I cheerily called Bashō's name, and tossed the earwig before him, he took not the slightest notice.

Then I knew something was terribly wrong.

I knelt and gathered him up gently in my hands, but he barely opened his eyes. Was this the same quail who had cozied down under my chin the night before, eagerly seizing selections of my supper off the tip of my tongue?

He felt cool too, especially his feet. I sat down, cradling him anxiously. I had to realize that Bashō, who had long outlived his siblings in the lab, was probably nearing his end.

Earlier in the year, he'd developed an odd twist to his left wing, and shown difficulty in operating the toes of his left foot – indications that he'd had a minor stroke. After resting, he often rose awkwardly, and would limp stiffly until he got limbered up. Then he'd limp still, but only slightly.

In my heart, I'd felt that our tiny elder was beginning to fail. Now I was convinced that he'd endured another stroke, a conclusion that was confirmed by the Animal Care Technician at the local university. His motor control was strongly affected, and he couldn't even manage a drink of water. Nor could he walk.

Housecleaning suddenly lost its importance.

For the rest of that day, and all through the night, Mack and I held Bashō by turns, providing warmth and contact to which he responded by snuggling cozily against us. His eyes remained closed in an aura of stillness – unless we shifted or spoke softly to him. Then he'd peer up trustfully at us, before sleeping again. When we tried to set him into a nest of towelling contrived beside the bed, he struggled insistently until he was picked up. Only then did he cuddle down contentedly.

He gave no indication of pain in any degree. He just seemed weak, partially disabled, and in need of being held. And held he was.

Bashō, our diminutive elder, was not going to be set aside as an inconvenience at such a crucial time in his life. Nor did we intend to have him put down by a vet in order to spare ourselves discomfort.

Somehow, running on three hours of sleep and a full tank of anxiety, we weathered six hours of filming the next day, either Mack or me holding Bashō cradled in our hands. He took no notice of the flurry of activities around him – of furniture being shifted, of the blaring lights. Instead, as though absorbing some of the energy around him, Bashō *began to rally*.

When Mack, on impulse, held up a glass of water to Bashō's beak, he – unbelievably – took *seventeen* short sips. Then, although his neck lolled awkwardly, Bashō conquered his motor control enough to eat several mealworms. Mack and I were ecstatic – and teary-eyed. Surfing buoyantly on hope and relief, I allowed Bashō to be filmed with me, snuggled in my hands during one brief sequence.

The interviewer, producer, and cameraman showed unexpected sensitivity and concern about Bashō's condition, having read about him in the book to the point that he seemed almost like a familiar friend. They hung over him at every victory, cheering him on softly, and they worried that their presence was intrusive at such a time – to Bashō, as well as to us.

I was touched by their kindness.

Throughout that night, the next day, and the following night, we continued to hold Bashō, snatching occasional hours of sleep by turns. We frequently offered him water, which he opened his eyes to accept, mysteriously aware of the proximity of the glass. He also struggled valiantly to eat mealworms, but missed often when he grabbed at them, as though his vision as well as his coordination had been affected.

And always, he responded to our presence, our touch, our warmth – even our heartbeats – as he'd lie on our chests, sleeping more soundly there than anywhere else. The sound of our voices passed unacknowledged, unless we spoke in gentle tones directly to him. Then this feathered stranger, so oddly inert and withdrawn, would open his eyes partway, and our familiar Bashō would twinkle up into our anxious faces.

But now a day dawned – which surely couldn't have been more badly timed – when we were committed to a full media day in Halifax. Though a trusted housesitter moved in to take care of the rest of the family, we knew we simply *had* to take Bashō with us. The housesitter held him until we'd collected our things together and lugged them out to the car. Then I leaned over Bashō, murmuring reassurance as I gently lifted him. He'd been lying quietly with closed eyes during all the confusion. But at the sound of my voice by his ear, and at the change of energies from other hands to mine, he lifted his head, unable to prevent it from weaving slightly, and stared up at me intently.

After so many years of eye contact, I understood the message: he wanted to stay with me.

Birds communicate much more by body language than vocalizations. And they read energies around them with ease. I was certain Bashō sensed our imminent departure. But when I tucked him in comfortably under my shirt, I also sensed his relief that there would be no parting.

I have always been amused at the ease with which the creatures I live with sense my intentions, and act accordingly. They seem to read my mind like an open book, whereas I find them fascinatingly unpredictable – a comparison I avoid dwelling on. They invariably know when I'm planning to leave the house. Even if I'm only going for a hike, it's often the general signal for pandemonium in my absence.

And if a long trip is involved, all hell can break loose.

One instance still glitters in the murk of my mental archives, like fool's gold in river mud. I had hugged the goats and exhorted them to be good while I was away, backpacking in Britain. I'd already double-checked the fences, although Goatlips and Noa hadn't broken out of the pasture for weeks – an unprecedented hiatus for me. Neighbours had agreed to care for them in my absence.

Apparently, I didn't even get as far as the train station – only ten miles away – before both goats invaded the hayfields across the road.

In more recent times, Mack and I have only to return from a two-hour hike to find even mild Edna contentedly digesting my cherished cape primrose, blossoms and all, though she'd never so much as *looked* at it in my presence.

But Bashō needn't have worried about this untimely trip. We would see it through together, all three of us.

During that long day, we were escorted in and out of radio and television studios, a public park, and two restaurants, with Bashō in a nest of towelling inside my shoulder bag. Knowing how important direct contact was, I kept one hand curled around or underneath him. And whenever I peeked down, out of the whirl-wind of tensions and traffic in which I was caught, I'd see Bashō dozing snugly in the curve of my fingers, warm, secure, and creat-ing an aura of stillness around him that seemed to be also an aura of protection, of inviolability.

His centred presence helped to centre me – as he had done for years – and his needs kept my priorities in proper order.

As I talked to interviewers, I tried simultaneously to send comfort and love to Bashō. As I ate hastily, I held my purse on my lap below the tabletop, and Bashō slept peacefully. He was unable to eat any longer, even when I decapitated a few mealworms with merciful speed, then squeezed their milky contents into the side of his beak. But he drank eagerly whenever I offered water.

No one seemed to notice me walking with my hand inside my purse. But whenever I was on the air, and Mack held my purse with *his* hand inside, he received glances from various technicians that ranged from curious to frankly speculative.

For me, the most unnerving session was the live television broadcast. Cautioned that I would be asked what prompted me to write the book, I was then rigged up with a hidden microphone and left in a small fake living room to create sweat for twenty minutes.

And to wonder just why, indeed, I wrote the book. In my agitated state, and my preoccupation with Bashō, no reason whatever seemed to suggest itself.

I watched headphoned aliens, with bulbous ears and protruding wires, scurry about, pushing cameras and operating lights as televising proceeded nearby. One alien in particular seemed determined to dissolve my shaky confidence by loudly intoning the number of minutes, then seconds, to air time.

Suddenly, light blazed around me in my quiet corner, and an animated vision, in white shirt and tie, wearing makeup and glossy shoes, slid into a seat near me. I surreptitiously rubbed my scruffy sandals on the backs of my socks, heard the final seconds tolled tonelessly in the same impassive voice, and braced myself for the ordeal. My host smiled smoothly into the camera's monocle, and his patter flowed like treacle. I paled like a dried rock at low tide, managed an appalling smirk, and wondered – now in desperation – why, *oh why* did I write that book?

It was the only question he didn't ask.

After the book launch that evening, at a bookstore called Frog Hollow, we returned to our hotel, wilted with weariness. And there, I distinguished myself by remarking sleepily to an inquiring guest that we'd just finished a frog launch at Book Hollow.

We slipped past the hotel desk to the deluxe accommodation that had been provided by the publishing house. Unknown to the staff, the real guest of honour in our room wasn't an author, but a quail.

Throughout that night, we held Bashō again by turns, trying to keep him comfortable. His favoured position was not prone, but standing, and his legs still possessed amazing strength. But he needed propping to maintain this pose, and he'd lean against our chests or hands or submit to a wadded towel to support him in my handbag.

During the following week at home, Bashō clung to each hour with us. I created a nest for him in the front of my shirt, and tied a cord around myself under my armpits, so he couldn't fall to the floor. With this unflattering contrivance, I was able to prepare suppers, as well as conduct other activities that required both hands.

When I absolutely *had* to put him down, I tucked him into a towelled nest in a box that I kept near me. In this, he dozed, and I often laid my face against him, murmuring softly. He always responded, sometimes peering up at me. If too much time elapsed between moments of contact, he'd struggle fretfully till I came.

About every hour, I'd dip my finger in water and release a drop against his beak; he'd swallow instantly, perking up for more until he was satisfied. His neck would weave uncontrollably when he tried to dip his beak in water, causing him sneezes to clear his nostrils, so it was easier for us to supply it.

For the last nine days of his life, he took no food. Like a leaf vibrantly full and pliable, then leaving the tree and gradually shrivelling, Bashō became lighter and lighter. Before our eyes, he faded a little more each day.

One morning during this time, Mack brought in a lima bean pod. He'd split it down one side and opened it like a book, in order to check on the maturing rate. But when he saw the beauty of the interior, he felt as if he'd intruded, and he brought it to me to see. Each bean, curved slightly like an embryo, tinted in the delicate, pale green of renewal, was still joined to the inner wall of the pod as though by an umbilical cord. The pod itself was canoe-shaped, reminding me of ancient soulboats from primal cultures around the world, bearing spirit passengers over the threshold between one level of existence and another. Rock carvings and paintings of soulboats, from Canada to Egypt, attest to endless visual variations. And here from our own vegetable garden, was one more.

Bashō's spirit, too, was crossing between two realities in a feathered soulboat, and one of the traditional attributes of feathers is flight to other spheres of existence. Bashō had arrived safely in another soulboat – an egg. He'd been twice born here – once into an egg. Again by hatching. Now, his journey was continuing, and soon his present vehicle would be discarded.

For what new vehicle? What new transformation?

All life is constant change.

As I gazed out the window, feeling Bashō's warmth nestled at my heart, I saw the bright glow of pumpkins – more soulboats. Bearing as passengers myriad seeds, embryonic pumpkins that, when disembarked, would hatch and begin new lives. Or, more correctly, continue their lives in new vessels.

Winter itself is a soulboat, a time when the seeds of autumn are protected by snow, that they may begin to grow in the spring.

I mused, sad but accepting, watching leaves in their fullness wind-dancing on branches. But soon they would follow others who were lying in a glow on the ground, already launched on the next stage of their journey. Like Bashō, they were fading away, dwindling, becoming lighter and lighter. They would grow increasingly frail, until their forms crumbled into nourishment not only for the hidden roots that had generated their own lives, but for seedlings in the spring.

As his egg vessel had already done, Bashō's feathered vessel would give back nutrients to the earth when its present voyage was done. But his consciousness would chart new seas, unknown to us here. Unknown, but not unguessed. Not unbelievable.

When so much that is miraculous surrounds us every day of our lives, in forms and ways we could never have imagined, how can we doubt the existence of more?

Mystery exists, whether we have proof to comfort us or not, and we are a part of it. We can analyse our outward forms, but what of the vitality all life shares? We are not only surrounded by mystery, we *are* mystery.

Embracing it, accepting limitations to our knowledge, accepting that water is wet without needing to know why, accepting eventually that wet and dry have no boundaries, generates inner cohesiveness. Accumulating diverse data, under the guise of being well informed, leads to fragmentation.

Our culture, however, is based on answers. Because answers constitute knowledge. And achievement. "I've got all the answers."

But what constitutes wisdom?

Accepting questions.

Birds and other creatures that I've cared for have been such marvellous examples of beings living fully in the moment. I've seen actions that obviously indicated anticipation, and others that indicated memory – just as I've noticed in humans. But mostly I'm impressed by their greater participation in the present moment.

We tend to clutter, or replace, our experience of the present with worries, plans, regrets, and endless variations on anxiety. So many marvellous moments brighten around us, then fade without our participation. Or pass with only a brief glance when someone else calls our attention to them.

But the wildlings I've known, and even the domestic creatures, like goats or chickens, can really teach us not to throw away such richness, but instead, to become aware of its existence.

Now Bashō was teaching us about dying fully, but gently, in each moment.

The prospect of death we avoid acknowledging, clinging to fashions and activities more suitable to young adults when we are entering middle or old age. We only admit to death when we are forced to. Yet it completes life, as night completes day. As fruit completes blossom.

We talk about a quality of living.

Equally important is a quality of dying. For everyone.

As I cradled Bashō's frail form, as I felt it diminish with dignity, surrounded by loving care, I realized yet again that *all* beings deserve such a gentle passing. But if our own species experiences that so rarely, what chance do others under our stewardship have?

What chance for us, addicted as we are to aggression?

What chance for those in slaughterhouses?

Almost as light as a breath, Bashō crossed that next threshold, dark as it is with mystery, yet bright with release – that threshold that equates all beings. Eleven days had passed since his stroke, days when he lived each moment *for* that moment.

When the last one came, he shifted slightly, and raised his eyes to mine once more. Then, like a leaf passing on the wind, he, too, passed on.

Leaving unavoidable grief behind. But grief mellowed by the recognition of Bashō's long life. Most Japanese quails live two to two-and-a-half, or maybe three, years – in cages. But our elder achieved five years, eight months, and three days.

A lengthy voyage.

In his lifetime, he must have calmed the anxious hearts of fifty to sixty wild birds who shared his garden until they were releasable. I could sense their rising fear pause, and return gradually to habitual wariness, as they watched Bashō trot past them to my hands to be cuddled or fed.

Now the empty indoor garden was full of Bashōs.

In my memory, I saw him with an overwintering ovenbird, preening and eating side by side. I saw him with evening grosbeaks, siskins, finches, sparrows – showing them by example how to find food and water in such unfamiliar places as dishes. I saw him in his role of pigeon parent to a young pigeon who followed him everywhere and insisted on imitating such unpigeonlike activities as dustbathing and eating mealworms.

I wondered anew at his rejection of young Miles. But then, maybe raising one pigeon is enough for any quail.

I remembered Bashō enduring Chip's sauciness, her tweaking of his tailfeathers, her thievery of his beloved mealworms – and yet still sharing companionship with her. I saw him cozied down in my lap beside the big roosters, Bubble and Squeak. Or on the floor beside them, pecking innocently at their great spurs, and as gently tolerated as a chick.

I recalled Bashō's eager delight for earwigs. His housecleaning of spiders and moths. The wild waxwing, another transient, that descended from the indoor trees each day to share the mealworms I tossed for Bashō.

Bashō also wrought a change in children whose only experience of birds was limited to plastic monstrosities activated in unbirdlike ways by springs or batteries. When Bashō allowed these children – under guidance – to hold him cupped in their hands, they responded with awe to his vitality, while we watched, hoping seeds of gentleness were being sown.

I smiled as I realized the ways in which Bashō had touched the lives of strangers – by appearing on CBC television, on the Discovery Channel, and in two books printed by a national publisher.

Truly, Bashō had been a "quail of an ambassador."

A fascinating teacher.

And a friend we were privileged to have known.

As I heard, in my memory, his strident calls at dawn, saluting each day, I thought of the quiet mornings to come.

And wondered how we'd manage without him.

We lay his head on a morning-glory leaf, and wrapped his body in two vibrant grape leaves from the garden vine. Then we dug a hole in the eastern wing tip of the robin garden, beside the patch of sweetgrass, and lined the hole with more grape leaves. Into this eggshell of leaves we laid Bashō with his beak facing into the east of renewal and refilled the cavity with rich earth from the garden.

On top, we placed an egg-shaped stone, mottled like Bashō's own colourful plumage.

And wished our traveller "bon voyage."

CHAPTER 23

WOOLLY PULL BUNS

Along the fenceline, the last apples pulled at the trees. One tree bore only a single fistful, like grapes suspended from a vine. Fallen apples clustered in hollows, bobbed down streams, rolled across roads.

Emerged hot from the oven in pies.

Deer haunted the apple trees, their hooves leaving apostrophes in the damp ground below. And although trees receded in every direction, in the mornings we often found fresh deer droppings among trampled apples close beside the house.

One evening I was returning late from a meeting. As I walked up the boardwalk from the road in utter darkness, having forgotten to leave on an outside light, I felt a tinge of familiar anxiety, that vulnerability ingrained – not surprisingly – in my gender, even though Mack was just inside.

Suddenly, a loud WHUFF! burst out beside me.

My heart exploded in my ears. And my knees dissolved.

A second WHUFF, followed by thudding hooves, restored the remnants of my reason. It was only some deer – more alarmed than I – who'd been eating apples in the dark.

With the blood-red trees in the fall come the blood sports – and deer, already high-strung from the added tensions of the rutting season, avoid even the possibility of a human encounter. They also devise ingenious methods for survival.

I remember one autumn night years ago when I was driving a country road. As I rounded a curve, my headlights swept a scattering of cattle that were grazing in a pasture. I casually glanced their way, and an antlered head rose abruptly out of the hornless herd, nervously watching the car.

A deer seeking safety among untargeted cows.

Though Ringo, too, sought safety still with us, he was also drawn to wild raccoons – who, in turn, were drawn to Mack. They clustered around our doorstep each evening waiting for his jovial greetings.

And, of course, his handouts.

As autumn reached its fullness, all the raccoons, including Ringo, reached another kind of fullness. They grew fatter and fatter, till I fancied that, if I unzipped their woolly parkas, it would be like unzipping a twenty-pound bag of dog food. I'd see endless heaps of tumbled kibble stored for the winter.

In Ringo's case, I'd expose neat rows of Fig Newtons. With his passion for them, I doubt if he'd allow them to digest and disappear. His Pudginess would hoard them forever.

Ringo's independence from us was steadily growing, however. For several weeks, we'd left the door between his pen and the natural world unhooked at the bottom, but latched firmly at the top. Though the door was closed to other animals, Ringo knew that he could squeeze out below whenever he wished. As well, he

could just pry it back and shoulder his way inside again, while it snapped shut behind him.

Of late, he had abandoned the pen altogether, and was living under the house with the wild raccoons, joining them at our door for communal feedings.

We were delighted. This was a major step towards re-integrating him with his own kind, and restoring him to his natural element – and also restoring his droppings to their natural element, much to Mack's relief. We were both astounded at Ringo's fall output. In the course of one day, when we were absent, he produced *seven* mounds of glistening excrement, all on the small floor of his sleeping shed.

Ringo, no doubt exhausted by his efforts, lolled lazily on his side high in his box, watching while Mack, tired after several hours of driving, scooped and washed. And *muttered*. Only after Mack was done did Ringo finally slither down his log to the floor, yawning and looking languidly relieved that the janitor had finally freshened his quarters – raccoon dens we've looked into have always been perfectly clean.

But even though Ringo had begun living with the wildlings, he still considered us his pals, which created confusion during feeding times. At dusk, hungry raccoons would huddle under the bird feeder, sifting through empty seed hulls. Then, when Mack opened the door to toss out dog food, the wildlings would all retreat, waiting for the door to close. The more nervous would crash through the bushes like woolly bulldozers, or lug themselves hurriedly up trees.

But not Ringo.

Dutifully heeding the communal alarm, he'd run *towards* Mack and climb him like a tree. From the safety of his dad's shoulders, Ringo would peer about at his horrified comrades, seeking the cause of their alarm.

Then Mack would sit down on the doorstep and the wildlings would watch in sheer disbelief as the fattest of them all would break all raccoon laws of decent behaviour and clamber eagerly into a human lap. There, His Pudginess would roll back comfortably against Mack's chest, his belly like a beach ball, and chew a Fig Newton that, to the envious noses of the other raccoons, undoubtedly smelled delicious.

There's no justice.

But hand-feeding Ringo had become a cautious procedure. As he matured, he became militantly protective towards food. A slight movement of a hand near him when he was eating would ignite sudden snarls. Even occasional bites. But once he'd finished the last crumb, his usual genial nature reasserted itself, and he'd be ready for cuddles.

We'd wanted Ringo to learn natural raccoon ways, which he was doing very quickly. Ways based on the drive to survive, when tasty handouts wouldn't be plentiful. Now, in turn, he was teaching us the rules of natural raccoon life – and we, too, had to abide by them.

Fortunately, being humans, we already understood about not sharing resources.

Meanwhile Ringo's girth had so expanded in preparation for semi-hibernation in winter that the usual raccoon entrance under the house grew a little wider each time he struggled through. It was beginning to look as if it would accommodate a small black bear.

The metabolism of raccoons during autumn allows them to store fat quickly against the coming cold. They're drawn to anything remotely edible, including excess zucchinis rotting in the compost, and they scoop everything up like furry front-end loaders. Their bodies swell so rapidly, and their coats thicken so luxuriously, that their faces and paws look two sizes too small. Their tolerant manners also shrink, and they become testier and grabbier with food. Sometimes as many as fourteen raccoons would be shouldering each other for every tidbit.

Now, on the brink of winter, the masked butterballs hauled themselves up trees with what seemed like difficulty, and we howled heartlessly one night as we watched Ringo from the kitchen window. He was wedged ridiculously into a covered homemade bird feeder, hanging out over all four edges and gorging on birdseed directly under his chin. The other raccoons on the ground were left with the hulls. Then Ringo spent ten minutes trying to extricate himself from the feeder.

His Portliness simply couldn't bend.

One night, we peered out at two smallish raccoons and a larger third one with its back to the door. Only when the large one turned aside, searching through birdseed, did we realize it *wasn't* a mother with two half-grown youngsters.

It was Ringo with two others the *same age.*

"My gawd," I breathed, "We've created a MONSTER!"

Whenever we lifted him up, we couldn't simply swing him up by his front legs – they'd have been dislocated by the weight. We had to haul him up with one arm curved under his bottom. Once up on our shoulders, his bulk pushed our heads forward like a hundredweight bag of feed.

Which he closely resembled.

But as Ringo became more of a raccoon than a human, interacting with us only every two to three days, someone else came into his life. And the two were seldom apart.

If Mack, bearing a special offering – like fish skin – knocked on the house wall above the den, and Ringo peered out sleepily, the face of a pretty little female pushed out beside his. They looked for all the world like a suburban couple answering a salesman's knock.

Initially, she was horrified to see Ringo waddle out and be swung up on Mack's shoulder – as was I, if Mack wasn't wearing a back brace for extra support. Retaining her natural wariness, she'd remain in the den, with just her anxious face visible.

Eventually, though, she began to draw nearer during these visits, coaxed by kindness – and, of course, by cookies. Before long, she'd be reaching up Mack's leg for a cookie, while Ringo overflowed Mack's shoulder, eating his.

During communal feasts, Ringo and his "girlfriend" ate side by side. Though he growled at the others, as is usual when food and raccoons combine, he never growled at her. One evening, to our astonishment, she timidly took a piece of coveted bagel away from under his nose. Then she turned her back and ate it daintily, while we still braced ourselves for a sudden uproar. But nothing happened.

Amazingly, His Greediness could actually *share*.

Mack enjoyed watching all the raccoons, and could distinguish many individuals. One enormous creature, far bigger than Ringo, and with a remarkably kind face, Mack called "Humphrey." He always backed down when growled at by others – even by youngsters – for reasons clear only to raccoons. But when dry dog food was distributed, Humphrey ruled. He chose the largest portion and plopped his bulk down over it, hiding it from the challenge of others. And, like an immovable boulder, there he remained, chewing stolidly, and backing up little by little to uncover more as it was needed.

No one could dislodge him.

Raccoon interactions were always intriguing. When one wanted to share another's food, he wouldn't confront the other. That would provoke instant snarls of defence, and was done only to drive the other away. Instead, he'd shuffle backwards into the food, and they'd push and wiggle together until both were settled and eating. After five or six raccoons had so wedged themselves into one tight furry heap, we marvelled that they could actually *find* any food beneath them.

Like masked musketeers, they were "all for one and one for all." Not only did each individual get fed, but with their backs together like musk oxen, each watched for danger from a different point.

Mack called them "Pull Buns," after one of Edna Staebler's famous recipes, in which lumps of sweet dough are dipped in

melted butter and brown sugar, piled in a heap, and baked. Then each sticky bun is pulled off and eaten.

But Edna had never dreamed of a variation called "Woolly Pull Buns."

Whenever the kibble was consumed to the last crumb, the insatiable raccoons returned wistfully to birdseed, their lifestyle evidently founded upon the survival of the *fattest*. They lounged back on their ample rumps and sifted hopefully through muddy hulls. Or they squeezed themselves ludicrously into the feeders, their thick ringed tails hanging down like bellpulls. Or they checked the latest deposit in the compost, leaving deposits of their own in exchange.

Meanwhile, in the den under the house, other raccoons had also moved in, recognizing a good set-up when they saw it. With justifiable irritation, we heard them tearing away the floor insulation for bedding. At times, they chewed the underside of the house so loudly, ripping and prying so determinedly, that I half expected to see them pop up through the floor like gophers.

For the first time, we felt no enthusiasm about Ringo learning raccoon ways.

CHAPTER 24

ANOTHER BILL ARRIVES

The chill hand of winter pressed against the land. A few determined leaves, faded and brittle, still spotted the trees. The rest lay curled in drifts, and dark spires of evergreens dominated the hilltops. The last flowers had fled, chased by nightly frosts. I crouched above my garden beds, planting bulbs.

I find this a special activity. To be surrounded by images of decay, to feel northwest winds probing under my collar with cold fingers, to hear not the rich music of summer songbirds, but a pervading silence broken only by the nasal bleats of nuthatches or the shrill queries of jays above me. Yet to hold a fat tulip bulb in my hand, or a daffodil – embryos of spring. To sense life within, life so indomitable that it can withstand winter in ways that I couldn't – that, in fact, *needs* winter for fulfillment. To anticipate the triumph of colourful blooms rocking in a warm spring wind, when sunlight grows stronger each day, and nearby perennials are cautiously emerging from the opening palm of the earth.

All this, to me, is magic. If, of course, the squirrels don't eat the bulbs.

Each day, the cold deepened. Down by the lake, the golden glow of tamaracks created an illusion of warmth, despite wrinkles of ice in the shallows. Only the reddest wild apples, small and hard, still brightened the drab trees. And when the first snow calmed the chaos of their branches, and quieted the restless, rustling land, red apples gleamed as cheerfully as holly berries in the white, muted world – as did vibrant rosehips, floating on the tips of dense twiggery beside the boardwalk.

Occasional migrants still appeared for a day, then passed on. Stragglers following the sun, riding the north winds south.

A lone robin dug energetically into the sun-touched snow by our door, her plumage rounded to hoard heat, her rich russet colouring intensified by blue shadows from the trees. I cautiously raised a window and tossed out thawed blueberries for her from the freezer. They sank almost out of sight in the soft snow, but clustered invitingly in the troughs of deer tracks. She left two days later, well fed, and taking the last warmth of summer away in her glowing breast.

But autumn resisted winter's early encroachment. Hurrying clouds blew out the stars one night, and noisily lashed the sleeping snow with dissolving rains. Winter awoke, and retaliated with plummeting temperatures, leaving us with slitherings of ice that plagued us for days. More rain followed before winter finally routed all resistance with volleys of snow. Once again, a victorious white silence muffled our clattering world with beauty.

But for how long?

While the seasons struggled for dominance around us, we tucked ourselves out of the way like the bulbs, and enjoyed indoor life with all our "creature comforts."

One of them – Beejay – paralleled the activities of the outside jays that he watched from the window. Lacking their resources, if not their resourcefulness, he too hid sunflower seeds. But buried them in various plant pots. Soon, leggy stalks rose everywhere, each bearing two leaves, with one leaf usually still trying to disentangle itself from a striped hull. We also discovered little hoards of seeds under carvings, behind couch cushions, and under magazines. Even under the rug.

With his crippled leg, Beejay had difficulty holding the seeds while extracting kernels, but he countered his disability with that ingenuity so characteristic of jays. One day, he watched as I set out one of my cherished rocks, pitted with small, circular dimples. Where I saw aesthetically pleasing texture, Beejay saw it instead as *useful*.

Later, the hulls of sunflower seeds lay scattered over and around the rock. Beejay had first wedged the seeds into the holes, then pounded the hulls apart. He'd also conquered whole corn and pigeon peas, which were particularly difficult, by the same method – except for a few that remained so tightly crammed into cavities that the hulls couldn't split. These seeds I was hard-pressed myself to pry out.

When, for variety, I dropped a handful of the raccoons' dry kibble into his dish, Beejay was so enthused that he not only ate several pieces, he secreted the remainder, anxious perhaps that I might not be able to resist their allure for a snack of my own.

Mack and I discovered hidden treasures everywhere. Our heels crunched down on kibble lurking in the fringes of the rug. We sat on kibble under chair pads. We stepped on it in our shoes. But whenever possible, we left it where Beejay had tucked it.

The kibble was too large to fit into the pits of the rock. So the hardest pieces he jammed into an outside angle of the baseboard upstairs, which he reached by hopping up, stair by stair, his throat bulging with dog food. The chipped outer corner of the wall created a gap behind the wood – unsightly to us, but to Beejay, a perfect vise for holding kibble. He'd unload his throat, place the first piece in place, pound and eat it, then place the second piece in place.

We were fascinated by his inexhaustible ingenuity.

We also felt obtuse by comparison.

Beejay's thriftiness with food reminded me of a large crow I'd rescued during my younger days. The crow's drooping wing prevented him from flying, and the midwinter season offered little foraging. The wing wasn't broken, fortunately, so all that was needed for healing was time and nourishment.

Because I felt we had to protect him from our two small cats – who, conversely, the crow could probably have eaten – and because of my mother's regrettable views on having a crow reside in the living room, he shared my bedroom. In a frenzy of enthusiasm, I dragged in boards and poles and created a monstrous arrangement of perches, leaving minimal walking spaces for humans.

The crow roosted each night only a few feet from my head, but my initial enchantment at this arrangement was soon dispelled. That first morning, when dawn could only have been a suggestion on the horizon, the crow burst out in a room-shaking CAW-CAW-CAW that skewered me through the ears, electrified my sleeping mother in the belief that the furnace had blown up, and – judging by later evidence – not only splayed both cats to the ceiling, but accelerated the sluggish bowel movements of the male.

Like Beejay, the crow, too, stored food in hidden crevices, in case leaner days returned. But his treasures were less benign. When one sleeps in the same room as a crow that hides meaty bones of all sizes – but retrieves only *some* of them – the prevailing aroma is that of an abattoir during a heatwave.

My mother was not amused.

For a convinced vegetarian, I handled a multitude of bones during that crow's convalescence. I was also in the first throes of my lifelong addiction to Henry Moore's bonelike sculptures. So I began returning home with various skulls or pelvises of creatures that I found, whitened and lichened, lying in the woods. To me, those osseous forms had an enduring beauty. And still do.

I recall my mother entering my room, then pausing before a pale sheep skull glimmering on my floor. As the blank eye sockets returned her perplexed gaze, she adjusted her bifocals and cited waggishly, "Alas, poor Yorick . . ."

Edna, sharing the upstairs studio with Molly, was adjusting, as we all were, to wintry days ahead. After feasting for months on prime wild greens, she sniffed disappointedly at the store-bought lettuce I laid before her. Though I'd tried to scrub off the sulphite wash from the supermarket sprayers, Edna was not impressed. With the reluctance of a hungry horse presented with a fish for supper, Edna finally nibbled the leafy edges, but found herself unable as yet to eat the thick spine. No doubt the flavours of fertilizers and pesticides were strongest in that watery shaft. After two days, we removed the spines – still disturbingly preserved, for freshness – and offered a few more leaves.

Edna's long ears, ever expressive, seemed to be asking just how long she had to wait for spring to bring her tasty, organic greens again, bursting with vitamins. Chastened, we returned from a trip to Halifax for other reasons, and laid a few leaves of organic lettuce before our gourmet rabbit.

In ten minutes, not a scrap remained, and she was lolling beside my chair while I rubbed her back, her pleased ears seeming to convey her delight that we'd finally come to our senses.

There are those who know quality when they see it.

Edna knew quality when she ate it.

As we drew closer to the yuletide season, abrasive bitter cold polished the stars to a piercing brilliance, and tightened the skin of the land till the living vitality of the earth we trod felt remote from our touch, as though withdrawn to a great depth. Our warm feet, enclosed in thick winter boots, crunched impersonally over a crisp, cold barrier between us and the warmth of hibernating chipmunks, the sleeping seeds, the bulbs – all the suspended life that would rouse and respond to the gentle prodding of the spring sun.

One morning, I looked out the upstairs window. A sudden rise of temperature overnight, accompanied by a quiet rain, had created a still morning with warm breath lying over the wilted snow. On top of the drumlin, rising like an island out of the mist, stood two ravens, sentinels in a silent world of mystery – a world primeval, as though newly created.

As I watched, the risen sun pierced the vapours with glowing shafts that kindled the top of the drumlin. One of the ravens croaked; they both opened their wings, and then sprang up. With gulping strokes, they pulled heavily through the moist air, like eagles swimming. Another single croak, and they faded out of sight into the mist. The sun meanwhile, as though summoned by the ravens, continued to strengthen, and the woodland world brightened and grew active.

Mack drew near me at the window, and we eyed the mild weather anxiously. In a few days, we would be joining other folk in town to create ice sculptures. The town would provide about ten blocks, two feet by four, and over a foot thick. All blocks would be set on top of small platforms placed at varying intervals along Main Street. A variety of intriguing ice carvings would be part of the festivities of the Christmas season.

We'd already designed an owl for our ice. But if rain persisted, how would we carve it?

"Change it to a reindeer," chuckled the unquenchable Mack. I groaned at the deplorable pun.

But the festive day dawned, cold enough to preserve the ice, yet warm enough to preserve us. We donned heavy sweaters with turtlenecks, long underwear, and thick socks, and packed home-made date turnovers for energy. We also added a couple of Thermoses of hot chocolate – liberally laced with a tasty, eighty-proof antifreeze.

At the site, we unpacked a battery of wood chisels, mallets, and hatchets, and were joined by Jeff, my art agent, who was looking for comic relief to lighten his busy schedule – and knew where to go.

As we plunged into our joint effort to create deathless, if transitory, art in the eye of a critical public, we chipped and hacked at the block, often with more enthusiasm than accuracy. With three of us surrounding the ice, we worked under a continual spray of flying particles from one another's tools, which stung our faces and melted under our collars. Our mitts soon became sodden, and we began to seek solace in the spiked cocoa, though the sun was still far from the yardarm. The drawing we followed as a guide became as saturated as our mitts, and so dog-eared as to be almost indecipherable. But our zeal could not be quenched, and a shape began to emerge under our relentless blows.

Curious strollers roamed up and down the street, pausing during their Christmas shopping to watch the carvers. Most of us were whacking at our blocks with hand tools. But two of the more confident artisans were slicing easily through their ice with chain-saws – tools that, although they shaped the ice with ease and speed, nevertheless created a hideous uproar that we felt negated their technical advantages.

Or so we told ourselves as we watched enviously.

The hours passed as quickly as our drams of cocoa, and recognizable sculptures began to emerge from their blocks. Wonderful pieces, with imaginative renderings. A dragon coiled and uncoiled in one spot, a great eagle lifted up somewhere else. There was a fish, a baby in a manger, a madonna and child. Even an Egyptian pharaoh.

We struggled on with our owl, stamping our chilled feet, pausing as needed to fortify ourselves with date turnovers and cocoa – especially cocoa. We also warned one another jocularly not to breathe on the ice directly after one of our fiery gulps lest the fumes create shapes we hadn't intended. The sun's warmth was enough to reckon with.

Then two little boys stopped in front of our sculpture and stared at it sceptically. We chipped on, engrossed, yet uneasily conscious of their analytical gaze. I watched them covertly.

Baffled, one child asked finally, "What is it?" But the other nudged him impatiently.

"It's an elephant," he answered decisively.

"One of us isn't following the drawing," I murmured.

"Or we're all having too much cocoa!" snickered Mack, pouring us another round.

A third child arrived, and peered curiously at our effort.

"Is it an angel?" he queried loudly, and an argument quickly ensued between the elephant- and the angel-theorists.

"My gawd, they sound like curators," I choked, hiding behind the ice for a furtive gulp. At that point, an adult stopped, and we braced ourselves for another devastating comment. Clearly, art was in the eye of the beholder.

"Are you Linda Johns?" he called out.

I leaned out warily from behind the sculpture. "The Tate Gallery? The National?" I muttered facetiously.

"Because there's a bird that can't fly, on the ground near my place."

Ah! Reality had intervened.

I dropped my tools – eagerly. I was used to hearing criticism *after* a piece was completed. Getting generous doses throughout the creative process was playing havoc with my feeble self-esteem, already high on the list of endangered species.

After a brief walk of five minutes down a side street, we arrived at the stranger's apartment building. There on the pavement was a bohemian waxwing, sitting up but motionless. He had struck the man's window the day before, but, although the man had run outside, he'd been unable to locate the bird. Another waxwing had struck later, but been killed.

As I gently gathered up the bird, who made no protest, a dog trotted around the corner of the building, nose to the ground. We'd arrived just in time.

The stranger kindly drove me home while I cradled the waxwing in my hands, trying to convey reassurance. There seemed to be no visible injuries, so I hoped rest, food, and protection for an indefinite period would allow the healing process to be completed.

I loosed him in the indoor garden and hastily thawed blueberries from the freezer. Then I added mealworms, but tucked them out of sight, lest Beejay steal them.

All seemed well between the two birds, and the waxwing calmly began to eat, so we returned to the sculpture fest.

Back at the site, I noticed several new viewers watching Jeff and Mack at work, and I sidled up behind this audience to listen to comments. The regrettable child who'd concluded that we were carving an angel had evidently routed those in favour of an elephant, and was now backing his opinion against a pair of little girls who were in hot disagreement with him.

"It is *not* an angel," argued the little redhead with the runny nose. Her companion shook her tasselled head vigorously in support. Then she pulled her thumb out of her mouth.

"It's a FRAW-W-G!" they shrilled in unison. And the redhead wiped her nose on her mitt for emphasis.

I looked at the sculpture with a speculative eye, my head on one side in the time-honoured pose of artists everywhere, and I had to agree with the little girls. At this stage, the thing *did* look more like a frog than an owl – though to suggest an angel was clearly ridiculous.

I wiped my own nose anxiously, but resisted using my mitt. Clearly, quick thinking was needed if this owl was going to fly and not hop.

Mack was chopping away at one wing, trying to release it from the head – although, if a live owl were brought to us with a wing that shape, I'd despair of the bird ever flying again. On the back of the piece, Jeff was burrowing into the tailfeathers, presumably under the impression that no owl needed a tail. Not this one, anyway.

But at the end of the afternoon, when our piece was finally finished – as was our cocoa, alas – and our legs were stiffening with cold, one last child stopped for a look. We continued to dry off our tools, but our invisible ears grew huge and leaned anxiously over the boy's head. He was determined, however, to examine our effort from every conceivable angle before committing himself. Then he ran back to his waiting dad.

"An owl," he said, firmly.

"Promising kid," I remarked to his father.

The waxwing continued to flourish in the indoor garden and, as his strength returned, he began flying around the house. He made only short forays in the beginning, but gradually ventured further from the garden. Finally – what is crucial to recovery – he flew up to the second level of the house with ease.

Though he devoured thawed berries each day, he refused mealworms. He'd pick up a mealie, shake it as though preparing it to feed a youngster, then toss it aside. We concluded that, since insects wouldn't form part of their winter diet, waxwings perhaps aren't able metabolically to handle them. Similarly, a deer's metabolism changes in winter, so that deer can survive by eating twigs and lichens after a summer diet of fresh greens.

The waxwing grew very knowing about my actions, as transient wildlings often did. When he sat on the windowsill in the garden, watching the outside birds, I'd approach bearing a jar lid mounded with thawing raspberries. He'd immediately show interest. Then I'd lower my gaze so as not to intimidate him, set the lid down in the garden, and back away. As I did so, he'd zigzag down the large root of driftwood, hop over to the berries and begin to eat – encouraged no doubt by Beejay's equally intrigued look above him.

Only five days after he'd arrived, Mack and I caught the waxwing on a windowsill, set him gently in a small, ventilated box, and drove him back to town. The short street where I'd retrieved him ended at a brook lined with huge trees, and there we released him.

As he soared up easily and settled lightly on a branch, I felt that familiar feeling of pleasure, of sudden lightness, as though I, too, had taken wing. As indeed part of me had.

As if in response, the waxwing remained for a few minutes watching us. The sky beyond him was a sullen grey, but sunlight suddenly brightened behind us and pointed a golden finger at the waxwing, kindling his rosy face with its striking black mask.

We watched, entranced by the beauty above us, and lulled by the melodious rippling of waters hurrying past, as they had for hundreds of years.

Then the waxwing, oriented to his familiar world again, flitted away to join his flock.

And the sun faded.

CHAPTER 25

An Unwise Fling Before Spring

New Year's Day opened with wonderful music when I rose before dawn to write. Close to the house, wild cries of a peculiar richness rang out from the trees surrounding the house. Interspersed with these were short bursts that ran rapidly up the scale to meld into a high sustained note with a tenor's vibrato before suddenly sliding down again. Excited squeals and barks interrupted one another continuously, while I listened, fascinated.

Given the time of year, these were probably courtship calls from barred owls – unless these particular owls had been celebrating New Year's Eve and were still carousing on their way home.

I woke Mack, and we crept out onto the balcony to hear them more clearly – maybe even see them. The night was polished to crystalline clarity by the crisp air. Stars flickered in a cold wind, great planets gleamed like watchful eyes, and an almost full moon created a blue unearthly world stripped of warmth and familiarity.

We stood encircled by the eerie cries of invisible owls, which sounded like primal spirits that had been roused. Below us, against the ghostly wings of the robin garden, three pale deer moved silently in the moonlight, nibbling on the last stalks of fresh chard. Under the feeder, a huddle of raccoons searched through fallen hulls and seeds for a few final mouthfuls before sleeping away the daylight hours in their den under the house.

But though owls called all around us, we never did spot their shadowy shapes – as if, indeed, we were hearing woodland spirits.

I was reminded of a hike into the woods that Mack and I had made with a friend in late summer. We were hunting edible mushrooms. Later, when we were heading home, we heard the call of a barred owl – not a common occurrence in the daytime. I cupped my hands, and delivered my best reply.

In a few moments, a gliding form slid through the trees and paused high in a maple. The owl called again. Again, I answered.

Then he flew once more, alighting only a few trees away from Mack, and peering down suspiciously at him. I stood twenty feet beyond Mack, and hooted anew.

The owl straightened up abruptly, stared at me, and swooped to a branch above my head. For several minutes we exchanged calls, with the puzzled owl cocking his head this way and that, and poking out his neck like a heron stalking a fish.

I, in turn, stifled my delighted giggles and continued to mimic the incredible variety of his calls, many of which were unfamiliar, while the owl almost danced with excitement. His barred plumage blended beautifully with tree trunks in particular, but his large, dark eyes burned with rapt intensity. As our interchange continued with fervid enthusiasm, I turned to Mack, whose eyes by this time were even bigger than the owl's, and murmured with a superior simper, "Why don't *you* ever tell me things like that!"

With regret, finally, I ceased, afraid that I might unwittingly be upsetting the owl. He was probably a young adult establishing his territory. I was also concerned that crows or jays might hear us, and arrive to harass the owl, as is their way. We left, therefore, pursued by his hootings, and could still hear him calling, though with dwindling enthusiasm, when we entered the house five minutes later.

Snow began to fall day after day, rising like a soft, white tide. It crept higher and higher, pulling down the lower branches of the spruce trees till their heavy burdens of snow merged with the white froth swirling below. The buried branches then created little caves, and soon the busy feet of snowshoe hares, squirrels, and mice wove communal trails in and out. Higher branches drooped, their long dark fingers hanging in helpless clusters under fluid shapes of sagging snow.

Below the hills, the lake was a whitened calm amid the jutting thrusts of receding treetops.

We watched five grouse from the window. They fed from fallen seeds below the feeder, then withdrew under the trees. There, two of them began digging their way down into the snow with elbowing actions that reminded me of little children awkwardly pulling on snowpants. Soon, only a pair of dark heads were visible, and barely so, as they settled themselves comfortably, insulated by snow for greater warmth.

The male grouse, having dined well, presented himself in full display for the delectation of his ladies, tailfeathers spread and erect, neck ruff fully flared. He gave his head a brief, abrupt shake to one side, then to the other, then to the first side again, over and over, gradually quickening his rhythm. Beak open, he shook faster and faster, then suddenly darted forward with tiny steps on blurred legs that then stopped short. His ladies, alas, seemed less fascinated then I.

Mack jogged my elbow insistently to get my attention. "So what's he got that I haven't got?"

I merely smiled and raised my brows – knowingly.

We walked out into winter silence, soothed and mesmerized by the falling flakes, the softening of all rigidity, the hushed calls of chickadees and kinglets. As snow rose, submerging and quieting the woods, peace rose within us, softening our splintering anxieties, hushing our internal clatter.

Winter, for us, is a time of cleansing, of re-establishing priorities – and of rest, the taking of a long breath before being drawn into the driving intensity of spring.

Winter is also endlessly fascinating with its variable beauty. All too soon, gusts swept the intricate tracery of fluff off the slumbering hardwoods. In the windless stillness that followed, we exchanged gentle beauty for one much more brash, as freezing rain stung the branches till they bowed, overcome.

As we stood on the drumlin gazing up, we felt as though we were on the brink of creation. Silence surrounded us, and, above, the elements of the cosmos were still in chaos. Clouds and blue sky created such an amorphous blend that neither could be distinguished, till finally, like the primal elements of earth and water creating the world, they began to separate. Distinct clouds formed against an awakening blue that slowly grew richer. Then sunshine suddenly burst through, and the icy crowns of trees on the hilltops shone in response.

We wandered through a crystallized world, skidding on light in the glittering fields. Raspberry canes, swollen many times their usual size by ice, arched over the crusty snow. Bent reeds in a marsh created an angular maze of triangles like a gigantic puzzle. Brittle stalks of tall, dried weeds were transformed to silvery wands.

Under the maples, we listened to branches tinkling musically as they swayed into one another, occasionally dropping sprinkles of ice that scattered lightly over the polished, undulating hillside.

But indoors, less harmony prevailed when strong winds began to blow and the power failed twenty minutes after I put a cake in the oven. Determined to save it, I lugged the cake up to the studio by candlelight and set it inside the woodstove near the glowing coals. But luck was against me.

After an hour, I ended up with a cake so charred on one side and raw on the other that I doubted if even the eternally optimistic raccoons would try eating it.

Domesticity, alas, is not my strong point. I cannot slice Mack's bread without undercutting till the loaf topples – though carving stone or whalebone presents no problem. My pasta invariably boils over and creates gummy sludge under the burners. My pies drool into pools on the bottom of the oven. And once the stove has cooled, I forget it needs to be cleaned – till the next time I switch it on. Then, I counter the inevitable odour of burned food with incense when I'm cooking.

My roasted veggies, though usually successful for Mack and me, prefer to cremate themselves rather than face guests. And my crackers either collapse in the hand when scooping up pâté, or bake crisp enough to slit throats – should the occasion arise.

Preoccupation with my writing or artwork adds another hazard. One evening I set a large dish of lasagna into the oven to bake, only to discover an hour later that I hadn't turned on the heat. I *had*, however, worked out a painting idea that, though nourishing in one sense, was a poor substitute for supper.

Then there was the time I was pondering a chapter while carefully squeezing out juice from two expensive organic lemons. I poured the juice down the sink instead of over the grain salad.

I remember, too, the day I discovered tiny white worms at the bottom of my raisins. I had opened the bag to shake out the last of these favourite treats for the roosters, who were circling eagerly at my feet. As worms and raisins in equal quantities tumbled into their dish, the roosters' passion for raisins became clear. Especially *these* ones with the succulent centres.

Thus, being domestically challenged, I tend to cook up three-day meals, thereby eliminating at least some disasters. Fortunately, the raccoons, being natural garburators, are wonderful supporters of my culinary catastrophes.

But when even *they* refuse my latest effort, I *know* I've struck an all-time low.

Despite my contributions from the kitchen, Ringo and his buddies spent a comfortable winter under the house. They slept during the bitterest weather, but emerged sleepily at every thaw to huddle on the doorstep, hoping for treats. A delighted Mack would stand among them, passing out cookies, while on his shoulder Ringo, still chewing, would grow so outraged that Mack usually offered him a second cookie as a pacifier.

But late in the winter season, calamity struck.

With every visit, we began to detect a disturbing smell from Ringo. A *reek*, as of rotting flesh. Though days often passed between visits, we noticed vaguely that he often licked under his belly. But his alacrity around Fig Newtons didn't diminish, so our vigilance was lulled.

Till one memorable day in late March.

Ringo emerged from the den looking decidedly listless. So we left the kitchen window where we'd been watching him with growing concern, and stepped outdoors. Mack swung Ringo up on his shoulder in the usual way, and in the blast of renewed stench that struck me, I caught sight of something very strange.

"Let's take a look at his belly," I suggested anxiously.

Mack obligingly pulled Ringo down into his lap and tipped him on his back. Ringo squirmed and twisted forward, licking frantically at his penis.

And no wonder.

According to the books we'd consulted, raccoons mature sexually in two years. Ringo, however, hadn't read the books. He must have tried to test his mechanism early – with disastrous results. Although the penis had projected to its full length, it hadn't retracted. The incident must have occurred some time ago, because the organ was filthy, infected, and swollen beyond any possibility of natural retraction. And Ringo's actions indicated severe pain. The appalling smell seemed to originate from areas of dead skin that were greyish, in contrast to the rosier inflamed parts.

We were horrified.

I phoned the vet, who suggested that we soak the member in cold water, then lubricate it and try to push it back inside – instructions that I felt from the first were beyond our collective expertise. And Ringo evidently agreed. He snarlingly resisted any interference, till he and Mack began to fight for the last word on the subject – a victory Ringo won temporarily by breaking loose and scrambling gingerly up a tree.

Worried that we might cause more harm, we made an appointment for him, and I used my old raccoon call – and a cookie – to coax him down. In the vet's office, Ringo, despite his malodorous state, created a sensation among clients and staff as he rode on Mack's shoulder. Even though he was less than a year old, Ringo loomed hugely over Mack's head, a woolly – if anxious – affirmation of the good life. The vet quickly injected a tranquillizer under Ringo's skin, and reduced one enormous, intimidating raccoon to a tiddly sop, yawning, drooling, and grinning as vacantly as a stuffed toy.

Then a shot of anesthetic into muscle rendered His Drowsiness unconscious, and we spread him out gently on his back. With his round belly and projecting penis, he looked like a compass with the needle pointing north. The stench, fully released, struck us all momentarily speechless.

Quickly, the vet cut away the rotting skin, cleansed the inflamed penis, and forced it back inside, probing deeply into Ringo's abdomen afterward. Even under anesthetic, the pain was so severe that Ringo bared his teeth and began shuddering continually.

But Mack leaned over him, rubbing Ringo's head and murmuring softly, till Ringo lay quietly once more. A shot of antibiotic followed. Then we carefully gathered up our precocious raccoon, drove home, and bedded him down warmly in his old sleeping box in the shed.

Because Ringo was a wild, not domestic, animal, the vet waived any charge, as has been his habit for years.

Would that all vets would so encourage people to help wild creatures in need.

Eventually, Ringo became groggily aware of familiar surroundings and of a caring Mack gently stroking him. When he was fully awake, he took a long drink of water, followed by a light meal of warm pasta and a hard-boiled egg. But he was more than content to stay in his box instead of climbing down. There he remained, resting, while Mack glided in and out of the shed, checking on him and rubbing his head consolingly.

Ringo obviously felt great discomfort, moving only when he had to, and then gingerly. But his condition was so vastly improved that, every time Mack came near, Ringo clung to him insistently and washed Mack's face and hands over and over. Only a faint reek still lingered, like a memory of his anguish.

By the next day, Ringo's eyes were clear, and his anxiety visibly relieved. He seemed almost lighthearted again, and compulsively affectionate, washing our faces repeatedly, as though earnestly conveying his release from pain. There was no doubt in our minds that he associated us with his returning health.

Many creatures in such a dilemma die from infection and self-mutilation. Ringo, lucky after losing his mother, was lucky again.

By the third day, His Luckiness was hurling himself at his suspended teddy bear with all his old enthusiasm, growling with mock ferocity and swinging through the air each time he grappled with the tattered bear. Ringo's fur, too, had regained all its usual freshness, and he'd scamper up our legs with his familiar zest. Soon, he'd be outdoors again with the wildlings.

Mack returned from one of his frequent visits with him while I was preparing supper.

"Penis Report: everything's working great!" he volunteered.

"Great!" I rejoined, tossing my salad.

Then added wickedly, "And how is Ringo's?"

CHAPTER 26

REMEMBERING

The last days of March slipped past, with shrinking snow hastened by the strengthening spring sun. On the south side of the house, I noticed fingertips of green pushing up cautiously from my hidden bulbs, new life leaving darkness and seeking light. The round, red eyes of rhubarb buds peered through the dingy moulting snow that was still blanching the wings of the robin garden.

At the feeders, the first grackles were swelling their iridescent chests and releasing the time-honoured calls of another triumphant migration. In my memory, Chip danced excitedly on the windowsills.

Across the awakening fields, flights of robins alighted and began their short runs, pausing with familiar cocked heads, then running again, returning to the cool north with the warmth of renewal burning in their breasts.

Ringo, sharing the den once more with the wild raccoons, nevertheless sought our company with almost the same anxiety as when he'd been a babe. Perhaps he, too, was haunted by the memory of his recent ordeal.

Mack, lured by the energies of the season, began lugging more rocks to strengthen the edges of the veggie garden. Ringo, equally enthused, "helped." He pushed between Mack and the rocks for more attention. He scampered through mud and wet snow before hurling himself all over Mack, climbing up his back and thrusting cold, wet paws under his shirt and down the back of his pants. He checked every pocket over and over for cookies, and left a sticky residue of mud in each one. By the time Mack returned to the house, even his ears were smeared with mud.

"Another male bonding ritual?" I murmured drily.

Luckily, our confidence about Ringo achieving full independence wasn't shaken by his ease around us. When other humans came near, he grew as wary as the wildlings – to our relief. We, however, were treated like *family*.

One evening, we sat on the doorstep playing with Ringo, who was obviously coaxing us for a treat. Beguiled again by those twinkling eyes, I offered him one of the muffins I'd baked that day. Clutching his treasure in greedy paws, Ringo quickly munched down part of it, then paused to lick his penis, ate more muffin, then licked himself again, alternating over and over till the muffin was gone.

Beside him, Mack and I howled helplessly, wondering just what sort of seasoning Ringo felt the muffins lacked.

Later that night, in a driving rain, Ringo peered in through the glass door. His magnificent coat was glistening with wet, and his tail had shrunk to a rope. However, when we opened the door to greet him, a breath-catching stench of skunk struck us broadside and we slammed the door as if he were a canvassing politician.

Despite his rejection – or perhaps because of it – Ringo still managed to appropriate a slice of bread, a scoop of our own leftovers from supper, and a Fig Newton, all thrown rudely out the door with a haste most unseemly among friends. But the sweet scent of his fur returned before our relationship suffered unduly.

A few weeks later, the den dwellers broke up and scattered, leaving a lone female to birth her young in seclusion.

And when the wildlings left, Ringo went with them – on his own at last.

Our raccoon parenthood had come to a successful close.

Such varied members coming and going in their season create an ever fluctuating family. We don't seek them out; instead, they seem to find us in their need, often through kind-hearted rescuers. From day to day, we never know what the house count will be.

I've often been asked if I've ever considered walking away from an injured bird on the road, a starving nestling, a baby raccoon mysteriously separated from its mother. People have suggested that perhaps I should just "let nature take its course."

This raises multiple considerations.

In the first place, the creatures I see are often suffering *because* of human interference, not because of natural hazards. They've been struck by cars, poisoned, mangled by fed housecats, shot, taken from unnoticed parents by human children (usually well-meaning, though not always). Birds have been brought that have struck windows with such an impact that they need days, even weeks, of convalescence. Single fledglings are often on their own too soon because a parent has been killed, *not* because they've been "abandoned." Ringo, a well-cared-for baby, certainly hadn't been arbitrarily discarded by his mother and siblings. But in an area affected by clear-cutting practices and hunters, a disaster caused by humans very probably separated him.

None of these is an example of "nature taking its course."

However, if I see a hawk trying to strike down a bird – and this will happen where birds gather near feeders – I don't interfere. The hawk is killing legitimately and efficiently for its own survival. Or that of its young. And that indeed is nature in balance. Life feeds on life.

But a fed housecat tormenting for pleasure is a different matter entirely, and if I can help the victim, I will. This is not to condemn cats as pets. It is, however, a plea for restricting their activities so as to eliminate the unnecessary sufferings of not only birds, but mice, rabbits, squirrels, chipmunks, garter snakes, and so many other creatures. We all share this planet.

Everywhere, wildlife is afflicted by human encroachment. Each one of us participates – however unwillingly – in this abuse. Driving a car, or building a house with windows, will always take a toll upon the original dwellers.

Our natural world and its creatures have taught me the real priorities of life, and have yielded insights that continually inspire my work – insights that I try to convey in my art and writing. Fortunately, I need reminding and reinforcement, so the wildlings keep coming, and the wilderness keeps calling. More and more, I feel that to help in any way is to give at least something in return, to repay a fraction of my debt.

Being with creatures is not only endlessly intriguing, it's humbling. They fully experience the richness of each living moment instead of hurtling through the hours in a frenzy of self-administered multiple stresses.

Because of their ability to be still, and to radiate an aura of stillness, they create a corresponding stillness within me that centres me amidst our contemporary chaos. And those daily moments of stillness enrich my life, whether spent in reflection before the hearth while holding a contented quail, or in sitting on top of the roof gazing into the immensity of a starry sky arching over ancient hills, or in holding an injured, frightened bird, transmitting the calmness taught me by other birds, feeling its fears fade, its hopes quicken. All such experiences give immeasurable reality to each day, involving me in those vital issues common to all beings: life, suffering, healing, and death.

Somehow, our technological trivialities pale in comparison.

But the basis of life is change. And acceptance of change. The creatures come, then go – often followed by our hearts. Though Ringo diminished our family by one when he left, tomorrow could increase it by two. Grateful for our blessings, we move over to accommodate each arrival, feel privileged to share what we have for as long as we can, and release them with our best wishes.

And always, the creatures leave their presence behind.

I have only to see a loaf of Mack's bread cooling on the counter to see Chip perched on top, her eyes gleaming devilishly as she digs out beakfuls. In the indoor garden, Bashō still crows a salutation to each sunrise. Sitting down before the studio fire, I feel the roosters jump into my lap and cuddle down with approving clucks for a visit.

When I glance over at Molly dozing on her shelf, she's joined by a shadowy young Miles, asserting his independence. As I walk familiar paths in the woods, I feel the warm backs of Goatlips and Noa under my hands as they stroll beside me.

Rubble still picks strawberries with me, quacking with enthusiasm, and getting more than her share.

When I rub Edna's back, feeling fur as soft as flour, I'm also feeling Ringo's unbelievably soft palms, seeing him asleep in my lap, watching him play in the canoe with Mack, laughing again as I see him roll back on his woolly haunches to savour his beloved Fig Newtons.

Sometimes I'm almost confused about the size of our current family since those that are gone still remain.

And if I were to have a retrospective show in a gallery, for me it would be like displaying a family album. Although I don't paint the creatures in a literal style, still each individual speaks to me out of my art.

The dying bird placed under imagery of transcendence in one painting brings back memories of a particular grackle – before Chip's advent. I hang another piece with a robin, and I see County on her nest, her delighted eyes, her babies. In a sculpture, the roosters are present again, with their magnificent combs, and the winds teasing their long tailfeathers. In another sculpture, a canvas, or a print, I rejoin an owl that has long returned to the woodlands.

I unwrap a framed painting on paper, and viewers see starlings blurred with movement, like night winds with stars. But I see one particular starling, feel her warm feet on the side of my head as I doze in bed, see her twinkly eyes peer out as she cuddles under my shirt, watch her bathing in my glass of water and spraying my unguarded drawing.

People flipping casually through this book will see merely drawings; readers will recognize portraits of the creatures they've

come to know in the text; but Mack and I see old friends caught in familiar poses.

Mack, peeking over my shoulder, watches a hawk he once knew emerging from a carving I'm working on, and we share a sudden spate of *remember when? remember when?* And I feel Ringo lying across my shoulders again, with stone dust coating his fur while he sleeps.

Even in the greenhouse he helped us build, now with April lettuce leaves swelling to the size of elephant ears, we see Ringo knocking over containers of nails. Ringo peeing his odour of ownership all over the hammer and saw. Ringo following Mack up the ladder to "help."

Mingled with the transience of our ever-changing family is their permanence in our memories.

We do live a privileged life.